STRAWBERRY CONCRETE

SCOTT MORALES

A Novel

Book Four

Strawberry Concrete

Copyright © 2025 All rights reserved.

ALL RIGHTS RESERVED: No part of this book may be reproduced, stored, or transmitted, in any form, without the express and prior permission in writing of Crossroads Publishing, LLC. This book may not be circulated in any form of binding or cover other than that in which it is currently published. This book is licensed for personal enjoyment only. All rights are reserved. Crossroads Publishing, LLC does not grant you rights to resell or distribute this book without prior written consent of both Crossroads Publishing, LLC and the copyright owner of this book. This book must not be copied, transferred, sold or distributed in any way.

Disclaimer: Neither Crossroads Publishing, LLC, or our authors will be responsible for repercussions to anyone who utilizes the subject of this book for illegal, immoral or unethical use.

This book is a work of fiction. Names, characters, businesses, organizations, places, events, and incidents either are the product of the author's imagination or are used fictitiously. Any resemblance to actual people, living or dead, events or locations is entirely coincidental. The views expressed herein do not necessarily reflect that of the publisher. This book or part thereof may not be reproduced in any form, stored in a retrieval system, or transmitted in any form by any means-electronic, mechanical, photocopy, recording or otherwise-without prior written consent of the publisher, except as provided by United States of America copyright law. This book is authentically written and designed. The author approved the final PDF of this book. This book may not be used for anything to do with AI, training, creating, etc.

Crossroads Publishing, LLC—620-204-1710
www.crossroadspublishingllc.com
ISBN: 979-8-9999528-6-8
Author Scott Morales
Cover by Jhea Dimog
Edited by Elizabeth Morquecho

ACKNOWLEDGEMENTS

No book is written in a vacuum. There are always people there to push you, prod and keep you on course. Some offer moral support, while others provide their expertise to help you create the best work you can put down on paper. It is for these people I wish to acknowledge and thank them for being there.

Angela, thanks for keeping me on track and listening to me rattle off plot points without context and shoving me out the door to fly to Dallas and Austin to do first-hand research of the sites I would write about in this story. Thank you for the support and compassion you showed me.

My sons, James and Karson. I know some of my creative juices flow in your veins and I am very proud of the young men you have become. To Jena, Scott and the kids. Thank you, guys, for making my life richer.

My Uncle Thomas Frensley. Uncle Tommy lived a very adventurous life, and he is the (highly fictionalized) inspiration for Ted Fielding. (As far as I know, he never was a party to the death of anyone.) Thank you for the stories Uncle Tommy. You helped fuel my imagination.

Doctor Wendy Vogel, (VET), Author of "Horizon Alpha" arc and the "Of Words" series. Beta reader extraordinaire and esteemed writer in her own right. Thank you for helping me fill in plot holes and beating me over the head with comma splices.

Elizabeth, "Mizz Liz," Morquecho. Author of the "Shattered Resolve", and "The Highshore Series". I can't believe how far and how fast we have come to be good friends and colleagues. You have kept me steady and forthright in my vision and have provided me with so many insights and alternatives. They made this book so much more cleaner, readable and fun. I cannot wait to see what the future holds for you.

Patrick Lane, Louisiana State Police Crime lab (Retired), who took the time to answer my questions and read through the manuscript, making sure that my science was accurate and plausible.

Detective Bradley Nickell, Las Vegas Police Detective and writer of the 2015 True Crime Story of the Year, "Repeat Offender." Thank you for giving me a kick in the pants and keeping me at the keyboard to get the story told. Forever Blue, Brother.

To the men and women of the Dallas and Austin Texas police departments for their assistance, taking me behind the curtain and allowing me to walk through two of Texas's most infamous crime scenes. Standing where Lee Harvey Oswald was shot and Charles Whitman fired from the University of Texas Tower gives you a rather unique take and perspective of history.

To the Police Officers in Fort Wayne, Indiana and Deputy Sheriffs of the East Baton Rouge Louisiana Parish Sheriff's Office, who were my partners, my back-up, my friends and my inspiration to become a writer. It was my honor to serve with you, my fellow Warriors.

To Tonya Andrews, Publisher of Crossroads Publishing, who gave this novel another shot and supported me in publishing it again. God bless you, Miss Tonya.

Finally, thank you to the federal government, for finally releasing the JFK files, which helped confirm and elaborate the plot points and evidence I have always known to be true,

DEDICATIONS

This book in its newest creation, has been a long time coming. Several people who influenced this story have gone from this world and they need to be acknowledged and remembered.

Mary Morales, my mom. Mom was always my strong rock to lean on and a person I could talk to. She was here when "Strawberry Concrete" was first released and when she told me she was proud of my work, I didn't need any other reward. God bless you, Mamma. Until we meet again.

Mary Hutchinson. Mary was a strong-willed and passionate person, who had her opinions and stood by them. She was wise and compassionate and raised her daughters well. She is missed by many.

Gerald K "Jerry" Simmons. Jerry was a Deputy with the East Baton Rouge Parish Sheriff's office, who was killed in the line of duty, November 21, 1988. (Ironically, John F. Kennedy, who this book centers around, was killed on November 22. But I remember Jerry's day in history more than JFK's.) Jerry was a good friend and brother to his family and me. I miss my friend. The town of "Camp Simmons, Indiana." is named in his honor.

Les Edgerton. Author, Mentor and very patient instructor, who taught me to write in my own voice and to be true to my writing. Thank you, Les and Rest Easy. Blue Skies.

FOR LORI.

PROLOGUE

NOVEMBER 22, 1963
DEALEY PLAZA
DALLAS, TEXAS

Secret Service Agent William Greer eased the limousine into the turn onto Elm Street and slowed it to a crawl. He saw the triple overpass directly ahead and knew they could speed toward the Trade Mart once they were under it, where the President would give his last speech before heading back to Washington.

"You can't say Texas doesn't love you today, Mister President." Nellie Connally, the First Lady of Texas, pointed toward the large crowd lining the motorcade.

John F. Kennedy nodded to her, flashing the trademark smile that had won him the 1960 election. He waved, then ran his right hand through his chestnut-colored hair. The autumn day had started with a drizzling rain, but now the sun was out, and the wet asphalt was starting to steam.

Kennedy glanced at his wife. Though still grieving the death of their newborn son, Patrick, from less than four months before, Jacqueline was as beautiful as ever. He noted that her face was a bit flushed, and knew they would both feel better once inside the cool interior of the Trade Mart.

The first two bangs sounded more like firecrackers than gunshots. Agent Roy Kellerman, seated in the front passenger seat, jerked his head to the rear. Kennedy raised his arms, his hands gripping his throat. Governor John Connally held his chest, his face twisted in pain.

"Oh my god. They're gonna kill us all!" Nellie screamed.

"Lancer is down!" Kellerman shouted. He grabbed for the two-way radio while watching Kennedy lean toward Jackie, his eyes etched in pain.

A second later, the President's head exploded in a crimson halo of blood and brain.

"Let's get out of here; we're hit!" Kellerman screamed.

Agent Greer accelerated toward the overpass, leaving the other vehicles in the motorcade. Kellerman looked back in horror when the First Lady jumped up on the trunk, her once pristine, pink dress suit now saturated with her husband's blood.

Secret Service Agent Clint Hill, sprinting for his life, made a desperate leap, grabbed a support bar on the trunk, and pushed the First Lady back into the limo. He climbed on top of her to protect her from other shots. Huddled in the seat, Jackie cradled the head of her slain husband, her body shaking with sobs.

Secret Service Agent Ted Fielding stood at his assigned post on the Elm Street sidewalk, scanning the crowd as the limousine slowly turned toward him. He tried to blend in, but his dark suit, sunglasses, muscular frame, and crew cut stamped him as Secret Service. Behind him, a grassy hill with a stockade fence separated the plaza from the Dallas railroad yard.

The former Marine instantly recognized the sound when the first shots cracked the still air.

People all around the plaza ran in panic. Fathers and mothers dropped to the grass, shielding their children with their own bodies. Motorcycle policemen laid down their bikes in the street and drew their revolvers, scanning the plaza and nearby buildings, unsure of what, exactly, they were looking for.

Fielding observed the chaos inside the car as the limousine passed in front of him.

Everything was a snapshot in his mind: the shock on Greer's face, the fear across Jackie's, and the pain in John Kennedy's eyes, right before the final shot extinguished that pain.

Drawing his pistol, Fielding glanced back over his shoulder at the stockade fence, sensing that the last shot had come from there. As soon as the President's limo fled the kill zone, Fielding spotted his partner, Agent Abner Wolfe, across the street. Fielding pointed to Wolfe, then pointed toward the schoolbook depository. He tapped his chest and pointed toward the stockade fence. Wolfe nodded his understanding and headed toward the depository.

Fielding sprinted toward the fence. A Dallas police officer, wearing a long black raincoat, emerged from the other side, pistol in hand.

"Drop the gun!" he shouted.

"Secret Service," Fielding said, raising his hands. "I have my ID in my inside coat pocket."

"Set the pistol down, and take your ID out slowly," the officer ordered. He kept the pistol level at Fielding's chest as several people joined them on the knoll. Fielding set his revolver down, then reached inside his coat and removed the leather wallet, holding it out for inspection. Satisfied, the officer motioned for Fielding to pick up his pistol.

"Find anything?" Fielding motioned toward the stockade fence area.

"Nothing." The policeman shook his head. "I was standing post when I thought I heard shots from here. It looks like everyone is heading toward the book building."

The cop made a furtive glance up the street as if urging the agent to go there. Fielding ignored him and jumped up to scan behind the fence. He caught a faint whiff of cordite in the air and looked at the officer, who stared, blank-faced, back at him. Seeing nothing suspicious behind the fence, he and the officer hurried toward the depository. Fielding spotted Harold Booker, a Special Agent assigned to the plaza, standing in the street, seemingly at a loss as to what had happened. A cigarette dangled precariously from his bottom lip.

When Fielding made eye contact with Booker, the man inclined his head toward the officer with him. Booker stared blankly, and as if awakened from a stupor, his eyes suddenly snapped clear, and he jogged over and joined them.

"Ted, what am I supposed to do?" Booker asked, fear pulsing through his veins.

Fielding read the fear and shock on Booker's pale face. Booker was thicker than Fielding, having accumulated his fat from years of sitting behind a desk. Although he was just three years older than Fielding, smoking and stress made him look much older. He sweated profusely and swallowed air like a guppy out of water.

He looked like he was going to pass out.

"Hey, I don't need you checking out on me!" Fielding said, placing a hand on the man's shoulder and shaking him. "We have a job to finish, and I expect you to uphold your part. Understood?"

Booker pulled a linen handkerchief from his suit pocket and wiped his face. "I'm fine." He pulled a cigarette from a crushed Chesterfield pack and lit it before realizing he already had one in his mouth. He flicked the older one out of his mouth and replaced it with the newly lit one.

"All right. This is what I need you to do." Fielding took the young officer by the arm. "Take this man out of the scene with you and speak to him privately. Make sure he tells you all he knows. Then, find out where they took Lancer, and check his condition. When we're done here, Wolfe and I will meet you there. Now, move!"

Spotting Wolfe, Fielding went to him, and the two moved closer to the front of the depository.

Booker escorted the policeman to a corner, where they would be undisturbed, and spoke with him briefly. Satisfied by what he'd learned, he motioned for an unmarked car, which pulled up next to them. Booker leaned in and spoke with the driver, who nodded. The officer climbed in, and the car slowly drove from the scene.

Booker jogged back toward the plaza. He was sure he could catch a ride to where the President had been taken, but paused to walk through the crime scene. He moved toward the curb opposite the grassy area and saw something shiny lying on the asphalt.

It was a cylindrical item about the length of his finger. Leaning down, he pitched the butt of his cigarette to the ground, crushing it with his toe, and picked up the item, holding it up to the sunlight.

It was a slug from a high-powered rifle and was sticky to the touch.

Booker realized it was coated with the blood of the Chief Executive of the United States. Looking around to ensure no one was watching, he pulled out his sweat-soaked handkerchief and wrapped it inside, tucking it away.

His eyes scanned the area for some form of transportation in the plaza. Noticing an officer sitting in his car near the rear of the depository, he walked over and flashed his credentials.

"I need a ride to wherever they took the President," Booker said.

"Parkland Hospital," the officer replied. "Get in."

Booker slid into the front seat, and the squad pulled toward the front of the building. Lighting another cigarette, he saw Fielding and Wolfe standing away from the other officers, looking down the street. He followed their gaze and caught a glimpse of a man walking toward a city bus. When the man glanced back, Booker recognized his thin features.

Lee Harvey Oswald was climbing onto the bus.

When Booker arrived at Parkland Hospital, chaos reigned at the Emergency Room entrance. Reporters, cops, nurses, and ER patients milled around, gawking and questioning anyone who arrived, trying to dig for any information on the President's condition. Two priests pushed past Booker and rushed into the ER.

Booker noticed the presidential limousine parked just outside. A motorcycle officer, his face a portrait of controlled grief, stood guard next to it, doing his best to keep the public and press away.

Booker showed his ID and peered into the presidential limousine.

"Oh, holy God," he gasped.

The backseat was thick with blood and brain matter, which dripped onto the floorboard and was now drying in the warm Texas sun. The jump seat, where John Connally had sat, was also coated in blood.

Dizziness overtook Booker, and his stomach lurched. He walked behind a car and gagged, fighting back the rising bile. He held his handkerchief over his mouth until the spasms passed, then lit a cigarette and smoked it absently.

I've seen too many autopsies and dissected too many cadavers to let this get to me.

Booker returned to the limousine and saw a news photographer leaning in with a camera, snapping photos.

"Hey! Get away from there!" the officer shouted. "Have some respect."

The man pulled his camera back but didn't budge an inch. "Hey, pal, I have a job to do, and this is news!"

Booker showed the photographer his ID. "This is a Secret Service investigation, pal! Now back off!"

The man took one parting shot and walked away from the car, cursing under his breath.

Booker looked toward the growing crowd. Another agent whom Booker recognized stepped toward the limo.

"Do we have keys to the car? Can we move it?" Booker asked.

"I have no idea who even has the keys," the agent responded. "And it's pandemonium inside the hospital right now."

Booker nodded, then came to a solution. "Look. As long as the car is as messed up as it is, people are gonna gawk and try to get more pictures. I'm gonna take care of this."

Booker walked inside the emergency room, packed with law enforcement and medical personnel. When an orderly passed by, he grabbed his arm.

"Hey, can you help me?" Booker asked. After telling the orderly what he needed, the orderly left and returned a few minutes later with a bucket filled with warm water and several towels, embossed with the hospital name.

Booker wasn't a small man and found it difficult to climb around in the back of the limousine, but he was determined to clean up the mess. As he scrubbed, sweat saturated the back of his white shirt until it stuck to him, his starched cuffs now stained with blood.

He lifted the First Lady's bouquet of roses out of the car, intending to set it on the trunk. He changed his mind when he saw the thick smear of blood on it and handed the flowers to the motor officer, who placed them on the hood. Booker swallowed the bile rising in his throat again as he wiped down the seat, pushing as much gore as he could onto the floorboard and soaking it up with towels.

He dug his fingers into the crack between the seat, forcing the gore to bubble to the top of the seat. The more he wiped, the more the blood seemed to smear. Booker wiped the sweat from his face, smearing the bloodstained rag across his forehead. His eyes stung from what he thought was more sweat until he caught a glimpse of himself in the rear-view mirror. Tracks of tears cut through dirt and blood that had caked on his cheeks. He wiped his nose and eyes and worked to keep his emotions under control, knowing this was not the time or place to lose it.

He paused for a moment when he saw a piece of the President's skull, brain, and hair still attached, lying in the center of the mess.

Booker thought back to his training as a psychiatrist. He'd conducted enough anatomical examinations to know which part of the skull the pieces had come from. He knew this fact might raise questions about whether there was more than one shooter. Questions like that could cloud the investigation, throwing up red herrings and conspiracy theories.

"How the hell did I let him talk me into this?" Booker muttered to himself.

This one piece of skull could determine history.

He put it in the pile of bloody rags but paused before throwing it out.

Booker held the rag and considered his options. He was nothing if not a realist. He knew there would be a full investigation into the killing of the President. Officials would be questioning witnesses and agents who'd been on the scene, which meant the investigators could come knocking on his door.

He also realized he'd need a bargaining chip if things went bad for him at the end of the day.

Booker plucked the piece from the soiled rags and wrapped it in a separate towel. He threw the other soiled clothes away but tucked this one into his pocket.

After the job was done, he went back inside and washed up as best he could. When he stepped out of the bathroom, Fielding and Wolfe walked through the doors, escorted by the uniformed officer from the plaza.

"What happened to you?" Wolfe asked, taking in the sight of Booker's bloodstained suit and shirt.

"I cleaned up the limo," Booker said. "It was—"

"I saw the shot," Fielding interrupted. "I can imagine how bad it was." He leaned closer to Booker. "Did you find anything?"

Booker stuck his hand in his pocket, his fingers closing around the saturated towel as he looked at the floor and shook his head. "No. Nothing. Just the blood."

Fielding exchanged a look with Wolfe and turned back to Booker as he looked back up. "Okay. But if you do, I need to know about it immediately. Understood?" Booker looked bewildered when Fielding grabbed his arm. "Understood!?"

"Yeah," Booker said. "Yes. I understand." He hunched his shoulders and walked toward the exit.

Fielding took Wolfe by the elbow and gave him a knowing look. "Watch him. We still need him. We can't afford to have him go rogue on us now."

"I told you I didn't trust him," Wolfe said. He cut through the crowd, searching for Booker.

Fielding headed toward the examination room but stopped short at the unmistakable sound of overwhelming grief. He spoke with Agent Kellerman, who confirmed his fear.

Fielding walked back to the entrance and stopped. Vice President Lyndon Johnson stepped out of a guarded room and looked at him. Fielding nodded.

"I'm sorry, Mr. Vice President. He's gone."

JUNE 6, 1968

"Make sure there's no moisture left before you apply the dust." Fielding blew on the drinking glass and saw that it was dry. Taking it into his hand, he squeezed it, leaving his fingerprints behind. Setting the glass on a pile of newspapers, he drew a camel-hair brush from his case and selected a jar of black print dust. After removing the top, he dipped the brush inside the powder, flicking off the residue before he passed the brush across the surface of the glass, lightly coating the oils from his prints. "Once the powder is on, you spin the bristles, cleaning out the excess dust and leaving a clean print."

Seven-year-old Jack Lefleur squinted to see the powder-coated ridge patterns of his uncle's prints. Fielding handed him a magnifying glass, which Jack moved back and forth over the prints. The loops and whirls that Uncle Ted had mentioned before came out clear and crisp.

Fielding pulled a length of clear tape from a roll and held the ends. "Now, take the sticky side and roll it onto the print, rubbing it down with your thumb." He pushed the tape down on the dusted print and lifted it. Once it came free, he held it to the light so Jack could see it. "Now, we put it on a clear piece of plastic, and it preserves it forever." He handed Jack the print lifts.

Jack studied the lifts with the magnifying glass before placing them in an envelope and running upstairs to put them in his drawer, where he kept his prize collections. As he walked back downstairs, he glanced at the television and looked at the young man on the small black-and-white screen—a man who so strongly resembled the President, who'd been killed five years earlier. Jack hustled down the stairs and sat in the center of the rug, his attention drawn to the screen.

"Jack, turn it up," Fielding instructed.

Jack leaned toward the screen and adjusted the volume, reseating himself on the floor in front of his uncle.

"*My thanks to all of you. Now let's go on to Chicago and win there!*" Robert Francis Kennedy, former Attorney General and brother of the murdered John F. Kennedy, gave a "thumbs up" and flashed a peace sign before stepping away from the podium.

Fielding leaned forward in his chair, staring intently at the screen.

"Do you miss it, Uncle Ted?"

"Hmm?" Ted asked, distracted by the TV. "Miss what?"

"The Secret Service," Jack said. "Ya know, protecting the President and stuff?"

"Not since Johnson took over," Ted said, his voice low. He stared off into space.

Kirk Lefleur shook his head and took a sip of his coffee. "That's all we need...another Kennedy in the White House. "I wonder how long it will be before someone puts a bullet in his—"

A shot pierced the revelry, and pandemonium reigned on the convention floor. A woman screamed as the camera panned to capture Kennedy lying on the floor. Someone held his head; another laid a rosary on his chest. A man appeared on the screen in front of the camera, putting his finger to his head and miming a gun firing into the head.

"Oh...my...God," Kirk said. "I didn't mean..." he sputtered.

Fielding leaned back in his chair and looked at the ceiling, shaking his head. He looked at Jack, who rose slowly, his eyes never leaving the screen, shocked by what he'd just witnessed. Fielding put his hand on the boy's shoulder and slid an envelope from his pocket, tucking it into Jack's.

He walked out of the room, not looking back at the screen. Feeling his nephew's eyes on him, Ted paused at the kitchen door.

"Mokroye Delo."

Fielding left the house, his mind reeling as he formulated what he would do next.

Jack watched his uncle leave and ran the words he'd heard him say through his mind, trying to comprehend them.
Mokroye Delo.

CHAPTER ONE
JUNE 15, PRESENT DAY

Jeffery Bailey was a creature of habit and not one to deviate from his normal routine. Mostly, he was exactly the type of person the management at the Hancock Arms Hotel, in Cincinnati, Ohio, wanted: steady, reliable, not one to lose his cool and aggravate a situation.

Boring.

After he clocked in at the start of his eleven PM shift, Bailey headed to the front revolving door that faced Fourth Street and greeted Charles, the doorman. Charles had been such a fixture at the hotel that local legend had it that he'd always been on the corner. They'd just built the hotel up around him.

"All quiet, Charles?" Bailey asked. He glanced at his watch and noted the time. 23:05.

"Yeah. I understand we might have the President visiting us for a bit?"

"Can't talk about it, Charles." Not much for casual conversation, Bailey left him and walked the outer perimeter, jotting down the time for each door he checked.

He strode down the marble steps to the downstairs hallway that led to the swimming pool. The pool closed at ten, so it was unusual to find anyone still swimming when he came on. Tonight, however, two kids were splashing away.

"The pool's closed. You shouldn't be in here," Bailey said.

"We just checked in and thought we could swim a bit," one of the boys explained.

"Let me see your room key." Bailey stared, expectantly, until the older of the two climbed out of the pool and pulled a key card out of the pile of towels. He read the room number, writing it on his pad. "Pool closes at ten. You have to leave."

Disappointed, the youths wrapped themselves in towels and made their way to the elevator, whispering about power-hungry security guards. Despite their discussion, Bailey walked with them. When they exited on their floor, he escorted them to their room and waited for them to bring their parents. "Pool closes at ten, folks." He nodded to them and walked off.

Back on his rounds.

The rest of the first half of his shift was uneventful, and it was now time for his dinner. He had a special time set aside each evening for dinner, and everyone knew not to mess with his time.

Seeing that mustard had fallen off his hot dog onto his tie, Bailey wiped it with a wet napkin. The napkin didn't help. Instead, it beaded up and made more of a mess than was already there. Aggravated, he unclipped the tie and reached into his locker to retrieve his backup, only to find that it had a bigger coffee stain than the yellow mustard one on the tie he'd been wearing. Sighing, he re-clipped the first tie onto his shirt and tucked the stained part inside his suit coat, doing his best to obscure it.

He looked at his watch. He had three minutes left in his lunch break, barely enough time to finish and get back on the job. He stuffed the rest of his hot dog into his mouth, washed it down with a swig of lukewarm coffee, and headed back out of the break room.

"Going 'on the walk,' Bailey?" Mel Keebler, the chief engineer, asked. Like everyone else who worked the third shift, he knew Bailey's routine.

And no one ever called him "Jeff" or "Jeffery." He was always Bailey.

"Yep."

It wasn't that he was being rude; he just believed in the simplicity of language and its use. Whenever Travis Goldstein, another guard on duty, and the security personnel would speak over the radio, he would listen in. If called by the dispatch center, their standard reply would be, "I copy," or just "copy." Bailey found that the response wasn't accurate or concise enough because he was not "copying" anything. He understood and was clear, so his response was either

"Understood" or "I'm Clear." He felt it was much more concise and to the point than the other responses.

After one more tour around the hotel perimeter, Bailey took the elevator to the top floor. From there, he walked down every floor until he reached the lobby.

The Hancock Arms Hotel was a landmark in downtown Cincinnati, Ohio. Boasting twenty-eight floors, it was one of the oldest hotels in Ohio. The oldest, the Netherlands Hilton, stood two blocks west. Like the Hilton, the Hancock was built during the height of the Great Depression. The construction employed thousands and helped keep Cincinnati afloat during the worst part of the era. After they were built, the two hotels competed against one another for guests and events.

Bailey had come to work at The Hancock Arms two years ago, after a not-too-successful career in the fast-food industry. He had applied to work at both hotels, and when a security position became available at The Hancock, had jumped at the chance.

"Have you ever worked in law enforcement or security before, Mr. Bailey?"

"No, sir, but I'm pretty sure I can do the job, given the chance. I'm very good with people and working under pressure."

It took a while for Bailey to fit in, but once he experienced the power and authority, even the minuscule amount afforded him by the hotel, the allure was almost overwhelming.

At least a couple of times a shift, he would enter the Hall of Reflection—a room covered from floor to ceiling with gold-tinted mirrors. Sucking in his gut, Bailey would walk away from the mirror, only to whip around and draw his radio from his hip. He would point the antenna like the barrel of a gun at each image of himself, imagining he was James Bond taking aim with his Walther PPK and blowing away various villains.

Around every corner was a terrorist or a gunman run amok, and it was up to him—Bailey—to use his superior training skills, intellect, and knowledge of the hotel to take advantage of the poor, outclassed criminal element that ran afoul of him.

And there was always a pretty girl who needed to be rescued. In every fantasy, he saved the day and got the girl. And in this one, she was being held hostage in the kitchen, just beyond that door.

He shoved the swinging kitchen door, causing it to strike the wall with a loud *smack*. This caused the three busboys who were washing dishes to jump. One dropped a glass but was quick enough to juggle it before his partner caught it, and it had a chance to smash onto the floor.

"Um...sorry," Bailey sputtered. "What a wonderful party. A shame I wasn't invited." He pulled off his best Bond imitation before closing the door and hurrying from the room.

His fantasies helped pump him up, making his walk more of a swagger and shading his confidence toward arrogance.

But the reality of the reflection was much harsher. No matter how much he sucked in his gut, he was still thirty pounds overweight, his girth straining against the button of his ill-fitting suit, which matched his scuffed shoes, and he walked with a slight limp, stemming from diabetic foot pain. He pulled a soiled handkerchief from his pocket to wipe his nose, the sudden exertion causing his sinuses to flare up. He coughed up thick mucus into the handkerchief.

Still, despite his many failings, Bailey was consistent in his work. His duties were simple: assist guests with problems with their rooms, pick up room service trays left in the hall, and collect the door hanger menus to go to room service for the next day's breakfasts.

Bailey carried the same equipment each day—a large set of keys clipped to his belt, each labeled to open every door in the hotel. Hooked to his front suit coat pocket was a laminated plastic carrier for his badge that read "Hancock Arms Security Officer." In that same pocket was a credit card-size pass key. His shirt pocket contained a notebook in which he would jot down observations on the floors as he walked, to be transferred to his written log once he finished the walk down. His manner of detailing his every move—his every *action*—bordered on obsessive.

"Dirty food tray outside room 2812, 0343 hrs.," he muttered to himself. He picked the tray up and placed it in the service hallway, only to note that two light bulbs were out in the main hallway. He scribbled the details down.

28th fl, Housekeeping closet unsecured, 0345 hrs.

28th fl, ice machine working.

On the twenty-fifth floor, he passed one of the maintenance workers. Bailey recalled that he'd seen the man before while making his rounds over the past few days, but didn't think he'd introduced himself or that Bailey even knew his name.

Oh great. Another new guy, Bailey thought.

On the twenty-second floor, he stopped in front of the Roosevelt Room. A plaque on the wall explained how President Franklin Roosevelt had stayed in the hotel back in 1942. The incident was so memorable that the Hancock Arms had thanked the President for staying with them. His visit had helped the struggling hotel to receive national recognition by naming a suite after him.

Bailey had even heard a rumor that, with the upcoming presidential election next year—and the party in power's national convention being held in Cincinnati in three weeks—the President, himself, might stay in this very room until his nomination was announced.

I hope I get to meet him. Maybe I can even get a picture with him, Bailey thought, even though he knew it was against hotel policy to take photos with celebrities.

The iconic photo of President Nixon and Elvis shaking hands came to mind. He wanted to have a moment like that.

Bailey imagined the President walking through the lobby, waving at the crowd. But, out from behind a pillar, a man with a pistol rushes forward. He levels the pistol at the President, when Bailey, with no regard for his own safety, leaps in front of the President and takes the shot meant for the Chief Executive. The Secret Service moves in and tackles the man as the president is hustled out. Bailey lies on the lobby floor, his eyes open, when he realizes that the bullet struck his plexiglass name tag, embedding itself. Bailey sits up and smiles, holding the name tag out to the adoring crowd, who overwhelm him with applause.

"For your unselfish actions and unparalleled bravery in risking your life for me," the President says, "I hereby present you with the Congressional Medal of Honor!"

Bailey smiled as he let the fantasy play out a little more.

And of course, a pretty girl was waiting for him in the wings to give him her own reward.

At least in his fantasies, he could make a difference.

Bailey approached the north fourteenth-floor stairwell with the warmth of the image still in his mind. He always looked forward to this part of the walk because the big, spacious stairway symbolized the halfway mark in his trek down to the lobby.

The door opened to the metal stairs, descending to a landing eight steps down. In the corner was a large concrete pole with a sprinkler valve, which was secured with a chain around the adjusting wheel to keep the valve from being turned. From the landing, the stairs made a turn to the left, six steps down to a second landing, then took a sharp turn downward until they reached the twelfth floor. Bailey had always thought the landing represented the thirteenth floor since it was about where the true thirteenth would be located.

Having never been a superstitious person, he never thought of thirteen as being anything other than a number.

Still caught up in his fantasy, Bailey waved to no one in the stairwell.

"Mister President, a ticker-tape parade, for me? Oh, sir. You shouldn't have!" he said.

"You've earned it, Jeff!" the President said, sitting next to him in the rear of the limo. *"I could use a good man like you as my Chief of Security. Interested?"*

Bailey smiled, realizing he'd allowed the President of the United States to call him by his first name.

He nodded at the imaginary offer as he pushed the door open and made his way to the first step.

The shove came violently and without warning.

He tried to brace himself as he pitched head-first down the metal stairway, throwing his right arm up to protect his face. The action did nothing to slow down his descent. His face caught the fourth stair, ripping open a gash on his forehead. His body pin-wheeled forward, slamming his back into the fifth and sixth stairs. As his body rolled, completing a somersault, Bailey's ribs snapped, and he cried out as pain shot through him. He was barely aware of the last thing he saw—the hard steel of a sprinkler valve. When the top of his head impacted the valve, his limp body tumbled down the next set of stairs until it rested on the second landing.

Bailey lay on his right side, the blood from his destroyed face and scalp running freely, dripping onto the grated stairs below.

As he fought to stay conscious, Bailey was vaguely aware of a pair of hands rifling through his clothing, moving aside his suit coat until the massive set of keys became visible. His assailant pulled out a small, square-shaped box, about the size of a mint case, and set it down on the landing next to Bailey's battered body.

His breath came in wheezes as the keyring was lifted from his waist. He heard the keys jingle in the hands of his attacker and tried to raise his head, but the effort caused a wave of dizziness, and he was forced back down. As he lay back, he caught a glimpse of the man's face.

"You just lay there, fat boy," the attacker said. "I'll be done here in a minute."

The attacker continued searching Bailey's clothes until he reached into his outer coat pocket and pulled out the credit card-sized universal key. He held it up for Bailey to see.

"Now, this makes it all worthwhile."

"Y-you c-c-can't..." Bailey mumbled, struggling to raise his head. The man slapped his hand over Bailey's mouth and nose, cutting off the air.

"Watch me." He pushed Bailey's head down, slamming it against the metal grating.

He examined the card. It had Bailey's initials written on it.

Bailey's vision was blurred as he watched him hold a duplicate card next to his. The assailant took out a Sharpie and duplicated Bailey's initials on the bogus card before slipping it back inside Bailey's coat pocket and patting it into place.

"You're probably trying to figure out why I did that." He sneered. "Well, ya see, if the hotel doesn't know that your master key is missing, they won't worry about changing the door codes and re-programming the locks. It buys me a whole lot of time to do what I was hired to do."

Having secured his find, his hands jerked away from Bailey's body when he heard the radio squawk into Bailey's earpiece.

"Switchboard to Bailey, a guest is locked out of their room. Twentieth floor, room 2015."

Calmly, the hands reached for the small microphone attached to Bailey's lapel and keyed it.

"I copy."

The attacker sat down next to Bailey's head. He looked at his watch.

"Looks like I have a couple of minutes. It's a shame you won't be around to see what's going to happen." He leaned in close to Bailey's blood-caked ear and whispered. "I'm gonna let you in on a little secret. I'm going to kill the President."

Bailey listened as the man told him his plan. His brow wrinkled in horror at the details and coldness of its execution. Hot tears pool in the corners of his eyes.

"I-I-ll s-stop you," Bailey cried. "I'll...s-save the President."

"Oh, son," the man said, "we both know that's not going to happen."

The assailant reached for Bailey's shoes. Bailey felt him unlace one and remove it. The cool air flowed across the hole in his sock, exposing his big toe.

"Just gonna do one more thing to make you look like the clumsy lout everyone thinks you are," he said.

Bailey strained to hear what the man was doing, but could only make out the sounds of something being ripped against the metal steps. The man then slid Bailey's shoe back onto his foot and laced it up. He tried to raise his right arm, but his broken bones wouldn't support it.

"Well, I appreciate your cooperation, Mr. Bailey, but I must leave. And you must die," the man said. He kicked Bailey twice in the ribs, guaranteeing they were shattered, and that the internal bleeding would do its job. Bailey moaned, coughing up pink, frothy blood. He thought the torture was over until the man punched him in the throat. Bailey gasped, and everything began fading to black. He held on long enough to hear the man climb the stairs and pull the door closed behind him.

An eternity of time passed before Bailey heard the feedback from the radio cutting through his ear, bringing him back to consciousness. Everything was red and blurry before his eyes. His breath came in shallow, quick puffs.

"Dispatch to Bailey. Come in, please. We need an ETA to unlock 2015. Are you clear?"

Bailey tried to move but felt like he was swimming through mud. He took a few seconds to collect his thoughts. He knew that his right arm wouldn't move, so he carefully tried moving his left. It moved but was pinned beneath him, and the pain in his shoulders and ribs knifed through him.

With incredible effort, Bailey took as deep a breath as he could manage and pushed off on his left arm, rolling from his side to his back. The action caused the jagged broken ribs to shift and puncture new organs and arteries. Bailey tried to scream, but his lungs felt as if they were no longer working.

He clawed at his radio mic, but it fell away from his lapel. Gathering his strength, Bailey shoved his hand into his coat, feeling for the notepad he kept there. Grasping it, he pulled it free until it fell onto his stomach. Blinded by blood, Bailey tried to lift his head but found the movement too excruciating. He dragged his hand across his gore-soaked shirt and felt a pen. Tearing his pocket as he pulled it away, he lay back, exhausted. Bailey felt his breathing getting more and more labored, and in his heart, he knew he didn't have much time left.

Grabbing a handful of pages, he opened the notebook and painfully started writing. Bailey was right-handed but tried his best to formulate letters with his left hand. His fingers trembled, causing the muscles to cramp and his hands to sweat.

Though not a religious man, Bailey felt the need to cry out for someone, for anybody, to hear and help him. *Oh, God,* he silently prayed. *Please let someone understand what I'm writing. Please! Jesus. If You're there, I'm sorry. I screwed up. Forgive me, please!*

Unable to see what he was writing down, Bailey only got a few letters written before he felt a sharp, stabbing pain in his head. Like a hot knitting needle, the pain lanced into the base of Bailey's skull. He arched his back, sending a piece of the fractured ribcage into his heart and lacerating it.

Bailey gasped, crying, as blood filled his abused lungs. Tears flowed freely as he realized what his attacker had said was true. There was nothing he could do to stop him from killing the President.

On the verge of death, Bailey imagined himself jumping in front of the President just as the assassin fired, the bullet striking his badge and saving the day.

A profound sadness gave his heart one last squeeze and stopped it.

"I really, really wanted that parade."

CHAPTER TWO

"'I KILLED HIM BECAUSE HE WANTED MY SANDWICH!'" Lieutenant Jackson Lefleur proclaimed loudly.

He tried to stifle a yawn. He'd only slept three hours before court, and it was finally catching up with him.

"Would you repeat that, please?"

"'I killed him because he wanted my sandwich,'" Lefleur said again, his voice emphatic and precise.

The prosecutor gave him a small smile and turned away, seating himself at the table. "No further questions for this witness, Your Honor."

Nelson Borders, Clayton County's lead prosecutor, flipped through his legal pad, satisfied that he'd covered all the questions he'd needed to ask.

Lefleur had been on the stand for the past day and a half, recounting how Sandoval Mendez had been captured and how he'd confessed to the murder of Roderick McCoy. Though twenty-five years as a cop had hardened him, it had still taken him aback when Mendez had explained why he'd killed his friend of three years.

All because Mendez had wanted two pieces of bread, a slice of baloney, and a piece of cheese—something he could've picked up at any corner deli for about two-fifty.

"Your witness, Mr. O'Doyle," the judge said.

Casey O'Doyle, defense attorney, rose from his seat and glanced down at his notes. He slipped the bifocals from his nose and tucked them into his pocket. Glancing at the wall clock, he approached the bench.

"Due to the hour, Your Honor, I move that I hold off on my cross-examination."

The judge agreed. "Let us reconvene in an hour."

Lefleur took a deep breath and rose from the witness chair.

Lefleur stepped into the hallway and slumped against the wall, looking at the ceiling. Borders stepped out of the courtroom and squeezed his arm.

"You did a good job," he said. "Just hold firm. You'll be all right."

"Who's next?" Lefleur asked.

"The pathologist, Doctor Reuben," Borders said. "She's to testify that Mendez stabbed McCoy forty-eight times, which was more than enough to kill him."

"Are you gonna bring up Mendez's intoxication level again?"

"I'm gonna make it a clear point that he wasn't as drunk as he tried to lead you to believe."

"O'Doyle is going to hit you hard on Mendez's interview," Borders said. "Once you're done, I'll still need you at the front table. It's not over just because you testified."

Lefleur bristled at the remark. "I know my job, Nelson. Just make sure you do yours, okay?" he snapped.

"What's that supposed to mean?"

"Just that I'm really surprised you decided to try this case yourself. I mean, isn't it your office's policy to plead out all the cases and give the smallest sentence you can legally get away with? That way, all those guilty pleas show up as a 'win' in your file so you can flaunt your statistics and show what a hardworking, hardline, crime-stopper you are and how many bad guys you've convicted when it comes time for re-election. Am I wrong?"

"Hey...we go with our best cases. If *your* people did their job right in the first place, we wouldn't have to be offering plea bargains to settle cases," Borders said indignantly.

"My people put together good cases, Nelson. The problem is that you have a bunch of rookie prosecutors over there who have never tried a case and wouldn't know which side of the table to sit on if it wasn't pointed out to them. And if your staff loses too many cases due to inexperience, the voters might have a serious issue with you come November."

"Look," Borders said, leaning closer to Lefleur so no one could overhear. "You gave me a shoddy case, and now you expect me to pull your fat out of the fire and a miracle out of my–"

His words were cut off when the door swung open and O'Doyle stepped into the hallway. Facing Lefleur, O'Doyle extended his hand.

"I'll apologize beforehand for going hard on you, Lieutenant. No hard feelings, I hope?"

Lefleur returned the handshake and shrugged his shoulders. "You're just doing your job, Casey, that's all anyone can ask of a public defender...especially the ones who get handed the worst possible cases to win."

"The judge gave us an hour, so I guess I'll see you back in the courtroom then," O'Doyle said. "I have to go talk to Mendez's family and feed them some bull crap about how well it's going for our side."

He nodded to the men and walked down the hallway, scratching the bald spot on the back of his head.

Lefleur looked at Borders, who appeared to be gearing up for another round of the blame game.

"Look...I'm sorry. I know you guys do the best with what you have," he offered.

"Yes, that's true. So, in the future, if you would, tell your people to stop sending me such feeble cases. I mean, just the other day–"

Lefleur stopped him with a raised hand. "I'll have my people work on it, okay?"

After a long, awkward silence, Borders finally spoke.

"Going anywhere for lunch?"

"I'm gonna check in with the office and see what's been going on for the past couple of days," Lefleur said.

"Well, beware. The media is camped out at the front door, just waiting to pounce on you," Borders said. "Might take the service elevator to the basement and go out the escort hallway."

Lefleur nodded and headed toward the far side of the courthouse, narrowly missing the camera crew and anchor person exiting the elevator as he passed. Avoiding the wait for the elevator, he slipped down the stairwell and hustled down the hallway in the basement, where they escorted the prisoners from jail to the court. He glanced behind him to see if anyone was following. When he turned back, he found himself face to face with Santiago Mendez, the brother of the accused.

"Well, hello, Lieutenant Lefleur," Mendez said. "I saw you testifying up there."

"That's right, Mendez."

"Is that yours?" Mendez pointed to an envelope on the ground.

Lefleur glanced down, his eyes narrowing. A thick pile of hundreds peeked out from the envelope. *There has to be ten thousand dollars there...*

Mendez picked the envelope up. Slipping it into Lefleur's coat pocket, he patted it. When he smiled, a single gold tooth caught the fluorescent light.

Lefleur paused for a long moment, thoughts of what he could do with the money running through his head at breakneck speed. *Mendez would own me.* The thought infuriated him. He grabbed Mendez's wrist and pulled the envelope from inside his pocket. He threw it in the man's face.

"I'm not taking your blood money, Mendez. You can't make me change my testimony or lie on the stand just for a few bucks." He moved close to Mendez and grabbed him by the collar. "And when this trial is over, I'm coming after you."

Pushing past him, he emerged a block away from the courthouse. He squinted against the bright sunlight and entered the Police Operations Center.

He entered the office and was forced to sidestep to avoid being knocked over by Richard "Ricky" Peterson, his second in command of the Special Crimes Unit.

"Whoa, Ricky. What did I miss? Did they indict the President yet?"

Two months before, the nation had been riveted to the news that the President of the United States, Alexander Kelly, and his Vice President, Donald Wells, had been implicated in providing nuclear weapons to Iran, which they immediately turned to use on Israel. The scandal broke when the device detonated prematurely, killing more than two hundred Iranian soldiers and citizens. Fortunately, it didn't have the nuclear warhead attached, so the radiation yield wasn't a factor. The Iranian Prime Minister renounced the United States and President Kelly, blaming them for purposely providing them with sub-standard weapons designed to wipe out the Iranian people. President Kelly and Vice President Wells were in full damage control mode and denied any involvement in the incident. The media speculated that the scandal may be enough to bring down the administration and that it wouldn't survive an open nomination at the upcoming Democratic Convention.

In the wake of the scandal, several assassination threats had been made against the administration officials, including the President. Lefleur's office, like many others in the country, had received several notices from the Secret Service, making them aware of death threats and asking them to be hyper-vigilant of rumors or any other threats.

"No, nothing that earth-shattering," Peterson said. He looked back at the squad room. "Hey, Garza! Bring me the clipboard!"

Sophia Garza grabbed the clipboard and hustled into Lefleur's office.

"Some guy went out to dig up a buried power line and found what might be human remains in a field behind his house," Peterson explained. "Looks like pieces of a skull and maybe some ribs. Uniform has it taped off, and the homicide team is heading there." He picked up the inter-office clipboard and read through it.

"Looks like it's human?" Lefleur asked, loosening his tie.

"Not sure. Still waiting on the initial report." He looked at Lefleur, taking in his suit. "You done in court? I could probably use a hand."

"I wish. I just dropped in to check my email. Gotta be back in an hour. Would you believe Mendez's brother tried to bribe me to lie on the stand?"

"Great values in that family," Peterson said.

"I don't think we'll finish the trial today," Lefleur sighed.

"Oh, okay," Peterson answered. "Well, I'll get with you later and tell you what we find."

Twenty minutes later, Lefleur was back outside the courtroom, waiting for the prosecutor and hoping they could get his testimony wrapped up before supper. Surprisingly, the cross-examination went quicker than he'd expected. He was soon off the stand, and the pathologist took his place. Once the prosecution rested, the defense called a witness and rested.

It took the jury only two hours to reach a verdict. It wouldn't have taken them that long, except they got one last free meal on the county's dime. Twelve dollars a day wasn't compensation enough. They ate their steaks and lobster, then emerged to announce the verdict.

"We find the defendant, Sandoval Mendez, guilty on the single count of second-degree murder, Your Honor," the jury foreman read.

Though the judge set the sentence at twenty years, Lefleur knew from past court convictions that Mendez would only serve ten because of the Indiana day-for-a-day sentencing guidelines. The system wasn't perfect, but he could live with its inequities.

Lefleur shook Border's hand and slipped down the stairway that led to the access hallway. He hurried down the corridor and exited out the side door, coming face to face with two news camera crews and his old friend, and one-time adversary from the *Camp Simmons Gazette*, Herman Cannon.

One of the anchors was primping his hair with a hairbrush, ensuring it was perfect, when he saw Lefleur. He picked up his microphone and held it in Lefleur's face.

"Lieutenant Lefleur, do you have any comment on the verdict in today's case?"

Knowing he was cornered, Lefleur took a deep breath and looked directly into the camera.

"I'm very pleased with the outcome and verdict. The people in this city should feel proud to have such dedicated civil servants as Chief Prosecutor Nelson Borders."

The anchor looked at his cameraman and made a cutting motion across his throat, stopping the tape.

"What're you doing, Lefleur? Running for office? That is one of the worst cases of sucking up I have ever heard," he said. "I thought you two were at each other's throats?"

"You're not getting any trash talk from me about Borders," Lefleur said. "The man has a job to do, just like I do."

"I hear you neutered a guy last night at some bar," Cannon said. "Anything going to come of it?"

Lefleur had stopped by to assist officers at a bar fight and had used his flashlight on a drunk as something other than an illumination device. In his defense, the guy had him by fifty pounds and had locked him in a headlock, so the most convenient place to strike was where he kept his brains...and not the ones in the guy's head.

"Probably. You know me and–pardon the generalization–the media. Anytime they can get me in their crosshairs, they will," Lefleur said.

"I'll try to lay down some cover fire for you if the need arises," Cannon said with a smile.

Lefleur returned the smile.

A few years ago, he would've seen Herman Cannon's smile like a cobra. But after they'd worked together on the bombing of the shopping mall, the men had healed the rift that had kept them apart, each gaining mutual respect from the other.

"Look, guys, that's all you're getting from me. Find Borders...I'm sure he'd give you a good quote," Lefleur said.

He walked off and headed to his car, which was parked on the top level of the city garage. On the drive home, he didn't bother turning on his car or police radio and relished the silence.

The next morning, Lefleur was at his desk, reading the story Cannon had written about the murder trial. He skimmed the piece and found his name. Cannon glossed over his quote, saying that Lefleur had praised Prosecutor Borders for his good work.

Borders, however, hadn't been so generous. He complained about how tough the case had been to prosecute and put the reasons squarely on the back of Lefleur.

"*We discussed the lack of quality of the casework being submitted to my office,*" the quote read. "*I plan on having my office draft recommendations to be submitted to Camp Simmons Police Chief Gray, on revamping the Investigative Bureau and their work ethic when it comes to filing high-profile cases.*"

Lefleur read the article through and shook his head at the inaccuracies in Borders' statement. He started to close the paper, but another article caught his eye.

"TROUBLED CAMP SIMMONS OFFICER INJURES MAN IN BAR FIGHT."

Lefleur scanned it, a sickening feeling rising in his stomach. The article was about his arrest of a drunk in the parking lot a few days prior. It went on to name Jack and listed his past department sins at length while detailing that several people who were on the scene accused him of excessive force.

He leaned back in his chair, tilting his head back and closing his eyes.

"Now what?" he said into the air. Lefleur crumpled the newspaper and tossed it onto the credenza behind him. He took a sip of his coffee, glancing up when Peterson came into his office. He looked at his cell phone. It was almost ten AM. Setting it on the credenza, he gathered the papers from his desk and set them next to the phone.

"Did you see the paper?" he said.

"Yeah," Peterson answered. "You've been down that road before. If there was anything to it, I'm sure IA would be pounding down your door to get to you."

"I just can't afford another Internal Affairs hit," Lefleur said.

Empathy pulled at Peterson's heart at the quiver in his voice.

"I saw Borders on the news," Peterson said, changing the subject. "What did you do to piss him off?"

Lefleur recounted the conversation he'd had with the prosecutor outside of court. "I thought we were cool after our little talk. I guess I was wrong."

"Ah, screw Borders. He just says that crap, because he knows he's in trouble and wants to be re-elected. Don't let him get to you, Jack. You're better than that."

Lefleur took a deep breath and let it out slowly. "You're right. Thanks, Ricky."

"Just call me 'Captain Morale'." Peterson flashed him a smile.

"So, what happened yesterday with the body and all?" Lefleur asked.

Peterson settled into the chair across from his desk and waved his hand.

"You remember a couple of years ago, some guy reported that his chimpanzee had escaped from a cage in his house, over in Willow Springs Addition? Well, guess whose carcass turned up in the field? Yep, the chimp."

Lefleur laughed and shook his head. "Well, have the Missing Primate Bureau close that one out...unless you think it was...a monkeycide...?"

"No...looks like he got his foot caught and starved to death," Peterson said. "I think the medical cause of death was ruled as 'Lack of Banana Syndrome.'"

Lefleur laughed.

"Oh. I need a case filed against Santiago Mendez for attempted bribery," Lefleur said.

"Who might the victim be?" Peterson leaned forward and picked up the Lucite paperweight on Jack's desk.

Lefleur pointed to himself.

"I hope you got a couple of witnesses to back you then," Peterson said. "You know, the last two cases we filed were 'denied on merits' because, without a videotape of independent witnesses, they feel it's a 'he said, he said' case."

He absently tossed the paperweight back and forth in his hands.

"Let's file it anyway," Lefleur said. "He offered me money to lie on the stand and it really pissed me off."

"Ah...I see. So, your probable cause is 'P.O.P.?' Peterson asked. "Pissing Off the Police?"

"Just file it, ok?" Lefleur said tensely. "I've been through enough. I don't need anyone thinking I can be bought or scared off."

Ricky saw Sophie Garza and waved her over. "Can you type this report up in case format and put it on my desk?"

"Sure, Rick." She paused before collecting the papers from the credenza and leaving the office.

"Be careful with that." Lefleur pointed to the paperweight. "It was my uncle's..."

"...badge and pin that he had when he was a secret service agent under Kennedy and Johnson...blah blah blah...that goes with the letter mounted on your wall...blah blah...and he was a crime scene photographer during the Texas Tower Incident in '66...blah blah...and your role model, and after he died, you decided to follow in his footsteps and be a crime fighter," Ricky said in one breath, a half-smile on his face. "Well, his and Batman's."

Lefleur smiled at Ricky's dissertation. "I might have mentioned it once or twice. Still...please, put it down."

"It's obvious you can't be bought because you buried that guy with your testimony." Peterson set the paperweight down. "I'll see that it gets filed. Can you have your report typed out by tomorrow?"

"Yeah. I'll get right on it," Lefleur said, adjusting the paperweight in its proper place. "Thanks, Ricky."

As Peterson walked back into the squad room, Lefleur's phone rang, and he looked at the caller ID.

St. Michael's Hospital.

He let his voicemail answer the call. He knew it was the collections department, regarding the bills that had stacked up from his heart attack nearly two years before. Ignoring the flashing light, he turned to his computer screen and began to type his case notes from the court case.

Twenty-five minutes and two half cups of coffee later, Lefleur finished the report. He leaned back in his seat and read over it, ensuring his recount of what happened flowed properly.

He stretched for a long minute, feeling the blood flow back to his limbs. Reaching into his pocket, he searched for his phone, but it wasn't there. He looked around his desk and the credenza, picking up papers and looking on the floor.

"Hey, Ricky," Lefleur yelled across the squad room. "Have you seen my phone?"

"Oh," Garza said, "Looks like I picked it up with the papers, Lieutenant." She crossed the room and handed him the phone.

His office phone rang a second time, frazzling his nerves further. Annoyed, he glanced at the caller ID and saw it was from the Three Oaks Nursing Home. Curious, Lefleur picked up the receiver.

"Lieutenant Lefleur."

"Is this Jackson Lefleur?" the voice on the other end asked.

"This is Lefleur. May I help you?"

There was some hesitation before the male spoke again.

"Lieutenant, my name is Donald Sloan. I'm a nurse for a man named Abner Wolfe, a resident here at the Three Oaks Nursing Home."

Abner Wolfe.

Something about his name nagged at his memory. Had he heard the name before? He couldn't remember for sure.

"What can I do for Mr. Wolfe?"

"Well, sir, Mr. Wolfe saw your name in the paper—you know, from that trial you were involved in? He asked me to get in touch with you and see if you could come out and see him on, what he says, is a 'matter of the utmost importance.'"

"Did he explain what the matter concerns?" Lefleur asked, jotting down both men's names, the nursing home name, and the phone number.

"No, sir. But I can tell you this...he told me you were the one he's been waiting for, and no one else can help him," Sloan said.

"Well, Mr. Sloan, I can't make it there today. I have too much catching up to do after being in court all week." Lefleur flipped through his calendar. "I have your number. I'll call you back early next week and see what we can do, or I can have one of my detectives..."

Lefleur paused at the sound of someone struggling for the phone, and then another voice—one much older and gruff—came on.

"No...I need to see you now!" an older man demanded.

"I take it this is Mr. Wolfe?" Lefleur asked.

"Abner Wolfe, yes, sir," he said. "Lieutenant, this is very important. My life, your life, and the nation's future may depend on it!"

Lefleur leaned back in his chair and thought for a moment. "You're being a little melodramatic, aren't you, Mr. Wolfe? How will my life, or yours, affect the state of the nation...such as it is?"

"You have to come here to find out," Wolfe said.

"It's not possible today, sir," Lefleur said, holding his ground. "Look, unless there is something else..."

"I'm not done here, son. Not by a long shot!" Wolfe interrupted.

Lefleur hung up and shook his head, clearing away the conversation and grabbing a file from a pile on his desk. Opening it, he slowly read through it while the grating voice of Abner Wolfe resonated in the back of his mind.

Lefleur pulled into his driveway after a mind-numbing day of paperwork and staff meetings. Before he could exit his car, his cell phone rang. Pulling it out, he looked at the number but didn't recognize it. He let it go to voicemail and stepped inside the apartment, or "The Dump," as he'd informally named it. He tossed his briefcase onto the ratty couch in the living room.

"I'm home," Lefleur said.

No one else was in the apartment to hear him. He threw a stack of bills on top of the pile already collecting in the little basket hanging on the wall next to the door. He kept the electric bill in his hand, sighing at the words typed in red. "DISCONNECTION NOTICE."

He read through the paper, his heart sinking with each word. It was a promise to shut his power off in three days if he didn't pay up. With payday five days away, he figured he'd better deal with this one soon.

Lefleur felt a momentary twinge in the knuckles of his right hand. He manipulated his fingers, and the joints popped.

It had been six months since he'd broken his hand on the jaw of the white supremacy member who'd tried to take his gun from him during a search warrant. When the gun had cleared Lefleur's holster, he'd hit the man so hard that he'd shattered his jawbone in two. In what should have been a clear case of necessary force, Lefleur had been blindsided by a junior uniform officer who'd given a different version of the events, painting Lefleur as overly aggressive. Lefleur had trained the officer when he was a rookie and, during his probationary period, had recommended that he have his probation extended because he was overly aggressive with prisoners. The rookie ended up getting an extra four months of training. After he'd become a full-fledged officer, he'd made mention to several of his classmates that the first chance he got he would "screw with Lefleur for screwing with me." At his first chance, the rookie went to a supervisor and made a formal complaint.

Already on Internal Affairs radar, it hadn't taken much for a full-blown investigation to be opened about the incident. Of course, the skinhead with the broken jaw was more than happy to weigh in on the false narrative, and when it was all said and done, Lefleur was handed a six-month unpaid suspension.

"You know, this is bullshit," Lefleur had told Dominick Gray as he pulled his badge from his belt and his gun from its holster, laying them down on the man's desk. "He made the whole thing up to get back at me for having his probation extended."

Gray, the Chief of Police, had picked up the gun and badge, putting them in his drawer. "Jack, in the current political situation, and considering the climate toward law enforcement officers, you should be grateful you'll still have a job after your suspension. Plenty of jurisdictions would have fired you."

Lefleur had bit his tongue and left the office, knowing he'd lost. He'd done whatever odd jobs he could to survive and keep his family afloat but ultimately, it was too little, too late. His wife had taken the kids and all their belongings from the house while he was working a twelve-hour shift doing construction on the Simmons Pointe Mall. When he'd returned home, he'd found a letter from the bank demanding he vacate the property by the end of the week. It was sitting on top of a pile of his things in the center of the empty living room. He'd received a text from Gretchen that evening, telling him she would let him know her new address when she got to where she was going.

Two weeks later, Lefleur had received divorce papers in his department mailbox. He'd read them through with a lawyer friend and signed them. Though saddled with all the leftover debt, he'd seen the divorce as a clean slate and a chance at a new life.

He was still waiting for the new life to come...

After a dinner of leftover Chinese food, the house phone rang while Jack was washing dishes. With all the collection calls he'd received since he'd been off work, he was hesitant to answer. Taking a breath, he decided to brave it and punched the button.

"Hello?"

"Lefleur, this is Abner Wolfe."

Jack was taken aback. "How did you get my home number? It's not listed."

"You'd be surprised what sort of information an old goat like me can get their hands on," Wolfe said. "You need to listen to me."

Jack was about to hang up when he heard Wolfe mention something that captured his attention. At first, it hadn't registered, but when it did, he needed clarification.

"This has to do with *who?*"

"Ted Fielding. He's your uncle, isn't he?" Wolfe asked.

"He was. He died when I was twelve. How did you know Ted Fielding?"

"We...worked together," Wolfe said quietly. "That's all I'm comfortable saying on the phone. We need to talk."

Jack looked at the clock and saw that it was nearly eight-thirty.

"Alright. Give me half an hour. What's your address?"

Jack jotted it down on the same piece of paper he'd written Wolfe's information earlier and hung up.

Ten minutes later, he was out of the house and on the road to the Three Oaks Nursing home, eight miles away.

President Alexander Kelly watched the uniformed Secret Service officer patrol the inner perimeter outside the Oval Office with his bomb-sniffing dog. Kelly looked over his shoulder at Anita, his wife, who was twisting a napkin to pieces on the couch.

Brett Sullivan, Chief of White House Security, who was in the Oval with the President and his wife, put his finger to his earpiece and nodded.

"All clear, Mr. President," Sullivan said. "No explosive devices found."

The First Lady let out a sigh of relief, which Kelly took as disgust.

"Anita, after all this time, you should have learned to expect something like this," he chided.

"I may be forced to endure it, Alexander," Anita snapped, "but I should not have to 'expect' it!"

Having grown up in Austin, Texas as the daughter of a prominent Texas politician, it was natural for Anita Rayford to speak her mind and form her own political opinions. However, she would never consider entering politics herself. She was content to stay away from the political arena, attend the University of Austin, and earn her degree in Chemistry. The degree had come in handy when she'd traveled to Tokyo in the wake of a gas attack on the Tokyo Metro. Twelve people had died, and over 6,200 had been injured. She'd seen firsthand the devastation the gas had caused and had considered dedicating herself to the elimination of such weapons, developing contacts and deep friendships with many of the chemists and scientists from around the world.

That was before she'd met Alexander.

His career in politics had pushed him from the local offices to the national spotlight after being picked out of obscurity to speak at the Democratic National Convention.

She'd hoped her degree would get her a job at a university as a professor, but Alexander had had other plans. For twenty-three years, he'd been involved in politics, dragging Anita along with him to every rally and every new position he was elected to. Being an introvert and not naturally one to put herself out there, Anita endured numerous campaigns and public appearances, even though the functions drained her emotionally. She hadn't thought she could physically endure another election until her husband was selected as the vice-presidential candidate on the ticket with President Hogan Rogers. Alexander took on the second seat, knowing that Rogers was in poor health. If nothing else, Anita knew that Alexander was one to seize an opportunity when it presented itself, to achieve a higher goal.

He was ruthless that way.

When Rogers had died suddenly, Kelly had been thrust into the presidency—a position he had coveted since first entering politics as a city councilman in Huntsville, Virginia. Anita had watched him move up the political ladder expertly, like a master chess player, captivating the board. She knew how vicious Alexander could be against an opponent, and even though his tactics sometimes sickened her, she stood stoically by his side at every victory celebration and every new opportunity.

And then, there were the affairs.

Alexander was handsome and charismatic, and used his charisma to bring men and women to his campaign and bed. He kept his bisexuality quiet, even though many suspected but were afraid to say anything. If Alexander found out someone was positioning to "out him" for his lifestyle, he used his money and power to either destroy them or cause them to go away—permanently. To Alexander Kelly, his power had to be total, and he diligently worked to obtain all he could.

His lust for power frightened her.

But she loved her husband, and like every other First Lady who had served before her, she stood with him, even when it was physically painful.

Anita recalled a conversation just a few nights after he had been sworn in, after President Rogers' death.

"I hate that people consider me an 'accidental president,' like Andrew and Lyndon Johnson or Chester Arthur or even Truman," Kelly had told Anita one night as they sat in the master bedroom sipping drinks. "Although these men fell into their positions by their predecessors dying in office, I have to show them that I EARNED this position. The people must see that I am the right person to be their president and that Rogers was not." Kelly swirled the liquor around in his glass, the fire reflecting off the amber liquid. "After I win, finishing out Roger's term, I can still run again, twice. I can be president for the next decade!" He looked at her. "Nothing will stand in my way."

"But, Alexander, when is enough, enough?" Anita asked. "Even Johnson didn't run in '68, because it took such a toll on him and his family." She hugged herself. "I-I'm not sure I can handle ten years as the First Lady. It's just...daunting."

Kelly stood up and threw back the Scotch in his glass. "I won't stand a quitter, Nita," he snapped, purposely using a demeaning form of her name. "I expect you to be there with me every step of the way." He softened his tone, slipping into what Anita had come to recognize as his "compassionate" face. He rose from his seat and knelt next to her. "Honey, I cannot do this without you. You know that, right?" He leaned in and kissed her. For that split second, when their lips met, the passion flooded back, and Anita remembered why she loved Alexander.

He broke the kiss and touched her face. "I need you, darling. You are with me, aren't you?"

Anita nodded, and he kissed her forehead and walked out of the room. "That's my girl," he tossed over his shoulder.

"I want searches increased as we approach the convention," Kelly told Sullivan.

His sharp tone snapped Anita back to today.

"I may have pissed some people off with the Middle East debacle, but I will not let some loud-mouth cowards in turbans dictate how I approach my agenda."

"Sir," Sullivan said. "We have just heard rumblings about an assassination attempt, and nothing points toward Islamic extremists. I have my people branching out and searching all social media and outlets, trying to find some handle on any information. So far, nothing. Perhaps you could cut back on some of your campaign stops until we know more."

"Hell no!" Kelly snapped. "I am currently four points ahead in the polls. I cannot afford to sit on my hands, allowing that bastard, Trevor Green, to pass me in the polls." Kelly poked his finger in Sullivan's chest. "I worked my ass off to achieve what I have, and I will not let some God-fearing, gun-toting hillbilly from Tennessee take it from me. You hear me? I earned this. I want to do a lot of things, and I can't do them in just four years. It's my time, now. It's my time."

Kelly took a deep breath and stepped behind the Resolute desk, leaning forward and resting on his fingertips. "Do you trust your people, Mack?"

Sullivan straightened his back. "I stake my life on them, sir."

"If you trust them, I trust them. And I trust they will do their duty and protect me when I am out there."

"Of course, sir. My people know their jobs." Sullivan struggled to keep the indignation from his voice.

"Well then, there shouldn't be any problems at any campaign stops."

The muscles in Sullivan's jaw jerked.

Anita Kelly took note.

"No, sir," he said. "No problem whatsoever."

"Good, good," Kelly said. He sat down behind his desk. "You're dismissed."

Sullivan stepped back and inclined his head toward Mrs. Kelly. "Ma'am."

After Sullivan left, Anita watched Alexander light a cigar. He smiled at the Secret Service Chief's discomfort and the power he could wield over those beneath him.

She rose quietly and left him alone in the office they'd both fought so hard for him to achieve.

CHAPTER THREE

The Three Oaks Nursing home was hidden from view. Situated off the highway about half a mile, Lefleur almost missed it. As he pulled into the semi-circular drive and cut the engine, his eyes took in the tall windows framing the ornate doors. The windows were covered in thick curtains that seemed to blow with the air conditioning he assumed circulated inside.

The nursing home's structure and design screamed of its ancientness, and Lefleur wondered how old it was as he approached the front porch. Pulling open the door, he stepped into a grand foyer. The marble floors had been well-kept and polished, so Lefleur could see his reflection looking back at him when he glanced down. A large reception desk was situated on the far side of the entryway.

Behind the desk was a nurse, her face framed in the light of a desk lamp. She was young, probably twenty-two, with black dyed hair and an anarchist "A" tattooed on the back of her hand. When she saw Lefleur, she put aside the book she'd been reading.

Lefleur glanced at it and recognized it as a health book from one of the local community colleges.

"What can I do for you?" she asked.

"I need to see Abner Wolfe," he said.

"You mean the creepy guy with the bugs?" She crinkled her face in disgust.

"I beg your pardon?"

"Bugs," she repeated. "I've never seen them, but I hear they're pretty gross."

Lefleur furrowed his brow. "I need to see him, please."

The nurse rolled her eyes before looking at her watch and then at Lefleur. "Well, it's past the normal visiting hours. Our residents are old. They need their sleep."

Lefleur pulled out his police ID and showed it to her. She looked it over, popped her chewing gum, and looked up at him, unimpressed.

"You're a cop. So? Our residents are still old."

"Nurse, Mr. Wolfe called me a couple of times today and made it quite clear that he needed to speak with me." He took back his ID. "Now, I'm sure you wouldn't mind if I spoke with him, especially if the conversation might involve the nation's security?"

The nurse snorted a laugh. "I couldn't care less." She leaned forward, resting her face in her hands. "This country can go to hell, as far as I'm concerned. I just need to do twenty hours at this place so I can get my practicals out of the way and get my degree."

Lefleur leaned in close. "Then you won't mind if I call Professor Davison in the morning and tell him you were less than cooperative? You know Professor Davison, right? The dean of the community college you're attending. You *do* know he has a direct influence over the Home Health Nursing course, right? The one that issues the certifications?"

Lefleur almost felt bad about bullying the girl to see Wolfe. Almost.

When she realized he was serious, the nurse sat up and shook her head. "No, sir! No need to call him!" She turned to her computer and typed in a few characters. "Mr. Wolfe is in the independent living section. He's in one of the little cottages across the courtyard. I guess the administrators wouldn't let him stay in the main building because of his bugs, but I heard he pays them a butt-load of money to keep them. He's in number forty-five."

Lefleur thanked her and followed her directions to Wolfe's cottage. He took a breath and knocked on the door. It opened a crack, revealing a large man dressed in a white smock peering out at him.

"Yes? Can I help you?"

"I'm Jack Lefleur. Mr. Wolfe wanted to see me?"

The man opened the door wider and stepped back. "Yes, sir, Lieutenant Lefleur. Mr. Wolfe is expecting you."

Lefleur stepped inside the apartment, taking it in. His eyes were immediately drawn to a terrarium set off to one side of the room. Inside, dozens of scorpions crawled around.

"I'll get Mr. Wolfe," the man said. He disappeared into the back.

While he waited, Jack's eyes roamed around the room. An extensive library lined the back wall. The shelves were filled with history books, with one shelf dedicated to the assassination of President Kennedy, as well as books about other well-known assassinations and attempts. But as fascinating as he found the library, Lefleur's attention was drawn back to the scorpion pen. He tried to count how many were in it, but lost count after twenty. They crawled over each other, stopping and raising their tails as if to strike him.

Lefleur had always been repulsed by arachnids—mostly spiders, but there was something about scorpions that made the small hairs on his neck rise in fear. He understood why the people who owned this place didn't want Mr. Wolfe in the main building. If those things ever got out...

"Scorpions are very predatory," said a voice behind Lefleur.

He turned and saw an elderly man walking with a cane. Other than the cane, the man seemed rather robust.

Abner Wolfe, no doubt. The orderly hovered a few feet behind him.

"They lie in wait for their prey and ambush them," Wolfe said, leaning closer. "The smaller ones are deadlier than the larger ones. Did you know that their bodies are composed of two parts: the cephalothorax, which comprises the head, pinchers, and legs, and the metasoma, which encompasses the telson, which contains the stinger?"

"That's very interesting, Mr. Wolfe, but..."

"You know, you look like him. It's the eyes," Wolfe said.

"I look like whom, sir?" Lefleur asked.

"Why, your Uncle Ted. I was telling Ted that just the other day. Wasn't I, Donald?"

Lefleur looked at Wolfe and then at Donald. The orderly looked at Lefleur and shook his head. He pulled him to the side and lowered his voice while Wolfe stared at the scorpion pen.

"Early stages of dementia," Donald said. "He gets conversations mixed up with people in the here and now from people in the past."

Lefleur nodded understanding before turning back to Wolfe.

"I've been keeping up with your career. After you solved that serial killing in Louisiana, you worked that mall bombing and wrapped it up, but not without catching hell from the Feds about it."

"Well...sometimes I don't work and play well with others."

"Then, this last bit of nastiness. Got what, six months' unpaid leave?" Wolfe's brows knitted as he shook his head.

"What's your point, Mister Wolfe?" Lefleur snapped. He'd endured enough public scrutiny from the media. They'd mercilessly dredged up the details surrounding his past, sparing no details when discussing his fiancée's death at the hands of the Louisiana serial killer known as "The Barber." As if that wasn't bad enough, they'd also dissected the battle between him and the Federal authorities during the investigation of the Simmons Pointe Mall two years before. And then they'd had a field day with his arrest of the skinhead, which had gotten him his suspension.

He gritted his teeth. He wasn't going to try to justify his actions again. Not here. Not to Wolfe.

"A bit touchy, aren't we? I expected a thicker skin from someone with Ted Fielding's blood," Wolfe said.

Lefleur remained quiet, waiting to see what else Wolfe would throw at him.

Wolfe saw he was getting to him. He took a deep breath before continuing. "How much do you remember about your uncle?"

"I was twelve when he was killed. I remember some stories he would tell...about his time with the Secret Service, and the Texas Tower shooting." Lefleur smiled slightly. "I got the impression that he loved Texas but hated Lyndon Johnson."

Wolfe's laugh was that of a harsh bark. "That's true. He hated that S.O.B. Although he never said anything in public, Ted said Johnson was behind the killing of Kennedy."

"You said you worked with Uncle Ted...what was your opinion?"

Wolfe snickered and wiped his mouth.

"My opinion doesn't matter...and neither should your uncle's. We were both on the ground in Dallas when the assassination happened, so anything I say would just..." He paused, staring remotely into space. "Did you know he was called 'Dodger?'"

"Who? Who was called 'Dodger?'" Lefleur asked, irritation rising.

"Your Uncle Ted. His Secret Service designation was 'Dodger,'" Wolfe said. "Mine was 'Dauntless.'"

Lefleur raised his eyebrows. "I didn't know that."

"John Kennedy was 'Lancer,' Jackie was 'Lace,' and LBJ was 'Volunteer.' We had code names for all the main players."

"Come to think of it, I do remember him referring to JFK as 'Lancer.'"

"What about Whitman? What did he tell you about Whitman?"

Lefleur gave Wolfe a puzzled look. It took him a moment to reconstruct all they'd spoken about. He didn't remember anyone in the Kennedy or Johnson Administrations with that name.

"I don't remember him talking about anyone he worked with in Washington, Dallas, or Austin..." Lefleur's voice trailed off.

The name suddenly clicked.

"Whitman? Are you talking about Charles Whitman? The Texas Tower sniper?"

"Of course, Charles Whitman. What did Ted tell you about him?"

Lefleur leaned forward on the couch and steepled his fingers before him.

He had heard of Whitman and how he'd killed his wife and mother before taking a footlocker full of weapons to the top of the clock tower on the campus of the University of Texas in Austin and opening fire on the people below, killing and wounding almost fifty of them. Hollywood had even made a movie about it back in the seventies. Kurt Russell had played Whitman.

"Uncle Ted was working with the Austin Police Department then. What year was that, 1966? He said he took photos of the bodies of Whitman and his victims. It seemed that some of the pictures were in Time Magazine or something," Lefleur said. "I was never really clear why he left the Secret Service and went to work for the Austin PD."

"Ted wouldn't work for LBJ and didn't want to be anywhere near the White House. I think he thought Johnson thought that he knew where too many of the bodies were buried back in Texas." Wolfe was quiet for a moment, scratching his scruffy chin as his eyes clouded over as if recalling something painful. "So many deaths," he muttered. He looked at Jack, his eyes clear again. "Ted took a leave of absence and went back to the Austin Police. He worked for them a while before returning to government service."

Wolfe stood quietly, with his head down. Thinking he might have fallen asleep, Lefleur leaned forward and saw that his eyes were moving as if he were trying to decide whether to speak. "He never spoke about a notebook or anything then?"

"No, not that I recall," Lefleur said quietly. "Mr. Wolfe, with yours and my uncle's history, I'm sure we could speak for hours about what you've seen and been a part of, but why am I here? What is of such urgency that it could be life-threatening?"

Wolfe raised his head and locked eyes with Lefleur. The intensity in his gaze was startling.

"Do you remember if your uncle ever mentioned the term...'Mokroye Delo?'"

Lefleur took in the term and let it run through his mind. A light, like a sunbeam breaking through the clouds, pierced his mind, and the memory tumbled forth.

"The night Robert Kennedy was shot. I remember him and my father arguing about what to expect with another Kennedy in office," Lefleur said. "When Kennedy finished his speech and was walking out, I remember hearing the shots and seeing the confusion."

He stood up and walked to the window. "I was a kid. I got scared because I saw that my dad was scared. That's when Uncle Ted stood up and cursed. When he was leaving the room, I heard him say something that sounded like what you just said, 'Mokroye Delo.' What does it mean?"

"'Mokroye Delo' is Russian. It means, 'wet dealings' or, more accurately, 'the spilling of blood.' It refers to the act of murder or assassination," Wolfe said. "Do you remember what I said about scorpions when you first arrived?" Wolfe walked closer to Lefleur and the glass enclosure. Lefleur noted that the effort seemed to tire him. "Probably not. You figured it was the prattling of a crazy old man. But I want you to listen to me and remember. Take notes if you must, because it's important!"

Donald had been standing quietly in the background, holding a wheelchair. He stepped up and positioned it behind Wolfe, who eased into it.

Once seated, Wolfe launched into the entomology and structure of the scorpion, breaking down its parts and their functions. Lefleur listened intently, jotting down notes as he went. He didn't exactly know why, but the urgency with which Wolfe explained it gave him the feeling that this wasn't just important to Wolfe to tell it, but vital that he understood it. When Wolfe finished, he slumped back in his wheelchair, as though exhausted.

"Do you have that? I'm too damn old and tired to go through it again," the old man said.

"Yes, I do," Lefleur assured. "But, how is 'spilling of blood'—this 'Mokroye Delo'—and the entomology of a scorpion related?"

"Assassinations—murder, to be exact. You must involve as few people as possible to get away with it effectively. The smaller the group, the less chance for information to leak out," Wolfe said. "Just like a scorpion is segmented into its smaller parts—each independent of each other—so must a conspiracy be separated into its own smaller parts. Everyone in one segment must do their job without knowing what the other part is doing. But the other part is equally as efficient, and equally as deadly."

Lefleur took in what the man was saying, but his purpose for saying it escaped him. He decided to ignore it and move on.

"Mr. Wolfe, you said something about your safety, my safety, and the nation's safety depending on what you told me. With all due respect, sir, how will learning the entomology of a scorpion keep any of us safe?"

Wolfe took a deep breath, the effort seeming to tax him. "Damn. I should have taken the injections when they were offered. Didn't want to be a guinea pig like Fielding. I don't care if it was supposed to extend my life."

"What are you talking about?" Lefleur asked. Try as he might, he was growing weary of the old man and his lack of ability to stay on subject. "My uncle has been dead for years, and you talk about scorpions and make cryptic statements."

"There are bigger things at hand here, boy. Bigger than just this little town...bigger than history itself. But I know that, once you understand the significance of what I told you, things will fall into place."

"Look, Mr. Wolfe, I really don't..." Lefleur began but was cut off by Wolfe's raised hand.

"'Mokroye Delo'... It's going to happen again...soon. Be prepared when the time comes."

"What do you mean, 'it's going to happen again?'" Lefleur pressed.

Wolfe waved him off, succumbing to a fit of coughing. After a moment, he wiped his mouth.

"One more thing..." Wolfe said, catching his breath.

Donald stepped forward again, this time more forcibly.

"Perhaps that is enough, sir. I mean, it's late, and I'm sure Lieutenant Lefleur has a family to go home—"

Wolfe spoke over Donald and continued.

"You know where Werling's Appliances is, on Ferguson Road?" Lefleur nodded. "Find the setting sun and take ten steps south."

"I don't understand. Why are you being so cryptic?"

"You're a smart guy. You'll figure it out. Just go down from there, and you'll start to understand what 'Mokroye Delo' means."

"Sir!" Donald exclaimed. "That's quite enough. I know Lieutenant Lefleur is too busy to go on some wild goose chase. Come on, you need your rest."

Donald turned Wolfe around and wheeled him toward the bedroom. Wolfe stopped him and turned in his seat, motioning Lefleur over. Wolfe leaned in close.

"Ted said that you would be the one to put everything together. It will be the case of a lifetime!" He locked eyes with Lefleur, his gaze penetrating him to the depth of his soul. "History demands it!" He held his gaze another second longer. "Ted Fielding demands it."

"Mr. Wolfe...Uncle Ted died...over forty years ago. I don't understand how..." Lefleur's words trailed off. He looked at Donald, who gave him a sympathetic look. Lefleur nodded, understanding the unspoken communication between them. Wolfe was remembering the past as if it were yesterday, due to his deteriorating mind.

Donald rolled Wolfe into his room.

"Find the setting sun," Wolfe said again. "Ten paces south."

Lefleur waited until the bedroom door closed before heading toward the front door. He paused to look at the photos on the wall. The pictures displayed a younger Wolfe, posing with various famous and unknown people, including presidents and heads of state Lefleur knew from history books. A framed piece of felt with the Marine Corps insignia and several military medals and recognition pins adorned the wall nearest the desk in the corner.

His eyes scanned the walls, taking in the enormity of life Wolfe had led when his gaze fell on something very familiar.

There was a handwritten copy of a letter from President Kennedy, addressed to Wolfe. It had been framed like the one in his office, and the words were nearly identical, except for who they were addressed to.

"...*Agent Wolfe, I wish to express my personal thanks to you and Agent Fielding for your professionalism in handling my security during our recent visit to Berlin.*"

Lefleur finished reading it, even though he knew the words by heart.

He glanced down and saw a slick black and white image in a scrolled gold frame sitting on an end table by the phone. Lefleur picked it up and recognized the three men in the picture. His eyes fell to a date that had been scribbled in the corner:

June 26, 1963

The photo was taken of a large group. Taking in the people and how they were dressed, Lefleur assumed the picture was taken somewhere foreign. In the center of the photo, President John F. Kennedy was smiling and fresh-faced, shaking hands and waving at someone in the crowd.

Flanked on his right side was Wolfe, eyes alert, watching the throng of people and their outstretched hands as they tried to touch the charismatic Chief Executive.

And in the foreground of the photo was a man Lefleur hadn't seen in over four decades:

His uncle, Ted Fielding.

He knew it was his uncle, despite the sunglasses shielding his eyes. He regarded the photographer as if he might have been a potential threat. His face was unsmiling, his expression grim.

Lefleur remembered watching that same look overcome Uncle Ted whenever he was confronted with a circumstance or situation that required his total concentration.

He replaced the photo and glanced back at the closed bedroom door before leaving.

Driving home, Jack replayed Wolfe's words in his mind.
"*Find the setting sun and go ten paces south.*"

The phrase seemed ridiculous, yet something about it, the way he was so emphatic about it, made him anxious for the following evening.

Jack sat on the edge of his bed, thinking about what Wolfe had said. He pulled his laptop from under the nightstand and logged on.

He thought back on one thing Wolfe had said: *"So many deaths."*

He typed *"deaths of witnesses involved in the Kennedy assassination"* into the search bar and watched it populate the page.

The list was quite long and covered nearly a decade and a half. Many of the deaths were 'unexplained' or 'mysterious,' while others were listed as unsolved homicides and suicides.

The first name on the list was Karyn Kupcinet. A few days before the assassination, Kupcinet attempted to make a long-distance call from Los Angeles. The operator heard her yelling into the phone that President Kennedy was going to be killed.

Her body was found on November 30, 1963, eight days after the assassination. Kupcinet had been dead for two days, strangled to death. Some researchers believed she was killed to keep her father, a prominent journalist, from talking.

Grant Stockdale was next. A friend of Kennedy, he plunged to his death off the thirteenth floor of a building in Miami on December 3, less than two weeks after the assassination. Although some said he was depressed about JFK's death, he left no suicide note and spoke with a friend the day before his death, saying that he believed the same assassins who killed Kennedy were going to come after him.

Gary Underhill, Mary Sherman, Davie Ferrie; the list went on and on. Friends, witnesses, hangers-on—all these people ended up dead, and the only connection between the victims was that they had been a part, even peripherally, of the assassination.

Jack leaned back in his chair, rubbing his chin. He thought about the toll the assassination had taken on his family. Ted Fielding had been tasked to protect the President and had failed. He died a little over a decade later, and after what Jack had read, Ted seemed as much of a victim of what he'd come to call "The Kennedy Curse" as everyone else on the list.

Logging off, Jack lay down in his bed.

But sleep escaped him as thoughts of death and snipers ran through his mind.

CHAPTER FOUR

After a morning that dragged with the mundane task of daily paperwork, Lefleur grabbed his fedora and coat and headed for the door. He'd decided that he would head out to Werling's Appliances and check out the area to see for himself if there was any validity to Wolfe's claim.

He was stopped by Dominick Gray, the chief of police, before he made the elevator.

"Lieutenant Lefleur, I was just coming to see you," Chief Gray said. "We need to talk in your office."

Lefleur escorted the chief back into his office and sat behind his desk.

Gray began without a preamble. "I'm planning on making some changes in your division. We will be shuffling some people around, and some assignments will change."

"How will that affect my investigators, exactly?" Lefleur asked.

"Specifically, you will lose three of your people from Special Crimes. They will be moved to the Domestic Violence section."

Lefleur felt as if he'd been punched in the gut.

"Chief, we just got this unit working how we wanted it. Everybody knows what to expect from one another. With everything going on, I need more people, not less." Lefleur fought the irritation rising in his chest. "I mean, how can I be expected to run a squad when..."

"You won't be running the squad," Gray said bluntly.

It took a few seconds for the chief's words to sink in before he reacted.

"I beg your pardon?"

"We're promoting Peterson and putting him in charge of your section. The memo has already been drafted. It goes into effect at the first of the month."

Lefleur put his fingers to his lips as he struggled to control his words. "And where does this leave me?"

"We're moving you to administrative duties...and demoting you to sergeant." Though the chief's tone displayed regret, his eyes spoke of the opposite. "You'll handle the court's paperwork and walk the criminal cases to the prosecutor's office."

"You can't demote me. Lieutenant is a merit rank. I earned it," Lefleur argued. "You try and bust me, and the Police Union will be all over you with grievances and lawsuits!"

"I already spoke to the union board," Gray said, keeping his tone even. "They're willing to accept my recommendation. They sided with me and said they would handle any heat you might want to bring."

Lefleur couldn't believe what he was hearing.

"The situation is this, Jack," Gray said. "I didn't want to take you back after your last suspension. You know I petitioned the Board of Safety to have you fired and they ignored my recommendation, taking into account all the cases you had worked, your dedication to duty, all that crap." He leaned forward and picked up the paperweight with Jack's uncle's badge inside. "Then you go and bust some guy's balls at a bar." He sat back in the chair. "The union's position is that it comes down to dollars and cents. It has shelled out a hell of a lot of money to pay attorneys to defend you in lawsuits and has had to pay out hundreds of man-hours to the union reps that have had to defend you in Internal Affairs cases. They feel that you're getting to be too much of a liability for them to keep covering. After the conversation I had with Deputy Chief Trumball about the other night at the bar and Prosecutor Borders' scathing ass-chewing he gave about you to the press, in the best interest of the department, I am removing you from the limelight, and by that, I am taking away your right to work extra jobs while in uniform and tucking you away someplace where you can't do the department any more harm."

"But I have rights, Chief. Just because you don't like me, doesn't give you the right to..."

"Right to what? Make personnel changes? Decide who can work part-time jobs? Who the hell do you think you are, Lefleur?" Gray asked. "Do you have any idea the heat I have had to endure from the mayor, the Civil Rights Coalition, and the citizen groups who want answers to why you still have a job? They see you as a bully—nothing more than a badge-heavy thug. In this day and age of modern policing, I'm not sure you fit in anymore." Gray leaned back in the chair and straightened his suit. "I can't fire you outright since I don't have the grounds...yet. But I sure can put enough pressure on you that you'll want to go on your own." He stood up and straightened his coat. "I think you understand where I'm coming from."

He tossed the paperweight into the air and caught it. Looking around Lefleur's office, he waved an encompassing hand. "I expect you to start moving some of your crap out of here soon." He dropped the heavy weight back on Lefleur's desk. As he walked out, he threw a thumb toward Lefleur's fedora and coat.

"And get rid of that stuff, will ya? You might think you look like Dick Tracy, but you just look pitiful, and it embarrasses me to see you at a scene wearing it. This is the twenty-first century, remember, not the 1950s!"

His gaze fell to his office phone, and Lefleur grabbed the receiver, dialing the union office.

"This is Jack Lefleur. I need to talk to whoever is in charge."

The voice on the other end became muffled, as though the speaker had placed their hand over the receiver. But even muffled, he could make out, "It's Lefleur. What should I tell him?" After a brief interchange, a new voice came over the phone. "Sergeant Lefleur."

Hot tears sprang to Lefleur's eyes at how they addressed him by his lowered rank, even though he had just found out himself.

"I've been advised to refer all inquiries from you to the union attorney's office," the speaker continued. "Hold please, and I'll transfer you."

There was a click, then the call rang once and went to voicemail. Lefleur was about to launch into a tirade that would melt the receiver, but thought better of it and hung up.

He sat back in his chair. He dropped his head to his chest and sighed deeply. Rubbing his forehead, he looked up at just the wrong moment. Through the window, he saw Gray shaking Peterson's hand and patting him on the shoulder. Ricky laughed at something Gray said, then turned and saw Lefleur sitting in his office. He covered the laugh with his hand and made a quick exit, following the chief out.

Lefleur felt as if all the strength had drained from his limbs. He gripped the arms of the chair tight enough to cause his knuckles to go white and took a deep breath, forcing himself to relax. After his heart attack two years ago, he knew overstressing himself would only hurt him. After all the stress he'd endured from his suspension, he didn't need to add any more.

Desperate for peace, he prayed—something he hadn't done since his divorce. After a few minutes of quiet communion with God, he felt his heart rate slow and his breathing return to normal.

Flexing his fingers to get the blood circulating again, he rose stiffly from his chair and gently removed the trench coat and fedora from the rack. Situating the hat on his head, the brim tugged down at an angle above his right eyebrow, he pulled on the coat as he walked out the bureau's door.

Only this time, he took the stairs.

Werling's Appliances on Ferguson Road was in an older part of the city. The building, built in the 1940s, was originally a haberdashery and men's store, selling double-breasted suits and stylish hats for the soldiers returning home from World War II. It had changed hands over the years, each a different type of business to keep up with the changing times. It had been Werling's since the late 1950s, selling and servicing the most modern appliances.

Lefleur had only been to the business once in his tenure with the Camp Simmons Police Department. He had responded to a burglary alarm early one morning. It had snowed that night, and the freshly packed snow showed signs of footprints around the windows, at the rear of the building. A window had been forced, which caused the alarm to sound. Lefleur and a K-9 officer had tracked the footprints in the snow across the field behind the business until they reached an access road. The footprints had ended, and tire tracks from a vehicle had been found leaving the area. Reaching a dead end, Lefleur had returned to the business, met with the manager, and taken the attempted burglary report.

Jack pulled into the store's parking lot and looked west. The sun was three-quarters of the way down in the sky. Going into the store, he found the manager on duty. He showed him his badge and identified himself.

"What can I do for you, officer?" the manager asked.

"This might sound a little crazy, but I need to walk around the back of your building at sunset. I'm…looking for something."

"Looking for what?"

"To be honest, I don't really know. It's kind of complicated, and if anything's found, I'll discuss it with you before I do anything about it."

The man scratched his head and looked at Jack, bewildered.

"Look. I have no freakin' idea what you're talking about. But, as long as you don't disturb my customers or damage my property, I don't think looking around would hurt anything."

"I appreciate your cooperation. I won't bother anyone or anything if it is at all possible. I'll just look around."

"Ok. Suit yourself," the manager said.

Jack stepped around the back of the building and turned toward the sun.

He reached inside his pants pocket and pulled out a worn, aluminum Mardi Gras doubloon he'd carried around for years. Flipping it across his fingers, the simple motions helped him concentrate and focus on the task at hand.

He turned back and tried to orient himself with where the sun was setting and decide from where he was to take the ten paces.

After four attempts, he grew frustrated and sat down heavily on a wrought metal bench behind the building, far enough away that the employees who smoked could sit and light one up. He thought about calling and asking Wolfe for more directions and a starting point to walk from, but after what had happened in the office right before he left, he wasn't in the mood to talk to the crazy old man again.

Jack stood up and turned toward the field, resting one foot on the bench.

Then, it dawned on him.

On the back of the bench was an iron representation of a setting sun, its rays spread out as it slipped below the horizon.

Jack ran his fingers over the image and then rapped the top of the bench. Turning around, he paced off ten steps. This put him about thirty feet from the bench. Marking the spot, he ran back to his car and removed the shovel from the trunk. He thought about telling the manager but decided to wait to see if it was worth the effort.

Once he returned, he pushed the shovel into the hard-packed ground. The earth broke up in chunks as he chiseled away.

He had dug down a little over a foot when the blade hit something substantial. He probed it with the tip of the blade, trying to find the outline. The sun had gone down, and darkness had descended on the area. Jack returned to the car and pulled his rechargeable flashlight from its holder. As he was returning, the store manager stopped him.

"Hey! I thought we agreed that you wouldn't damage my property?" The man followed Jack to the dig site. "Find something?"

"Yes, but I'm not exactly sure what it is yet."

"Need some more light?"

"Sure," Jack said.

The manager hurried back inside the store. Jack rounded the building and was instantly blinded by the outdoor spotlights mounted on each corner of the building. It bathed the entire area in light, reaching out to where Jack was digging and beyond.

"We normally don't use this part of the lot for much. Maybe an office barbeque now and again," the manager said. "About a month ago, the owner had us remove a concrete slab that had been there since the 80s. Heck, he even had that bench brought in for us to sit on during our breaks."

Jack dug a little further to establish the perimeters of the area, and once they were fixed, he began digging with his hands.

His fingers slid inside the eye holes of a smiling human skull.

Repelling in horror, he backed away, rubbing his fingers on his pants. He reached into his pocket, pulled out his cell phone, and dialed 911.

"This is Lieutenant Jack Lefleur," he said without preamble—and without using his title of demotion. "I need a couple of uniform cars, a detective, and a crime scene sent to my location. I have a body."

Jack provided the dispatcher with the address and hung up. Returning to his car, he pulled out a roll of yellow crime scene tape and began securing the area as the first sirens could be heard approaching in the distance.

"Oh, my Lord," the store manager said. "I'd better call the owner."

CHAPTER FIVE

The sun pierced the eastern sky as the final bits of bones were excavated from the ground. After the manager had signed permission for them to dig and a judge had been disturbed at home to sign a search warrant, Lefleur handed the paperwork to the lead crime scene investigator and stayed out of their way.

The excavation revealed the skeletal remains of a male, about six feet tall, wearing what was left of a black suit, white shirt, tie, black socks, and lace-up shoes. From the condition of the body and clothes, he appeared to have been buried there for at least forty or fifty years. A cursory examination of the body was unable to determine the cause of death, mainly because of the dirt packed hard around the skeleton, but circumstances seemed to add up to a murder.

Lefleur sipped another lukewarm cup of coffee. He had lost count of the cups he'd had, and at this point, the caffeine proved ineffective. He rubbed his hand across his face as Peterson pulled up on the scene. Taking a deep breath, he stepped over to the coffee carafe and poured another cup for himself and one for Peterson. He made his way over to the car just as Peterson was exiting.

"So, your 'confidential informant' panned you? I take it this isn't another monkey carcass?" Peterson asked with a nervous laugh. He accepted the cup of coffee and ducked his head.

Lefleur had called Peterson the evening before to inform him of the find since he was now his commander. Not yet wanting to drag Wolfe's name into the case, he'd just told Pete that he'd gotten a call from a confidential informant.

"No, sir," Lefleur said, acknowledging his friend's promotion. "Looks like we have a human body. I'd say he's been down forty-five, fifty years."

Peterson moved in front of Lefleur, creating a private area between them. "Jack, I'm sorry. I had no idea that Gray was going to pull that stunt. I..."

"Ricky, you told me before that you were looking for a promotion," Lefleur said tensely.

"You're right. I did, but not in our section and not over you. I thought they might kick me back to Uniform. I respect you too much to go over your head or behind your back." Peterson gave him an earnest look. "In fact, I told Gray that if that was my only option for promotion, then I didn't want it. He told me that this was it. So, I told him I had to think about it."

Lefleur nodded absently, hearing but not listening to Peterson. He hooked a thumb over his shoulder. "The victim has no ID on him. We're gonna get him to the lab and see if we can work on finding out who he is."

Peterson nodded and glanced around the scene. "So, they're about ready to wrap it up then?" he asked, sipping his coffee.

"Probably another half hour. Just waiting on the hearse to transport the body to the morgue." Lefleur glanced over Peterson's shoulder and saw the blacked-out SUV approaching. "And...there they are."

Lefleur and Peterson watched the hearse back up to the scene. Two of the funeral directors stepped to the rear and pulled out a stretcher, draped with a heavy, black, plastic body bag.

Lefleur noticed a car pulled up and park well outside of the crime scene tape. From this distance, he couldn't tell who the new arrival was.

"I'm going to go talk to Abn—my informant. I want to know how he knew this guy was buried there and if he can tell me who he is," Lefleur said.

"Okay," Peterson said, catching Lefleur's reluctance to name his source. He poured his cold coffee onto the grass. "Let me know what I can do to help."

Lefleur nodded as Peterson got back into his car and started it. "And, Jack?"

Lefleur glanced at him. "Yes, sir?"

"You call me 'sir' again, and I'll deck you!"

He closed the door, and Lefleur stepped away from the car, raising his coffee cup in a salute.

Herman Cannon walked up to the edge of the scene and took a couple of photos, nodding to Lefleur. "Lieutenant Lefleur."

"Herman," Lefleur said. He didn't feel now was the time or place to tell Cannon about his demotion, even though he considered Herman a friend.

"So, what's going on here?"

"Received a tip on a buried body," Lefleur answered. "Found a male. Looks like he's been buried for maybe thirty or forty years, near as I can determine."

Cannon jotted down a few notes. "You think you can fill me in on what the autopsy determines?"

"Sure, Herman. I'll see if I can get you something before your next deadline," Lefleur said. "Tell Carol I said 'hello.'"

The store manager walked over to Lefleur and leaned against one of the squad cars. "We've never had anything as exciting as this happen here."

"Were you able to get in touch with the owner?" Lefleur asked.

"I left a message with Mr. Wolfe's nurse," the manager said. "He's in a rest home and isn't in the best of health."

"Mr. Wolfe?" Lefleur asked, "Abner Wolfe?"

"Yes, that's him. Why? Do you know him?"

"How long has he owned this place?" Lefleur asked, avoiding the question.

"Since the late 70s, I believe," the manager said with a shrug. "I don't know the details, but apparently, he threw so much money at Mr. Werling–the owner, at that time–that he sold the business and retired. Wolfe kept the name 'Werling's' on the store and paid yearly royalties to Werling for the name, until Mr. Werling died in 2002."

"We should be wrapping it up here soon," Lefleur said, purposely changing the subject. "I appreciate your cooperation." The manager shook Lefleur's hand and headed back inside the business.

Lefleur's mind now raced with a barrage of new questions, and there was only one person who could answer them.

CHAPTER SIX

Lefleur pulled up in front of the Three Oaks nursing home and parked. Striding by the nurses' station, he walked directly to Wolfe's apartment. When he arrived, he banged on the door and was surprised when it slowly opened. He drew his pistol and peered inside before stepping through the door. A dim yellow glow lit the room. Lefleur pulled out a flashlight and it shone across the room.

In the corner, he saw that the terrarium had been overturned. He heard a noise like a crab skittering across the tile and looked down to see a large scorpion run across his shoe and scurry out the door. Startled, he jumped back and saw several more scorpions emerging from the corners of the room and climbing on the furniture. As he darted the light back and forth, the flashlight beam caught a pair of slippers sticking out from behind the couch. Moving slowly across the room while pushing the arachnids away with his toes, Lefleur looked over the couch to see Wolfe lying face up on the floor. Several scorpions ran across his chest, scared away by the blinding light, and disappeared under the furniture. Wolfe's hands and face were covered with puncture wounds and were noticeably swollen.

Abner Wolfe appeared to have been dead for hours.

Lefleur did a quick search of the apartment for any other victims. When he found none, he walked outside, pulled his cell phone from his pocket, and dialed 911 to request a team to the scene. Closing the door, he returned to the nurses' station and notified them of the situation.

"Do you know where Donald Sloan might be?" Lefleur asked. The nurse flipped through a logbook and ran her finger down until it stopped on a line three-quarters of the way down.

"Mr. Sloan should be with Mr. Wolfe. He wasn't in the adjoining bedroom?"

"I didn't see him in there."

"That's odd. He's always with Mr. Wolfe. He's Donald's only client."

At the sound of sirens approaching, Lefleur walked out to meet the team. A large black SUV, driven by workers with the coroner's office, pulled in shortly behind them. Lefleur guided the paramedics and coroner's people to the apartment and stopped them at the door.

"Watch yourselves. There are scorpions all over inside," he warned.

With raised brows, the paramedics nodded and looked around before carefully stepping inside. Several scorpions scattered toward the door, finding the heel of Lefleur's boot before getting too far.

The paramedics acted quickly, but it only took a moment to verify that Wolfe was dead. Walking back into the hall, they shook their heads, and the coroner's office personnel took their place. Although Wolfe was old, he wasn't frail or a lightweight. The coroner's people struggled, enlisting Lefleur's help in getting him into the body bag.

Hoisting the awkward load through the apartment, Lefleur bumped up against a closet door and heard a moan. He set down his end of the bag and pulled the door open to find Donald Sloan. The man was semi-conscious on the closet floor, and his head lolled back and forth.

"Get the paramedics back in here!" Lefleur yelled out the open apartment door. The paramedics scrambled back inside to assess Sloan. Once they knew it was safe to do so, they removed him from the closet and laid him on a gurney. They palpated his arms and legs and found several insect stings.

"Severe overdose of venom," the lead medic said. "I'm going to have to stabilize him before we can move him."

After setting up an IV, the paramedics loaded him into the ambulance and sped toward St. Michael's Hospital.

Spotting the sergeant in charge of the scene, Lefleur approached her.

"I want that man under guard 24/7," he said. "Have the hospital call me when he's conscious."

"That's going to tie up our manpower," Sergeant Janice Randall argued. "I'll have to clear it through my command."

"Do it," Lefleur said. "With Wolfe dead, Sloan is the only person who might know what happened to him and where that fifty-year-old body came from."

Randall nodded, pulled out her phone, and dialed her boss. Lefleur was focused on the scene until he heard her say, "Lieutenant Lefleur requested it." When he glanced at her, she cupped her hand around the speaker and walked off, continuing to speak. Once she'd hung up, she spoke into her lapel mic and then walked back to Lefleur.

"I didn't realize you'd been demoted, Jack," Randall said.

"I didn't know it was public knowledge yet."

Randall smiled and shook her head. "This administration sucks. What did the union have to say about it?"

"The union has gone along with their recommendation," Lefleur said bitterly. "They didn't honor my merit rank of Lieutenant. If I could afford an attorney, I would sue them over it."

"Look, Jack," Randall began, "I know you've had your problems, but those of us who know you know you're a good cop. The department and union doing this to you shows that they can do it to any of us, based on their personal bias, not on merit."

"I appreciate that, Janice," Lefleur said. "What about guard duty?"

"Well, Chief Trumbull wasn't too happy about it, but he approved it. I have Devlin, from the southeast quadrant, heading that way."

Lefleur took one last look around the apartment with Randall. Walking into the bedroom, Randall checked the closet while Jack looked at Wolfe's dresser. He spotted a pin that he recognized. He had seen the same pin in the Lucite globe, which sat on his own desk.

A Secret Service pin, specifically issued for a historic event. Noting that a letter hanging on Wolfe's wall was identical to the one Uncle Ted had received, Lefleur figured it had to do with the Germany assignment.

He yawned long and deep.

"I can take care of this, you know," Randall said. "I mean, you did train me right."

"Thanks," Lefleur said. "It's been a long twenty-eight hours. I'm going to head home and grab a nap."

"We've got this, Jack. Go home and see your family."

Jack snorted. A nod was his only response.

CHAPTER SEVEN

Six hours later, Lefleur was awakened by his phone buzzing. He had turned the ringer off to try and get some rest, but the constant buzzing told him he had several voicemails waiting for his attention. He picked up the phone and scrolled through the numbers. He recognized one from dispatch, another was from a private number, and two were "1-800" numbers. He listened to the messages and got out of bed. After showering and shaving, he dressed and headed out the door.

Lefleur flipped back through the messages. Dispatch had called to let him know that Donald Sloan was still in a coma. The "800" numbers were bill collectors—figures. The fourth message was from Lara Reubans, the county Coroner and Chief Pathologist. They usually passed each other in court, but Lefleur never paid her much attention. However, he'd heard enough about her from the people who'd dealt with her to know that she was green and inexperienced but had a keen intellect and a drive to learn the truth. She had been tasked to conduct the autopsies on both Abner Wolfe and the John Doe corpse they'd found behind the appliance store. The autopsies were due to start at ten AM, and Lefleur was intent on being there.

He stepped outside and was pelted by a steady rain. Pulling on his trench coat and fedora, he drove downtown, thinking about Wolfe. When he walked into the office, Reubans was there, along with a younger man who, he assumed, was her assistant. Before he could make his presence known, he heard creaking in the corner of the room. A man dressed in maintenance overalls was climbing down from a ladder. He was older than Jack, tall, with a thick, greying moustache. The man glanced at him, tossed him a nod, and packed up his toolbox.

"I changed the ballasts in both lights, so you should be good," the mechanic said. Lefleur detected a slight Southern accent but couldn't pinpoint where he might be from.

Reubans waved at him and glanced over her shoulder. "Thank you," she said. "They need to keep you around. This is the first time I've called in a problem and seen it fixed within twenty-four hours."

He flicked a couple of fingers to her in a salute and walked past Lefleur, who stepped to the side to let him pass.

For a brief instant, the two men locked eyes, and Lefleur was momentarily drawn in by the intensity of the other man's stare. Then, he was gone.

"I heard you dressed the part of a detective. Dick Tracy, right? You must be Jack Lefleur," Reubans said.

"That would be me."

Lefleur took the time to notice Reubans since he figured he would spend some time with her on this case.

She was about average height, an inch or two shorter than his five-nine. She was a little thick in the middle, and her hair, which Lefleur could barely make out since it was tucked away in a hairnet, had streaks of gray. He would put her on the low side of forty, and she had a hint of wrinkles around her eyes. He noted a wedding ring forming a slight bulge under her latex glove.

"By the way, good job on that Mendez case," Reubans commended him. "You sure made my job easier."

"I wish the prosecutor shared your opinion," Lefleur said bitterly. "He made sure the entire town knew he wasn't happy with my caliber of work."

"Typical political posturing," Reubans said with an eye roll.

She stood next to the cold metal drainage table, where Wolfe's naked body lay. Wrapped around Wolfe's toe was a small tag documenting his name, weight, height, location, and case number. A thick stream of saliva had run out of his mouth and dried on the side of his face. The smell of decomposition and death hung thick in the air. His chest had been opened, and his organs were in separate scales positioned around the table.

Reubens was garbed in a face mask with a splash screen, surgical gown, and latex gloves. "I would shake your hand, but-" She held her gloved hands up for him to see the blood covering them.

"No problem," Lefleur said. He tugged the trench coat off and shook the rain from his fedora, hanging it on a coat rack. He pulled on a pair of gloves and pulled out a digital camera. After adjusting the camera, he looked in the old man's chest cavity. "Find anything interesting?"

"Well," Reubans began, "I can tell you that he probably died of an overdose of venom. There are numerous punctures from what look like arachnid stings."

"He was stung by scorpions. They were crawling all over him when we found him," Lefleur volunteered.

"Where was he, in the desert or something?" Reubans asked with a raised brow.

"No. For some reason, he collected them in an aquarium in his apartment."

"Seems like a strange creature to keep as a pet. Any snakes or spiders?"

"No," Lefleur answered. "Just the scorpions. They seem to hold some significance for him." He didn't think to mention the biology lesson Wolfe had given him about the entomology of the scorpion.

Lefleur walked around the table, taking numerous photos of Wolfe and his injuries. He zoomed in on the puncture marks, noting the symmetry of the wounds and how the barbed tails had struck the flesh, leaving small holes resembling question marks, which were surrounded by puffiness and reddish skin discoloration.

"I'll run a toxicology report on his blood to confirm the cause of death," Reubans said. "I'm going to be looking for the levels of Chlorotoxin and Maurotoxin in his bloodstream."

Lefleur zoomed in on Wolfe's face and neck and took a few more photos. Taking the camera from his eye, he leaned closer and looked at Wolfe's neck.

"Do you have a magnifying glass?" he asked Reubans.

Reubans reached up and swung a large swivel light around to him. The light surrounded a magnifier in the center of it. Lefleur brought the fixture close to Wolfe's neck.

"Look at this," he said. Reubans stepped beside him and craned her neck to where he was looking.

On the jugular was a small puncture with a minute drop of blood crusted around it. The mark differed from the scorpion stings covering the old man's body. Lefleur took several photos of the mark.

Reubans picked up a cotton swab and dipped it in sterile water before swabbing the area around the puncture. Slipping it into a storage tube, she sealed it and noted the time and location from which it was taken.

"I've found other injection sites on the leg and shoulder. These correspond with insulin and dementia medications. But in the jugular? I don't know of any medication that is injected directly into the jugular." Reubans' eyes narrowed as she mulled over their latest finding. "Something's going on here. I'm starting to believe Wolfe's death was not an accident."

Lefleur pointed to the skeletal body on the other table. "Wolfe told me where that guy was buried." He snapped a couple of photos of the body. "I'd be really interested to learn whatever you find out about him."

"Hey, Paul?" Reubans called out. Her assistant walked in from the outer office. "Can you finish the post on Mr. Wolfe?"

"Sure," Paul answered. He pulled on a clean gown and latex gloves and surveyed the process of the autopsy. Producing a scalpel, he picked up where she had stopped.

Reubans changed gloves and did a cursory examination of the mysterious corpse. She walked around the body, speaking into an omnidirectional microphone positioned midway down the table, dictating notes and observations. "For identification purposes, I'll call him 'John Doe.' So, tell me, Jack. What do you see?"

Lefleur reached into his pocket and pulled out his worn aluminum doubloon, flipping it over his fingers while he walked around the body.

"I agree with your observations. The victim looks to be a male, about six-foot, six-foot one. From the heavy bone structure, he appeared to be a good-sized man." Lefleur leaned down and looked at his shoes, removing a tape measure from his pocket. "Shoe size, approximately twelve. Barely any wear on the soles." He looked at Reubans. "These shoes were new at the time he wore them."

He continued up the body, pausing at the top shirt pocket. His brow creased as he pulled out a silver pocket watch.

"Watch still intact. Looks like it stopped at eleven fourteen." He stopped at the skull and turned it gently so it wouldn't dislodge from the spinal column.

"Looks like I found the cause of death," Lefleur said. He pointed to a small hole on the back left side of the skull. "Gunshot, it looks like."

He looked closely and took several photos. "From the diameter of the hole, I would say either a .22 or 32. caliber." He looked around the front of the head and neck area. "I'll bet it's still in his skull."

"I agree with you," Reubans said. She looked at the man's death smile. "Teeth are in good shape. Should be able to get a match if his dental records are on file."

Reubans positioned an X-ray machine over John Doe's skull and took several photos inside and outside of his mouth. The images were transmitted to her laptop, where she downloaded them to a file.

She began undressing the body while Lefleur took a photo of the man's tie. He noted the tiepin had a symbol resembling a Marine Corps emblem. Reubens slipped the tie and pin off the body and placed them into a paper bag. Opening his coat, she found a faded label, still readable, that listed "Wolf and Desseur" as the manufacturer. The coat was a forty-six regular.

"'Wolf and Desseur?' Any relation to our recently deceased Mr. Wolfe?" she asked.

"No," Lefleur answered. "Different spelling. 'Wolf and Desseur' was a clothing store based in Fort Wayne. I understand they went out of business in the late '60s after a huge fire. The suit had to come from that era."

As Reubans continued to remove the suit from the body, she patted the right coat pocket and found a crushed cigarette package. Handing it to Lefleur, he straightened it and saw the brand was Chesterfields. Two crumbled cigarettes were inside.

Moving down the body, Lefleur found a bulge inside the victim's right sock. When he removed it, Lefleur saw it was a small, cylinder-shaped, wrapped in a worn and crumbling rag. He unraveled the item to find that it was a jar, a little smaller than a pickle jar. A dark-stained cloth was stuffed inside the container, and the lid had been tightly sealed. He took numerous photos before picking it up. When he shook it, something moved around inside. He looked at Reubans for direction.

"Don't open it just yet. Whatever is inside may crumble away if it's exposed to the air after all this time," she warned. "Let's preserve it, and we'll open it in a more controlled environment."

Lefleur nodded and placed the jar in a bag, setting it on the floor. As Reubans continued, she checked the man's pockets.

"Twenty-four dollars in bills, a pocketknife..." she rattled off, trusting that the video camera was documenting every part of the autopsy. She picked up the pocket watch again and held it to the light. "Looks like a stylized 'B' on the back. Could be an initial." She turned the man on his side and checked the back pockets. "No wallet or ID."

Next, she removed the man's shoes.

"Well, this guy is just full of surprises," she said. She slowly removed his left sock, and a metal object fell out.

It was small, about the size of a tie pin. It was faded, but Lefleur could make out the space in the middle, separating the red side from the white. It resembled a "Good Conduct" medal issued by the Army. He took several photos, twisting it in the light to pick up the highlights. He continued to turn it around and examined it slowly.

"What?" Reubans asked.

"I've seen something like this."

"Why in the world would this guy hide something like that in his sock?"

"I don't know," he answered. "Maybe he wanted to keep it a secret..."

JUNE 6, 1968

Nine-year-old Jack Lefleur sat on the living room floor, his attention riveted on his uncle, Ted Fielding. Jack had rushed through dinner to spend the evening listening to his uncle tell his stories.

Uncle Ted held up a letter and an envelope to the lamp and read the words on the paper:

"Agent Fielding, I wish to express my personal thanks to you and Agent Wolfe for your professionalism in handling the security during the recent state visit to Berlin. Knowing that men of your caliber are willing to defend me, and in extension, my family with your lives, if need be, is gratifying, and I am honored and humbled by yours and your families' sacrifice. God bless you. I am privileged to have you on my team. With gratitude..." *Fielding paused before he finished reading.* "John F Kennedy, President of the United States."

He put the letter down.

"Wow!" *Jack exclaimed.* "A real letter from President Kennedy." *He reached out and touched the paper hesitantly, lightly passing his fingers over the words as though revering a part of history. He looked at the envelope and saw his uncle's name scrolled across the front and the postmark, dated June 30, 1963.*

"The President's secretary told my supervisor that the President personally wrote the letters to me and my partner, Abe," *Fielding explained.* "I remember my boss saying that we should feel fortunate. 'It's not every day the Leader of the Free World takes the time to lick a stamp and mail you a thank you letter.'"

The letter was placed next to Fielding's Secret Service badge, as well as a lapel pin he'd worn in Dallas on the day Kennedy was assassinated.

"Wow," Jack said quietly. "Uncle Ted, do you think I can be a cop like you someday? I mean, I really wanted to be Batman, but since we're not rich, I don't think I can afford all the neat gadgets he has. But, with all the stuff you've done, you're way cooler than he is."

Fielding scooped Jack up and hugged him tightly.

"Jack, since I don't have a family of my own, I'm going to teach you everything I can about how to be a good investigator."

A lightbulb went off in Lefleur's head. "I know where I've seen this before. It's a Secret Service pin worn by agents assigned to the presidential detail. My uncle had one similar. It's on my desk, in a paperweight."

"Seriously?" Reubans asked. "How would this guy get his hands on a Secret Service pin, unless..."

"...he WAS Secret Service," Lefleur completed the thought. "He would have had to have been on the detail between '60 and '69. That means, he would have worked under Nixon, Johnson...and Kennedy."

"The Secret Service would have to have records on all their agents, especially ones that may have come up missing," Reubans said, catching Lefleur's excitement.

"The question that begs to be answered, then," Lefleur began, "is how a Secret Service agent from the mid-1960s ended up dead in a small Indiana town. And how did Abner Wolfe know he was buried here?"

CHAPTER EIGHT

Reubans placed the jar in an enclosed box with a vented hood. She'd donned a full-body containment suit–complete with an independent oxygen supply–and had made Lefleur put one on, too, though both had their hoods off.

"I don't know what's in this jar, but I'm determined to make sure no toxins or other nasty critters are inside waiting to ambush us," Reubans said. She introduced cyanoacrylate to the container, resting it on a sheet of aluminum foil.

"Our John Doe may be skeletal, but I'm willing to bet he's the one who sealed the jar. If he was, his fingerprints are probably still on the glass or the lid."

While she waited for the chemical to adhere to the glass, Reubans collected the bullet from inside the skull. She dropped the spent projectile in Lefleur's gloved hand.

"Looks like you were right," she said. "Small caliber."

Lefleur bagged the bullet, and they returned to the fuming box. A white mist had descended on the glass, coating it with a chemical residue. Reubans reached in and held the jar to the light, turning it. "There we go." She pointed to three full, milky white, latent fingerprints on the glass and one on the lid. Lefleur snapped pictures before adding powder to the prints to enhance the ridges and make them more visible. Once the excess powder was removed, he lifted them with transparent tape. "One looks really small. Like a partial, or the side of a finger."

"If this guy has been dead as long as it appears he has, he died long before AFIS, and he probably won't be in that file. Our best bet is to run the prints through the federal and military databases, which means we have to go through the Pentagon," Lefleur said.

"All right." Reubans picked up the jar. "Let's see if we can open this thing."

She turned on the overhead vent fan. It rattled and creaked before kicking on and began sucking out the dust and residue from the superglue. Reubans put her hood on, fastening it tight, and motioned for Lefleur to do the same. Once they were ready, she picked up a wide-mouthed wrench and carefully placed the jaws around the outside of the lid. She crimped it slightly and slowly began turning it. The lid stayed closed, but after a long, tedious moment, it began to turn. Once it loosened, she removed the wrench and turned it by hand. When it came off, it left a rubber gasket around the inside of the threads. The gasket crumbled with age and fell away.

Inside, the jar was stuffed with a thick, white cloth, tinted dark brown.

"Looks like dried blood," Reubans observed. She prodded the cloth with a pair of tongs. "Something's wrapped inside it." She held the jar out to Lefleur. "Be my guest."

Locking eyes with Reubans, Lefleur reached into the jar, slowly removed the cloth, and set it on the examination table. He unwound it and pulled the item out.

It was a jagged, flat piece of bone.

"Looks like it came from a skull," Reubans said. She picked the piece up and turned it one way, then another. She ran her finger along one of the edges, noting a semicircular hole. "Smooth, not jagged like the other part of the bone."

"Like a gunshot wound," Lefleur offered.

"That's what I'm thinking." Reubans' brow furrowed in concentration as Lefleur laid the bone piece down and took photos of it from several angles.

When he picked up the jar, something rattled inside it. He reached in and pulled out a rifled slug. It was tainted dark, with dark rivets that filled the ridges. "Looks like a high-powered rifle slug. Maybe a .30 caliber or a .308."

"I think it's safe to take off our suits," Reubans said. They shed the protective garments and slipped on a fresh set of gloves.

Reubans set her laptop on the table and brought up a schematic of the human skull. She looked at the bone piece and held it to the computer screen. After turning it a few times, she settled in on one position.

"From the orientation, I would have to think that it came from the right parietal region," she commented. "From the position of the smooth hole, I would say that this person was shot in the right front of their head."

"And the caliber would have been enough to blow this section of the skull away," Lefleur said. He motioned to the dark, stained rag. "There must have still been brain matter attached and a lot of blood to have soaked the rag so thoroughly."

Reubans picked up the stiff cloth and held it in front of her. "The blood and brain matter have dried, so we have a decent shot at getting a DNA sample from this."

"Wouldn't it have degraded after all this time?"

"Somewhat," Reubans said, "but if the sample was dried and then stored in this sealed jar to keep out the air, it could have slowed the degradation. And once he was buried, the coolness of the ground would have kept it at a constant temperature over the years."

Lefleur looked over at John Doe. "It still doesn't tell us who he is and why he was carrying around a baby food jar stuffed with a piece of skull and a spent round."

"No." Reubans sighed. "It doesn't. It just adds more questions."

As she continued to unwrap the cloth, she noticed something partially obscured by the blood on it. "What does that look like to you? Letters?"

Lefleur held the cloth up to the light and agreed.

"Looks like a P, something, something, maybe a K, something, something, something, D. The second word looks like something, something, S, something, something, T, something, L. That's the best I can do right now," Reubans said.

Lefleur examined it closely and picked out an L after the K in the first word. He wrote the letters on a piece of paper.

P_ _ K L _ _ _..._ _ S_ _ T _ L

"A name of a hotel, maybe," he said. "Maybe a place he stayed. He may have used the linens from the room he was staying in to wrap the skull piece in."

"Going to be tough finding a hotel from that time in history, much less where it is. We don't even know if the place still exists."

"Well, let's assume he's a local—or at least from an area between here and Fort Wayne. That will be a good starting point." Lefleur walked around the table, rolling his doubloon around his fingers.

"Let's just take it one thing at a time," he said. "First, we have a man buried in a suit from the 1960s. He has no ID or wallet; the only thing to identify him is a lapel pin, signifying that he may have worked with the Secret Service at some point, and a Marine Corps tie pin, meaning he had served in the Corps. In his sock, we find a jar containing a blood-soaked towel that has a piece of skull inside it and a spent rifle slug."

"Well, we do have possible fingerprints, dental X-rays, and I'm pretty sure I can get DNA from his bone marrow," Reubans said.

"Ok, we have that," Lefleur agreed. "We also have a possible name on the towel to research and see if we can find where the towel came from."

"So, we have several avenues to pursue," Reubans said. "I'll work on DNA and dental records and have ballistics check the spent slugs while you check out any possible hotels and see if the Secret Service can tell us anything."

"All right, Lefleur agreed. "I'll get back with you in a couple of days to tell you what I've discovered. If you find anything, call me."

"Will do." Reubans turned back to the skeleton, eager to uncover the secrets within.

CHAPTER NINE

Lefleur returned to the Special Crimes Unit and made his way to the cubicle that now served as his office.

He decided to call Herman Cannon and give him an abbreviated briefing on what they had found so far, leaving out any mention of the items found on the John Doe's person.

"Jack, I know you're not telling me everything," Cannon said, his tone impatient.

"I'm telling you all I can right now, Herman." Lefleur hoped he'd let it go. "You just have to trust me to give you the full story when the time's right. For now, just put it down as a cold case we're investigating."

"All right, Jack. I'll trust you, but don't leave me hanging too long."

Cannon hung up, leaving Lefleur alone with his thoughts. He picked up the Lucite paperweight that held the Secret Service pin and compared it to the digital photo of the pin found in John Doe's sock. Other than the wear and tear of age, they appeared identical.

Looking at the pile of worksheets and case logs from the other detectives, Lefleur knew that, as the admin sergeant, his job was to upload their paperwork into the investigative database. But that knowledge did nothing for his lack of enthusiasm about having to do so. He missed being actively involved in the cases that desperately needed his attention.

Sighing, he began separating the sheets by detective but quickly bored of the chore. Abandoning the task, Lefleur scrolled through his phone in search of a contact: Clarence Pierson, Indianapolis office of the Secret Service.

Lefleur had met him two years ago, when a bomb destroyed much of the Simmons Pointe Mall. Since then, he and Clarence had cultivated a friendship and would get together with their families from time to time.

The memory of his family rushed back to him, and the loss of it was bitter in his mouth.

"Don't go there, Jack," he admonished himself. "Focus on the task."

He drummed his fingertips on the desktop as the line rang.

"Hey Jack, what's going on?" Pierson's voice was cheery—a stark contrast to Lefleur's current mood.

"I need your help, Clarence," Lefleur said. He gave Pierson a rundown of the past few days' events, including his meeting with Wolfe and the discovery of the pin in John Doe's sock. "If I email you a photo of this pin and the information we have on the body, will you check him out and let me know what you find?"

"Sure," Pierson agreed. "I can contact the chief archivist at the Treasury Department and see if he can research that specific time, and maybe even the particular assignment, that the pin was worn."

"I also have some latent prints we lifted and dental records on this guy. If he worked with the feds, I'm sure there are records somewhere that might help us find out who he is." Lefleur thought about telling Pierson about the skull piece and the partially deciphered towel, but he held that in reserve.

"If you can, please research two other agents and their length of service. An Abner Wolfe and a Theodore Michael Fielding," Lefleur added.

"Send me what you've got, and I'll see what I can do."

"Great," Lefleur said, his mood lifting a bit. "I'll get it to you directly. Thanks, Clarence. I owe you one."

Lefleur hung up and sent the information in an email to Pierson.

"Lefleur!" Dominick Gray's voice bellowed across the squad room.

"Chief." His enthusiasm vanished.

"What are you doing?" Chief Gray walked up to Lefleur and shoved a finger in his face. "I thought I told you you're to do nothing but admin duties. What's this I hear about you being out on a cold case last night?"

"I received a call from a source who gave me information on where to find a body," Lefleur said, working to keep his cool. "Once we got him to the morgue, we found some questions that needed to be answered. But when I went back to talk to my source, he was dead."

Lefleur spent the next ten minutes filling Gray in on what they had taken from John Doe's body and what the findings could mean. Gray stood with his arms crossed and listened intently before stopping him.

"Assign the case to someone else." Gray's tone was not to be argued with.

Lefleur felt as though he'd been hit in the stomach.

"Sir, I was specifically asked by my uncle's partner to investigate this case. I do not feel comfortable betraying his trust in me," he argued.

"You just said that he was dead," Gray said. "He won't care if you work on it or not. Give it to someone else."

"No." He looked Gray square in the eyes, his jaw tense.

Gray blinked first.

"What did you say, Sergeant?"

"I said no, sir," Lefleur repeated. "I have wondered what happened to my uncle since I was a kid. And then, out of the blue, Abner Wolfe tells me things I never knew about him. Wolfe and my uncle were involved in one of the most historic and controversial events that ever happened in this country. I know that era. I've studied it because of my uncle's involvement in it. If anyone can figure out why this secret service agent ended up dead in Indiana, it would be me."

"You're too personally involved," Gray said.

"You're damn right, I am," Lefleur snapped. "And that's what's going to keep me focused on the case. I won't take the chance of taking shortcuts or not following up on a lead. I want to know the hows and whys. I *need* to know. For Abner Wolfe's and my uncle's sakes."

"This case means a lot to you?" Gray asked, frowning.

"More than any other case I've ever worked," Lefleur confirmed. "Come on, Chief. You have to admit that it is an intriguing case. I mean, when was the last time this department worked a case this cold and had the actual possibility of solving it?"

"If you waste all this time and can't solve it, what then?"

"I don't understand," Lefleur said, creasing his brow. "What do you want me to say? There are never any guarantees when it comes to a case, you know that. But...if nothing comes of it, then..." He took a deep breath. "I will resign."

"You don't mean that," Gray scoffed.

"Yes, sir, I do," Lefleur said pointedly.

"Alright, Jack," Grey said, "I'll agree to your terms. This case had better be earth-shattering, or you are gone."

Gray walked out, leaving Lefleur to ponder the weight of his decision.

Lefleur cursed himself for allowing Grey to put him in that position and then cursed Grey for pushing him there. He couldn't let this case spin out of control with "what ifs" and "maybes."

He sat back in his chair, wondering what had pushed him toward poor choices and bad judgment calls. Was it his feelings toward his uncle? Or was it his failed marriage? He sighed and tossed a pen onto his desk. It could even be the difficulties he'd experienced in this job. Maybe he just subconsciously needed to solve "the big case," once again, like the "Barber Killer" in Baton Rouge, or the Mall Bomber two years ago, to get back into everyone's good graces.

If he was honest with himself, he knew there might not be anything to this case. Maybe he was reading more into it than he should.

He was a good detective; he knew that. But he was concerned that being good wasn't going to be good enough this time.

He hadn't noticed that his ears were ringing louder than normal. The tinnitus he suffered from, stemming back almost twenty years before when a gun went off next to his head while fighting with a drunk, was usually at its loudest when he was alone. He felt a tightness in his chest and immediately flashed back to the heart attack he'd suffered on the job a couple of years back.

Lefleur hadn't realized he'd taken the doubloon from his pocket until he felt the aluminum coin slip from his fingers and fall to the floor.

"Oh, grow the hell up," he said. "You've got a job to do."

He picked it up and looked at the file on his desk. Concentrating on the case at hand, he was determined to answer all the questions before him, consequences be damned.

He placed a call to the local Marine Corps recruiting station to find out who he should direct his inquiry to, as well as DNA, dental records, and fingerprints. Once he'd contacted the appropriate division, he sent them off and picked the phone up again. The phone rang while he was still holding it. He glanced at the number and saw it was Dave Nance, his money manager and stockbroker.

Lefleur had invested more than half of his pension into the select stocks, anticipating that when he retired, which he planned to do in three years, the investments would help supplement his income. Money had been set aside in savings accounts for the children's college funds, but had been tied into the investments as well.

"Dave," Lefleur began, "what's the good news?"

The line was quiet for a long second before Nance spoke up. "Jack—I wish there *was* some good news for you."

"What's going on?" His throat tightened. How much more bad news could one man take?

"I'll be straight with you, Jack. Your stocks have taken a dive," Nance said. "As of right now, you're worth about half of what you were yesterday."

The impact of his words hit him like a throat punch.

"Don't tell me that," he stammered. "Wh-what happened?"

"It's the market, reacting to the presidential campaign," Nance explained. "President Kelly's actions at the G-20 Summit have left the market shaky and unsure about how the Middle East will react to his perceived insult."

"I was depending on those stocks for my retirement," Lefleur said, as though expecting Nance to retract what he'd just said. "What am I supposed to do now?"

"Just ride it out and hope for the best," Nance said. "I'm sorry I don't have better news."

After Nance had hung up, Lefleur tapped the phone against his lip and thought. It seemed like the hits just kept coming. He couldn't catch a break.

Lefleur wrote the last figure down on the scratch pad. He'd been figuring numbers ever since he'd received the phone call from Nance. If he closed out all his stocks, he would have to pay a ten percent penalty and would only be able to live off his savings for about four years. Running his hands through his thinning hair, he glanced at his ringing phone. Almost afraid that it would be more bad news, he saw that it was from Doctor Reubans.

"Please tell me you have something good," Lefleur pleaded.

"Well," Reubans began, "I don't have anything bad, so I hope that works for you."

Lefleur chuckled. He could hear Reubans rustling papers.

"I've identified the calibers of the slug recovered from John Doe's head and the round found in the jar. The slug is from a thirty-two, and, as you guessed, the rifle slug is a .30 caliber. Seven point six two millimeter."

"Any luck on identifying John Doe?"

"I haven't gotten anything back on the DNA yet, but," Reubans said, "believe it or not, I got a hit on one of the prints we lifted from the jar."

"Just one?"

"Yes. The one that looked like a partial print, or the side of a finger? Turns out it's a child's print, so I don't think it's going to be our guy," Reubans said. "So, I had to be creative. I considered the approximate age of the child that would be fed baby food at the time, which is anywhere from one year old to eighteen months, and from there I postulated what their approximate age would be now, which would be in their mid-fifties." Reubans held up a printout. "The print came back to a Matthew Booker, a convicted rapist who is only fifty-three years old. That would mean that he was only a toddler during the sixties."

"You said he was a convicted rapist?" Lefleur confirmed.

"Yes. He's currently incarcerated at the correctional facility in Plainfield."

"Give me his information," Lefleur said. "I think I need to take a trip to Plainfield."

It was another full day before Lefleur could make the trip to see Booker. In the meantime, DNA results had returned. The sample taken from John Doe had family traits that, when compared, were found in Booker's DNA, which meant they had been directly related—a sibling or parent, perhaps.

Lefleur ran all the information he could find on Matthew Booker. After getting permission to drive the hour and a half to the state facility, he called ahead and set up an interview with the inmate.

Plainfield Indiana Correctional Facility was located a short distance from Indianapolis. Lefleur pulled into the double-fenced enclosure and checked in with the administrative offices. After signing in and locking up his pistol, he was escorted to the cell block interview room. Two wooden chairs and a Formica-covered table were in the center of the room. He set his file folder on the table just as the door opened and a man in a blue denim work suit walked in. He wore handcuffs attached to a waist chain and shackles around his ankles.

Time had not been kind to Booker. He was in his mid-fifties, with stringy grey hair and glasses. His large stomach pressed against the front of his blue denim shirt, stretching the buttons almost to the point of popping. He was unshaven. His face was red with broken capillaries, indicating that he'd been a heavy drinker. There was a slight yellow color to his complexion, displaying early signs of Cirrhosis. Lefleur assumed the man was probably suffering from hypertension and liver disease.

Ironically, his going to prison for the next twenty years would probably extend his life.

Lefleur stood up and extended his hand. "Lieut—I'm sorry—Sergeant Jack Lefleur, Camp Simmons Police Department."

The man ignored his hand and sat down. "Matt Booker. I've never been in Camp Simmons," he said coldly. "If you think you got a case on me, Sergeant, you can shove it up your—"

"Let me explain why I'm here," Lefleur interrupted. He opened the file folder he'd brought and pulled out Matt Booker's criminal history and fingerprint card. Next, he withdrew a color photo of the fingerprint he'd lifted from the glass jar. "A few days ago, I was told where to find a body buried behind a building—"

"Hey, man," Booker loudly interrupted, pushing away from the table. "I told you I ain't never been to Camp Simmons, and I sure as hell ain't killed no one there."

Lefleur stared him down, unwavering. "Sit down, please, Mr. Booker. I am not here to accuse you of murder. When this person was murdered, you were a child."

This revelation intrigued the inmate. He was quiet for a moment as if what Lefleur had said had meant something to him.

"Then what are you here for?" Booker asked. He stood defiantly, still seething.

"I'm hoping you can shed some light on who the victim might be," Lefleur said. "Please sit down, Mr. Booker."

Booker hesitated for another few seconds and then re-settled himself in the chair. "Tell me."

"The victim was a tall man, wearing a suit from the early nineteen-sixties." Lefleur slid a photo of the body of John Doe toward Booker. "When we checked his body, we found some interesting items on his person."

Lefleur showed him the photos of the baby food jar with the rag inside. "There was a piece of skull inside that jar." He pulled out the photo of the pin found in the man's sock. "This is a Secret Service pin." He finally laid the photo of the tie pin before him. "And this tie pin had the Marine Corps emblem on it."

Booker looked at the photos, and Lefleur noted that his hands were shaking before he buried his face in them. Lefleur gave the man a few minutes to collect himself before he placed his hand on Booker's shoulder. Booker shook it off and raised his head, wiping his face with his shirt sleeve.

"My father was Harold Booker. He was a Marine." Booker stared off into the corner as he spoke. "I was only about a year old when he left us, but when I was around fifteen, I asked my mom what happened to my dad. I guess Mom finally felt I was old enough to know the truth, so she told me. One day, my dad, who was supposed to be on active duty, showed up at our house in Fort Wayne. My mom was surprised to see him until she noticed he was in a new suit, not his Marine greens or dress blues. She said that he told her he was involved in something that he couldn't talk about and was afraid that, if he did, bad things could happen to him or our family." Booker wiped his nose and roughly ran the back of his hands across his eyes, embarrassed by the tears clouding his vision. "Mom said they fought, and Dad snatched a baby food jar from my hands and poured the food in the sink. He washed out the jar and stuffed something inside it. Mom said whatever it was, it was bloody."

"Do you know when this was?" Lefleur asked.

"My mom said it was sometime in November. The day after President Kennedy was killed, I think. Mom said he was gone the next morning."

"What happened then?" Lefleur's interest was piqued.

"Nothing. We never saw my dad again." Booker's jaw twitched. "Some Marine officers came by a week or so later, asking Mom some questions. She told them what Dad had told her. They left, and we never heard anything else after that." Booker paused. "One other thing happened. Mom said the banks were all closed on the day of Kennedy's funeral."

"That would have been, I believe, November 25," Lefleur said.

"Ok, whatever," Booker said, brushing him off. "The day after the funeral, Mom was cleaning up my room. Tucked under my pillow was an envelope with twenty-five thousand dollars inside. She figured Dad must have hidden it there the night before he disappeared."

"The Marines listed him as AWOL?" Lefleur asked.

"Yeah. He skipped out on his post without telling anyone."

"Do you know what his duty assignment was?"

Booker scratched his chin and thought for a minute. "I think he was like the base doctor or something. He didn't show up for work, and they started a search for him."

"So, your dad was a doctor?" Lefleur double-checked. "Do you know what base he was assigned?"

"Somewhere in North Carolina."

"Lejeune?"

"I think so," Booker said, shrugging.

"Do you know what kind of doctor he was?"

"I'm not sure. I think he might have been a shrink."

"Do you know if your father ever worked for the Secret Service?"

"No." Booker scratched his chin. "Mom did say that he did some work for President Johnson."

Lefleur noted on his notepad where he could find out more about Harold Booker.

"There's only one sure way to know if this is your father's body," he said. "I need to get a DNA sample from you."

"Don't you have my DNA on file from when I was transferred here?" Booker questioned.

"Yes, but to get an accurate comparison, I need to get one directly from you." Lefleur pulled out a sterile cotton swab from a plastic tube. "It's standard procedure."

"How do I know you aren't trying to pull a fast one? Just trying to get my DNA because you've got something cooking and trying to cross me up?" Booker eyed him suspiciously.

"Look, Booker, I've read your record. You're in here for the next forty years. You did this to yourself, and you should make peace with that. I don't need to bury you anymore, but maybe I can help you get a small amount of peace by finding out what happened to your father and who killed him," Lefleur said. "Isn't that worth a little spit on a cotton swab?"

Lefleur looked hard at Booker and saw a twinge of pain in the man's eyes. After a moment, Booker nodded and opened his mouth. Lefleur ran the cotton against the inside of Booker's cheek and sealed the swab inside the container. Standing up, he gathered his files. "As soon as I find out his identity, I'll let you know." He walked to the door and knocked, summoning the guard.

"I have a sister. Gale Travers. She lives in Huntington. If you find out your John Doe is my dad, will you let her know too?"

"I will," Lefleur assured him.

Booker reached his hand out as far as he could with the handcuffs on. Lefleur crossed back to him and took his hand, shaking it.

"Thank you," Booker said.

Lefleur pulled out of the prison, his sample secured in an envelope on the seat next to him. He pulled onto Moon Road and aimed his car back toward Camp Simmons, hope blossoming in his chest.

He didn't pay any attention to the late-model Ford parked just down the road from the prison or how it pulled out and followed him back to Camp Simmons.

CHAPTER TEN

Travis Goldstein, security supervisor at the Hancock Arms Hotel in downtown Cincinnati, jotted down a note about two lights being out on the fifteenth floor before continuing down the east stairway toward the fourteenth. He checked his watch; it was three-twenty-one. Once he emerged, he checked the housekeeping closets and elevator foyer, looking for anything out of the ordinary. He spotted a food tray outside room fourteen eleven and scooped it up. He opened the maintenance hallway door and deposited the tray near the elevator so Room Service could pick it up on their hourly pass.

Arriving at the north stairway, Goldstein pushed the door and took a deep breath before slowly descending. He paused on the landing, halfway between the fourteenth and twelfth floors. The halfway point was the thirteenth.

It had been here that Goldstein had found the body of Jeffery Bailey just two weeks before. He'd always considered Bailey an odd employee but had valued his work ethic and thoroughness on the job.

Bailey had acknowledged the call to respond to a room but never showed up. When he hadn't answered a radio check, a search began, involving security, maintenance, and housekeeping. Since Bailey's routine was well known, it hadn't taken Goldstein long to find him.

He hadn't been dead for too long. Goldstein had called for an ambulance and the police and then stood guard until they arrived. Mel Keebler had joined him and stood by his side until emergency crews had arrived and loaded Bailey onto the stretcher. Goldstein had removed the pass key and keyring from Bailey's pockets and handed them to Walter Hudson, the hotel manager. That night, Hudson had looked more haggard than his fifty-five years.

"If you don't mind, I'd like to ride along in the ambulance so I can complete my investigation," Goldstein had petitioned Keebler, who'd agreed.

They'd ridden in silence until Goldstein looked at Bailey's feet, protruding out from under the sheet.

"Did you notice Bailey's shoe?"

Keebler had leaned down and examined Bailey's footwear. "The toe's all torn up," he'd observed. "Looks like it's stubbed all to hell."

"He must have tripped on the stairs and fallen," Goldstein had said, looking at the body. "That would explain the damage to his face and skull."

Goldstein had continued to look around Bailey's body. His service in Afghanistan, with the 82nd Airborne, had hardened him to death—even the deaths of his friends. He'd looked at Bailey's fingers and seen the blood-stained notepad in one hand and his pen in the other. He'd pried the pad from his stiff fingers and flipped through the blood-soaked pages.

Goldstein had always thought Bailey was intense about his habit of meticulously documenting his walk-downs, making note of some of the most banal and useless bits of information in his reports.

Armed with this knowledge, the last page Bailey had written on stuck out to him as odd. He'd turned back to the page before and seen where Bailey had documented entering the fourteenth-floor stairway with the notation, "03:46-N Stwl." He'd known that it meant Bailey had been at the north stairwell.

He'd turned back to the last page Bailey had written on. The scrawl wasn't written on a line, and there was no time indicated. Instead, it was scribbled sideways across the page. Though blood had obscured some of the letters, the words looked like, "UMBEN...ROSLELLT...SUTE."

Returning to the manager's office, Goldstein had sipped a cup of coffee with Hudson and Sergeant Dannie Byrnes of the Cincinnati Police Department. Byrnes, an attractive woman in her mid-thirties, had read through Bailey's employment file and jotted down several notes.

"So, there were no indications that he was missing until he didn't show up at the guest's room, correct?" Byrnes had asked.

"Yes," Goldstein had said. "That was at 03:48 hours."

"Did he respond to the call?"

"Yeah, he said 'I Copy.' I responded and took care of the problem, and when he didn't show up, I called for him on the radio. After I called, the operator called, and then maintenance. When he still didn't answer, we started a search." Goldstein had sat quietly for a long minute, capturing Byrnes's attention.

"Is there something wrong?"

"He said, 'I copy,'" Goldstein had said, his voice distant as he stared at the wall. "Bailey never said, 'I copy.' He once told me that sounded stupid, and he would never answer like that."

"How would he answer, then?" Byrnes had asked.

"He always said, 'I'm Clear,' or 'Understood.'"

"You know," Hudson had said, "now that you mention it, that sounds right. He would always answer differently from everyone else. That's how I knew it was Bailey responding."

Byrnes had written a note.

"Is that significant?" Hudson had asked.

"You tell me," Byrnes had said, glancing his way. "When you have a death investigation, any change or deviation, no matter how small, can be significant."

Byrnes had pulled out the notebook Goldstein had given her, which was lying on Bailey's chest. She had bagged it in a plastic bag, along with the pen. She'd held it out for Goldstein to see.

"I think he was trying to write something when he fell," Goldstein said. "I don't know what it means, but apparently, it was important enough for him to use his last amount of strength to get it down.

Byrnes had looked at the writing.

"UMBEN...ROSLELLT...SUTE."

"Any ideas?" she'd asked.

Both Goldstein and Hudson had shaken their heads.

"Where can I make a copy of this?" Byrnes had asked.

Hudson had taken her to the copier in the front office, and Byrnes had made several copies of the note, handing them to Hudson and Goldstein. "Show these around to some of the employees. Maybe they can decipher it," she'd said, walking toward the door.

"Are you ready for the Democratic National Convention?" she'd asked.

"I hope so," Hudson had wearily replied. "We have three weeks to make sure everything is in order. The Secret Service has been here and inspected the property. We're keeping the Roosevelt Suite unoccupied until the final inspection the day before and the President is moved in." He'd rubbed a hand through his unkempt hair. "We're going to be hard-pressed to provide security, now that we're a guard short," he'd said absently, his gaze drifting to Byrnes. "We can handle it. We've handled similar things before."

"I don't doubt it," Byrnes had said. She'd handed Hudson and Goldstein her business card. "If there is anything I can do, please feel free to call me."

As Byrnes had walked out the front door, Hudson had turned toward Goldstein. "I'm going to get a shower and shave in the break room." Since he was always on-call, Hudson kept an extra suit and a change of clothes in a locker. "I'll get everyone together this morning and explain what happened and what we know."

"Understood, sir," Goldstein had said. He'd looked at the clock. The day shift should be here any minute, but Goldstein had known he wouldn't be going home anytime soon. He'd left the lobby and walked down the grand stairway toward the security office, located on the hotel's ground floor.

Two hours later, Hudson had stood before the assembled employees and told them about the accident. There'd been some tears and gasps of surprise, but as professionals, they'd absorbed it and continued with their jobs.

Goldstein had gone home for a fitful rest when the day shift security officer relieved him.

Now, two weeks had elapsed, and everyone had slipped back into their routine, except for Goldstein. He still felt compelled to pause on the landing, reflecting on that night.

Zack, one of the newer maintenance guys, sat in the break room, eating a Snickers and sipping a Coke, listening to Goldstein and Mel Keebler discuss politics. He didn't care who won the upcoming elections. As far as he was concerned, he was more concerned about the convention and when the President would be staying there.

"...so, the Secret Service does one more inspection the day before the President is scheduled to deliver his acceptance speech. Once they're on the property, only Maintenance, Security, and the housekeeping supervisor are allowed on the two floors above and below the Roosevelt Suite on twenty-two. The floors will be swept with bomb dogs and metal detectors, and anyone going on the floor will be searched."

"Will anyone be staying on those upper and lower floors?" Keebler asked.

"Yes. But only the President's staff and security detail," Goldstein answered.

"Anything new on Bailey's death?"

"No. Toxicology came back. No drugs or alcohol in his system." Goldstein shifted on his feet. "Hate to say it, but it looks like he was just clumsy."

"And no one has any idea what that scribbling in his notebook meant?"

"Well, seeing that the first word might have been 'Uber' misspelled, Detective Byrnes said that she contacted Uber to see if Bailey had any connection to them, but they couldn't find any record of him working for them or being a passenger," Goldstein said. "So, they have no clue."

Zack crumpled up the wrapper and finished his drink.

"Hey, Mel. I'm going to take care of the lights out in eighteen twelve and twenty-one sixteen," he said. Keebler nodded and went back to eating his frozen dinner.

"Zachary 'Zack' Weller," the name he was going by on this assignment, knew exactly what Bailey meant when he'd scribbled his last words. The poor lug had tried to spell out, "Under Roosevelt's Suite," alluding to what he had told him right before he died.

With the copies of keys in hand, Zack pushed his cart down the hall on the twenty-first floor, stopping at twenty-one sixteen. Using Bailey's pass card, he tripped the lock and opened the door. Glancing around once more, he slipped inside the room.

The room located directly under room twenty-two sixteen, The Roosevelt Suite, where the President would be staying during the convention.

He pushed the cart to the center and looked at the ceiling. He looked for the four small Xs he'd drawn on the corners of the ceiling when he was in the room a week prior. Once he located them, he reached into the top drawer of the cart and removed the drill and twelve-inch bit. He set up the ladder and went into the bathroom, turning on the water to mask the sound of the drill.

The bit reached the floor of the room above, slightly penetrating the carpet. Backing the bit out, Zack shined a penlight inside the hole, making sure it was clear all the way up. Satisfied, he stepped off the ladder and retrieved a small, lined box. He reached inside and removed a slender aluminum tube. The tube was as long as his index finger, with the metal thinner on the top and bottom. He slid the tube into the hole, the width just wide enough to hold it snugly. Pushing it gently with a rod, being cautious not to drop or rupture the thin metal, he felt it touch the floor above. Once it was seated, he slowly backed the rod out. Opening a drawer on the cart, he removed a radio-controlled detonator and checked it to make sure the extended plunger worked. Satisfied, he affixed the detonator, centering the plunger on the bottom of the tube. Once in place, he spackled over the hole and touched it up with some paint, sketching a small X back on the new paint.

He continued to the other three holes, repeating the action in each one. Vacuuming up the dust from the drilling, he looked up, satisfied that his work would pass any inspection.

He unscrewed two of the light bulbs from the lamps and placed a thin remote-control plunger, designed to pierce the specially designed bulbs he'd brought with him. This was so he could remotely blow the bulbs when Housekeeping checked the room. Once the housekeeper saw the lights were out, Zack would use that as an excuse to enter the room and change the bulbs.

But in the event the housekeepers were kept away from the room, he had a backup plan to get in. The plunger would rupture the filament, causing it to spark and smoke. The smoke would activate the smoke detector, and the alarm would sound.

Loudly.

Zack had altered the alarm siren so that it was ten times the normal volume of the other smoke detectors. Once the alarm was activated, it would be so loud and annoying that the Secret Service agents assigned to the floor would have to call maintenance to have it silenced. Zack would take the call and enter the room to reset the alarm.

And once inside, he would activate the remotes that would pierce the aluminum tubes into the ceiling.

Once the tubes were ruptured, the contents would go upward, soaking into the carpet above.

The Sarin gas, which was inside the tube, would then efficiently kill everyone in the room above.

The Roosevelt Suite. The room where the President would be staying during the national convention.

Zack took the service elevator to the twenty-eighth floor. Pushing the cart off, he pulled out a 305-foot length of rope. He removed the set of keys he'd made from the wax impressions of Bailey's set and found the one that opened the door at the end of the service hall. He picked up the coils of rope, removed a drill and bracket from the cart, and walked up two flights to the thirtieth floor. Once there, he found the auxiliary trash chute and unlocked the heavy metal door. He shined his flashlight down the hole, the light disappearing about ten floors down.

He drilled into the top of the chute and mounted the bracket in place, then attached the rope to the bracket and reached inside his work jacket, adjusting another remote-control device. Wrapping it around the coils of rope, he touched the remote in his pocket. The device opened, allowing the rope to unravel and drop free.

The rope would fall the length of the trash chute, over three hundred feet down, and land in the dumpster in the basement.

Zack's escape route was secured.

Getting back into the elevator, he pressed the button for the eighteenth floor and continued to room eighteen-twelve, confident his planning would go unnoticed...and the President would be dead.

CHAPTER ELEVEN

Santiago Mendez tossed back the fourth scotch of the night. The coarse liquor had ceased burning his throat. Instead, it dulled his ever-depleted senses and lowered his inhibitions. Javier Santos and Miguel Gonzales quietly sipped from their glasses; their eyes fixed on their companion.

His brother's trial had not gone as they had hoped. Sandoval had received a twenty-year sentence, which meant he wouldn't be released for at least ten years. But in the family business of running drugs, guns, and prostitution, ten years can be a lifetime

"Bastard Lefleur," he mumbled, "got my brother twenty years. Then, he files a charge against me?"

He slammed the shot glass down hard on the table. The Camp Simmons Gazette was open to the story Herman Cannon had written about Abner Wolfe and the unidentified body that Lefleur had uncovered. Seeing Lefleur's name enraged Mendez. He crumpled the paper and tossed it into the fireplace. "He should have to endure his own twenty years of hell. I'd make sure his body wouldn't be found for a few decades."

Santos nursed his drink. He had come by Mendez's house to discuss the operations of several bars that the Mendez Corporation owned. When the discussion turned to Lefleur, the liquor started to flow.

He glanced up at Mendez. Even though the man's eyes were bloodshot and lidded, Santos could see the blood lust there: the same blood lust he displayed when he executed an enemy or beat down a prostitute.

"Lefleur has to go. He went after my family, and he will pay for it." Mendez's grip tightened around his glass as though it were Lefleur's throat.

"All talk," Santos mumbled. "You can't touch this guy. If you do, they'll have the full weight of the police department come down on you."

"Oh, there are ways," Mendez said. "I know people on the inside who can bring him down." He slowly stood and walked over to Santos, a Scotch bottle in hand. "And I don't think you want to insult me in my own house."

"I'm not insulting you, Santiago," Santos said. "I just said that the man's hard to touch."

"What you mean, you 'know people on the inside,' Santiago?" Gonzales asked, pouring himself another drink. "You got someone who can get close to Lefleur without leading it back to you?"

"Si," Mendez said. "With the right leverage, I can bring Lefleur down to his knees, both in his career and life."

"If you can do that," Gonzales said, lifting his glass in a salute, "it would make all our lives easier."

"Give me a few days," Mendez said, taking a long pull off the liquor bottle. "Lefleur will no longer be a problem."

CHAPTER TWELVE

"Lefleur."

"I think you need to come see me about John Doe," Reubans said. "And bring an open mind."

"I'll be right there." Jack hung up and wasted no time jumping into his car. The moment he pulled out of the driveway, his phone rang. It was Pierson, with the Secret Service. Without preamble, he told Lefleur about his findings regarding the body they believed to be Harold Booker.

"Are you absolutely sure?" Lefleur said.

"It's been confirmed by the director of the Archives," Pierson said. "Both the photos you sent are accurate for the time and assignment."

"Thanks, Clarence." A glimmer of an idea began to grow until he knew what he had to do.

Turning around, Lefleur drove toward the Three Oaks Nursing Home. Once he completed his task there, he stopped by the detective bureau before meeting Reubans.

He had a dozen thoughts running through his head by the time he arrived at the coroner's office, foremost being what Pierson had said.

Taking a deep breath to collect his thoughts, Lefleur pushed the door open.

Reubans stood before a large screen with her arms crossed. On the screen was the bloody rag. She glanced over her shoulder at Lefleur and pointed at the image.

"Not only was I able to retrieve live DNA from the cloth, but I think I also deciphered the name on it." She pulled up an image of the letters. Once they were on the screen, she magnified the picture.

Lefleur squinted at the screen, and the letters came into focus.

P—A—R—K—L—A—N—D H—O—S—P—I—T—A—L

"I did a location search. There are three Parkland Hospitals in the US. I then checked to see which ones were in service during the early to mid-sixties," Reubans said. "One in Derry,

New Hampshire, founded in 1984, one in Farmington, Missouri, founded in 1995, and–"

"One in Dallas, Texas, which was in service in 1963. The same hospital that treated President Kennedy, Lee Harvey Oswald, and Jack Ruby," Lefleur said solemnly. His eyes snapped to Reubans. "Could it be... could this John Doe..."

"John Doe is Harold Booker. DNA confirms it." Reubans' smile spoke of her triumph.

"I called and spoke to the director of the National Library for the Marine Corps Archives at Quantico. I asked him to see if he could find a missing person's report on Booker."

"This just opens up more questions," Reubans said. "Why was he AWOL from Camp Lejeune? How did he end up with a bloody rag wrapped with a piece of skull from a hospital in Dallas, a Secret Service designation pin, and a grave in Indiana?"

"I think I may have some of the answers, though I scarcely believe they are true," Lefleur said. "Excuse me for a moment."

He pulled out his phone and dialed Pierson, giving him Booker's information.

"It just so happens that I have the historian on my other line," Pierson said. "Hold on."

Lefleur only had to wait a few minutes before Pierson came back on the phone.

"Good news/bad news, Jack," Pierson began. "The good news is that the historian searched his records and found Wolfe and Fielding. Fielding served from 1959 until 1965, while Wolfe served from 1959 through 1980. The bad news is that he couldn't find 'Harold Booker' in their records."

"You're sure?" Lefleur pressed.

"Up to 2001, each agent had a hard card generated when they were hired that documents their employment and assignments. It was a pretty efficient filing system for the time. There's no Booker."

"Thanks, Clarence. Lefleur hung up and looked at Reubans. "Pierson confirmed that Booker wasn't in the Secret Service."

He pulled the doubloon from his pocket and began pacing. "If I remember my history of the assassination, there were stories about people claiming to be Secret Service Agents, but when they were investigated, none of them were found. Perhaps there is some truth to that theory, and Booker was one of them."

"To be honest with you," Reubans began, "I wasn't born when it happened and haven't given it a thought. Just not something I've ever been interested in."

"I've always had questions about it," Lefleur said. "I was never comfortable with the notion that Oswald was the lone assassin."

"So, you buy into the whole 'Second Gunman' conspiracy theory?"

"I think there are enough questions to warrant another look at the whole thing. Even if we prove it, it will be hard to cut through the static of a thousand websites, each espousing their theories. The Cubans, The CIA, aliens, heck, there's even a theory that Kennedy's own driver turned around and shot him!"

"Well," Reubans said, "let's concentrate on one piece of the puzzle at a time."

"Agreed," Lefleur said. "Right now, we're trying to figure out why Booker ended up dead in my town."

"So," he refocused his mind on the investigation at hand, "Abner Wolfe, who was with the Secret Service with my uncle, knew–"

"You had an uncle who was in the Secret Service?" Reubans asked. "I didn't know that."

"I'm sorry. I thought I told you."

Lefleur told Reubans his uncle's history with the Secret Service and the Austin Police and how he had been involved in JFK's assassination and the Texas Tower Incident.

"Your uncle sounds like Forrest Gump. Except every time he turned up, someone got killed," Reubans said sarcastically.

"He died when I was 12. His death was the push that made me want to go into law enforcement."

"Sounds like he was an extraordinary man," Reubans said.

"He was," Lefleur said. "The way Wolfe talked about him, recalling conversations they had years before, and learning that Uncle Ted talked about me to him... it all just makes me wish I could have known him more."

"Those must have been some interesting times to be alive."

"Yes, they must have been," Lefleur said, standing up. "So, it would make sense that Wolfe, Booker, and my uncle knew one another and were all in Dallas in 1963. However, Booker was supposed to be at Camp Lejeune, working as a base doctor."

Reaching into the bag he'd brought from home he picked up the Lucite paperweight from his desk and placed it next to the photo of the pin they'd retrieved from Booker's sock.

"Both pins were used once, for one security detail," Lefleur said. "The one in the paperweight belonged to my uncle, and as you know, the other was taken off Booker." He then produced a third. "This was taken from a display in Wolfe's house."

Reubans nodded her head in agreement. She walked over to a chalkboard and drew three columns, placing Booker's, Wolfe's, and Fielding's names at the top of each column. Under each one, she wrote "S.S. pin," then, "Dallas, November 22, 1963."

"OK, what else do we have?" she asked, poised and ready to write.

"Under all, put 'US Marine,'" Lefleur said.

She jotted it down.

"Under Booker, put 'Camp Lejeune,' 'skull piece,' and 'Parkland Hospital.'"

In his mind, Lefleur reviewed the conversation he'd had with Wolfe, seeking out anything that might have been significant.

"Wolfe mentioned 'Charles Whitman,' as if that had some significance to my uncle," he said. "Put 'Whitman' under Wolfe and Fielding." Lefleur glanced at the table Wolfe had been lying on. "Also, put 'Scorpion' under Wolfe and Fielding."

"And," Reubans began, "we can put 'murdered' under Wolfe and Booker."

Lefleur was pacing, then stopped. "What? Wolfe was murdered?"

Reubans picked up a report and handed it to Jack. He scanned the paper.

"Three times the amount of venom found in his system, compared to the stings," he said.

"That injection point in the jugular. They shot him up with enough venom to kill three healthy men, much less a frail eighty-four-year-old."

"Donald Sloan, his caretaker, is still in a coma," Lefleur said. "If he pulls through, he may shed some light on who did this. Or, it could have been Sloan himself." Lefleur continued to pace. "Wolfe wanted me to find Booker now, for some reason."

"Regardless of the reason, Booker has brought some fifty-year-old mystery to the surface. And I think the key is the piece of skull." Reubans brought up an image of the skull portion on her screen.

She looked at Lefleur, who studied the image. She superimposed a human skull diagram and fitted the piece to it, as she had done a few days before. "You're the one who believes in the 'Second Gunman' theory," Reubans said, "What do you think this piece of skull proves?"

Lefleur began ticking off the points on his fingers.

"For starters, we have three people wearing Secret Service pins in Dallas on November 22, 1963. Two we know, for sure, were verified agents, while one is an impostor." He held up a second finger. "The impostor was in Dallas. Whether he was in Dealey Plaza at the time, we don't know. But we do know that he was close enough to the President's motorcade to recover a piece of skull, whether from the plaza or from the car itself. He wrapped the piece in a towel from the hospital where the President was taken. His son confirms that he went missing the day after the assassination."

Lefleur pointed at the screen and clicked off a third finger. "The skull piece is the front parietal region of the right side of a person shot in the head." Another finger. "Booker, who was a Captain in the Marine Corps and supposed to be working at Camp Lejeune as a doctor, disappears from Dallas, makes his way to Indiana, where they executed him and buried him in Camp Simmons." Lefleur held up his thumb. "At some point, Abner Wolfe relocated to Camp Simmons, armed with the knowledge of Booker's burial site. He was either told, or he executed Booker himself."

Reubans acknowledged all the points Lefleur had enumerated and stood, staring at the piece of bone that was the key to the whole thing. "If this leads to what I think you are saying...."

Lefleur pointed to the screen. "You said you recovered DNA from the bone and the blood-soaked towel, right?"

"Yes. But without something to compare it to, your theory is just that. A theory," Reubans concluded.

"Maybe we can contact the Kennedy family physician and enlist his help in getting a sample of the family's DNA," Lefleur thought aloud.

"I can try, but I'm sure they're pretty secretive about the family history."

"If we can show that this piece of skull belonged to President Kennedy..."

"Then you can prove your second gunman theory," Reubans said. "This is important to you, isn't it?"

"It's the most important mystery of the twentieth century," Lefleur corrected, arching a brow at her. "Shedding some light on the most sought-after historic secret in the last century would be satisfying, to say the least.

"The internet is rife with theories and opinions about who was involved that day, ranging from the Mafia to time-traveling aliens. If we find the truth, it will be hard to penetrate the static of theories that have run rampant for the past fifty years. So, we had better be one hundred percent right."

"Agreed," Reubans said. "Let's see if we can make some history."

"I need to make a call," Lefleur said.

He contacted the Marine Corps in Arlington, Virginia, and spoke with the Assistant to the Commandant. After a couple of transfers, he ended up with Sergeant-Major Emmett, the command of the Chasers–the unit designated to find Marines who were listed as Away Without Leave. Lefleur explained the reason for his inquiry and asked if they had records to verify that Booker was at Camp Lejeune in 1963 and if an AWOL order was issued.

After an extended period on hold, with Lefleur resigned to listening to the Marine Corps Band playing patriotic music, Emmett returned.

"We normally don't get requests from so far back, but I have a hound dog of a company clerk, and he was able to find it quicker than I expected," Emmett said. "Looks like Captain Harold Booker went AWOL, 24 November, 1963. He was on staff at Lejeune as a Camp Psychiatrist, as well as a Special Assistant to President Lyndon Johnson."

"He worked for Johnson?" Lefleur asked. The information matched up with what Mattew Booker had told him at the prison. "Does it say what capacity?"

"No. Just 'Special Assistant.'"

"Anything else?"

"They have his logbook here, which shows his patients' appointments."

"Can you tell me when his last appointment was? Maybe I can narrow down the time of the last time he was seen."

"His last appointment was on 23 November, where he interviewed a patient who had suffered a head injury and was in the brig, being held in solitary confinement." Emmett went quiet for a moment. "Well, this is interesting. His patient was a Lance Corporal Charles A. Whitman. That name probably doesn't mean anything to you, son, but—"

"Austin, Texas, August 1, 1966," Lefleur said. "I'm familiar with him. If I send you an official request through department channels, is there any way I can get a copy of Booker's AWOL report and anything you might have between Whitman and Booker?"

"I'll have to run it through our legal department first," Emmett said. "No promises."

"Whatever you can do, Major." Lefleur hung up. He walked to the chalkboard. Under Booker's name, he wrote "Whitman."

Reubans looked up as he wrote it.

"What did you find?"

"Booker was treating Whitman while he was locked up in the brig," Lefleur said. He drew a line from Booker to Johnson. "And he worked on Johnson's staff." With that, he drew lines to Wolfe and Fielding. "They are all related somehow. And whatever it is, it culminated on November 22, 1963."

Reubans took this in and picked up the phone. "I need to get on this."

She spent the next two hours calling and seeking out the family doctors who had treated the Kennedys. But after being told it wasn't available, she reached a dead end.

"That's it," she said. "That's as far as we can go with this."

"How about if we contact the National Archives?" Lefleur asked. "They have to have the President's suit or shirt or something related to the assassination."

"Wouldn't they have his brain?"

"No," Lefleur said. "Believe it or not, they somehow 'misplaced' the brain. No one knows where it ended up."

"The National Archives seems as insurmountable as the Kennedys' doctors," Reubans said. "I can try, but I don't really have a lot of faith that they will help."

"Then what?" Lefleur asked. "We can't have gotten this far and found out so much, only to be stopped now."

He paced around the office, flipping the doubloon across his fingers, thinking. He paused at the Secret Service pins, weighing the paperweight in his hand.

He thought about his uncle and the photo of him and Abner he had seen on the old man's wall. And the stories his uncle had told him about Kennedy. Then he stopped.

And a knowing smile crept across his lips.

"I know where we can get a DNA sample," Lefleur said. "I'll be right back." He raced out of the coroner's office and covered the two blocks back to the Detective Bureau and his office. He recovered the item he needed and rushed back to Reubens. He pushed into the office and handed her the framed letter from President Kennedy.

"There should be saliva on the envelope flap and the stamp from JFK," he said. "Will that suffice?"

Reubans was already disassembling the frame. "Oh, hell ya. If there is enough quantity on the flap and stamp, we should be able to match it with the towel sample."

CHAPTER THIRTEEN

Santiago Mendez looked at the incoming number on his phone and smiled before answering. "Hello. How's my favorite niece?"

"Waiting to find out when the money will be deposited in my account, Uncle Santi," Sophia Garza said.

"You did it."

"I did it," Garza said. "The Chief has put him on administrative duties. He's restricted his handling of cases, and the one case Lefleur is working on—some cold case involving a dead guy from fifty years ago—Lefleur told him that if he doesn't solve it, he'll resign."

"Well, I guess I'll just have to make sure he doesn't solve it," Mendez said. "But losing everything isn't enough. I want to personally beat him to the ground. I want him to feel my fist break him up like that testimony broke up my brother."

"Maybe I can get him alone somewhere and you and the family can show up and exact a bit of revenge."

"I can't go to jail," Mendez said. "If I do this, Lefleur can't walk away. We need to make sure it looks like a random act. Nothing can come back on me or my people."

"Let me see what I can do, Uncle Santi," Garza said. "I'll get back with you."

Mendez hung up and tapped the phone against his chin. He then dialed another number, starting a chain of conversations that would lead to the permanent removal of Lefleur as a problem for his organization.

CHAPTER FOURTEEN

Lefleur was in Dealey Plaza, waving at the presidential limo. John Kennedy was waving and looked right at him.

"You know what to do," Kennedy said.

Then his head exploded in blood and brains.

"Jack?"

He woke with a start and looked up to see Reubans standing over him, gently shaking him.

"Jack. Are you okay? You dozed off there for a moment."

"Yeah. Sorry, did you say something?"

"The DNA is back. I... think you need to see this."

Lefleur crossed the office and joined Reuban at her computer. She typed in a command, and a schematic came up.

"The diagram on the left is from the envelope and stamp you provided," she began, sliding her finger along the readout and pointing out several sets of numbers on the screen. "The one on the left is the sample from the towel."

Lefleur was not an expert in reading and understanding the complexities of DNA coding, but he took his time looking back and forth at the separate screens and markers.

They were identical.

He looked at the piece of skull, resting in a solution to keep it moist.

"This is actually a piece of President John F. Kennedy's skull," he said reverently. "For years, I have read the stories and seen the video of Jackie climbing out of the back seat, crawling onto the trunk of the limo, and how she almost fell off, trying to retrieve the part of the President's head that was shot away. And, now, to see it in person... to handle it... it's like...."

"Like a holy icon? A piece of the Original Cross?" Reubans offered. "Yes, it is. We are looking at a piece of history that has never been made public. And it's finding offers proof that there was another shooter involved in his killing."

"It's more than that," Lefleur said. "This ties me to my uncle and the most profound crime artifact of our day and age."

"We need to be careful," Reubans warned. "This secret has been buried for over fifty years for a reason. If we get it out there, some people may come looking for us for disrupting their narrative." She crossed her arms and leaned against the desk. "Even though I'm sure all the involved parties are dead, I'm not ready to endanger my family over this whole thing."

Lefleur sat quietly, taking in what Reubans had to say. Was it possible some of the original conspirators were still out there, and that they were the ones who killed Wolfe? Could they be monitoring what he and Reubans were investigating? If they decided to release their findings, would this person—or persons—silence them like the dozens of others who were witnesses and spectators of the original event?

"Let's keep things under wraps for the time being," he finally said. "Until we can figure out all the pieces and players, we won't be in any position to make our findings public. We still have to figure out the connection between Booker and Wolfe. Once we tie this together, we can think about going public."

Lefleur looked around at the blackboard and the evidence spread out on several tables. "We need to consolidate all of this into one place, preferably under lock and key," he said. "Take photos of the blackboard and wipe them clean, then take another set of all the evidence."

"My office has a safe in it," Reubans said. "We can lock the evidence away there. I'm the only one with the combination."

Lefleur looked at her and began to say something, but bit back the reply.

"What?"

"Nothing. Just... maybe you should let me have the combination. In case...."

"In case something happens to me. Is that what you mean, Mister Optimistic?" Reubans said with a smirk.

"I'm just being tactical."

"I can work with tactical," Reubans said. "Just as long as you don't take my collection of Las Vegas shot glasses, we'll be fine." She jotted down the combination and handed it to Lefleur.

"Deal."

The man leaned back in his chair, watching the video feed from the coroner's office and taking in the exchange between Reubans and Lefleur.

The video cameras and omni-directional microphones he'd installed while changing out the burned-out ballasts he'd caused to fail picked up everything, including the combination to Reubans' safe. It would be easy enough to sneak into Reubans' office after she and Lefleur were gone for the day. They would remove the evidence, and like so many other things, their crime would go down as one of those mysteries no one could explain. And the case would remain in the realm of the unsolved.

He couldn't do anything about the digital photographs they'd taken. His best bet was to steal the cameras when he got the chance and delete the photos, then send a computer worm into their joined systems, seek out the photos, and purge them from the hard drive.

His attention was drawn back to the video feed. Lefleur's phone was ringing. He looked at the screen and saw that the number was blocked.

Lefleur answered, listening for a long minute before looking up at Reubans. "I understand." He glanced at his watch. "I can be there in twenty minutes. Yes, I'll come alone." He hung up.

"What is it?" Reubans asked.

"An anonymous caller. A woman. She said she has information about who killed Abner Wolfe." Lefleur pulled out his keys. "I'm supposed to meet her at the Dos Amigos bar on Fifth. Alone." He thought for a few seconds. "That's one of the bars the Mendez brothers own."

"The same family whose brother you put away?"

"Yeah," Lefleur said. "And I filed a case against the other for trying to bribe me into changing my testimony."

"Now, I'm no cop," Reubans said, "but that sounds like a set-up."

"I agree," Lefleur said. "So, do me a favor. Give me forty-five minutes. If you don't hear from me, call my phone. If I don't answer, call dispatch and send a couple of cars to check on me."

"How will I know it's you answering the phone? I mean, you could have something dastardly happen to you, and when I call, someone pretends to be you."

Lefleur thought for a moment. "Let's have a code word. I'll say, 'Butternut.'"

"'Butternut,'" Reubans repeated. "I can work with that."

"Yep." Lefleur nodded. "Butternut."

"And in the meantime, I'm going to lock up all this stuff."

"Alright." Lefleur looked at his watch. "Forty-five minutes."

Lefleur pulled into the parking lot, scanning for any occupied vehicles or areas of possible ambushes. When he didn't notice anything odd, he moved to exit his car, but paused. Sitting back in the driver's seat, he picked up the radio microphone. "902 to Central."

"Central, 902, go ahead," the dispatcher answered.

"Put me out of service at 890 Fifth Avenue, the Dos Amigos bar, on a follow-up."

"Clear, 902."

He clicked off and walked to the front of the bar. An older man was leaning against the wall, trying to balance himself as he urinated. Lefleur stepped away from him and his splashing mess.

He pulled the door open and stood in the foyer, giving his eyes a few seconds to adjust to the dim lighting. He took in the scene before committing himself to enter all the way.

When Lefleur worked third shift patrol, he'd responded to several calls at this location. Most of them had just been disorderly drunks who tried to skip out on paying for their drinks, or picked a fight with the bartender. The crowd could be rough on some nights, but it seemed mild tonight. Lefleur attributed this to the fact that it was the middle of the week.

Letting his eyes pass over the room, he saw a couple deep in conversation, their table covered with empty beer bottles. A rough-looking guy with a leather vest and forearm tattoos sat in a corner. An older man was hunched over his drink in another corner, nursing his misery.

Standing by an old-style jukebox, a young woman glanced toward him and locked eyes. She inclined her head toward the back of the bar, which was hidden from view of the front door. Walking toward the back, the woman glanced over her shoulder to ensure Lefleur was following.

She moved to the far wall, toward an empty table. Stepping behind the table, she smiled as Lefleur approached.

Lefleur never saw the two men hiding behind the wall, nor the pool cue that cracked him across the back of his head. Going down hard, he rolled into a ball and tried to reach for his pistol, but the pool cue came down on his hand.

He screamed and cupped his hand just in time to see a boot come down, aiming for his head. Putting his forearm up, he deflected the kick, which was followed by a second, connecting to his jaw. Through bleary eyes, Lefleur saw that both guys wore bandanas over their faces.

Strong hands grabbed his arms and snatched him to his feet. A third male, also wearing a bandana, slugged him in the stomach, knocking the wind out of him. A hard slap and a punch followed, stunning Lefleur. His head lulled back, and when it rolled forward, the crack of a bottle sounded. The bruiser in front of him brought the bottle to Lefleur's eye level and twisted it.

"I hope this causes you as much pain as you caused my family, puta!"

Lefleur pulled against the arms, struggling to avoid the jagged glass. The bottle dropped to the floor, right before the man holding it. The thug on his left was snatched away from

Lefleur's arm, and the lack of support caused him to fall forward. Lefleur heard a sickening crack of bones and a cry of pain. Then, a second cry, followed by a moan, and a thud on the floor.

A pair of hands grabbed him under his arms and helped him to his feet. He barely remembered being put in the back seat of a car before he slipped into darkness.

He was roused back to consciousness by the ringing of his phone. Lefleur struggled to reach for the phone, but a hand reached from the front seat and took it from his pocket. Lefleur's strength ebbed away as he heard the front seat driver speak into the phone.

"Yes, this is Jack," the man said. "I'm fine."

Jack realized that it was Reubans calling and checking on him. But since the man didn't give the predesignated code word, Reubans would–

"I'll be here for a while," he said. Then after a pause, "butternut."

CHAPTER FIFTEEN

Lefleur woke to a throbbing headache. He lifted his head but fell back when a wave of nausea washed over him. Reaching up, his fingers brushed an ice-soaked towel on his head. He tried to close his fingers around it, but felt a sharp pain in his hand.

Slowly, he opened his eyes and surveyed his surroundings. He was in a darkened room, which, for the most part, appeared to be Spartan. Other than the small couch he was lying on, there was a recliner, an end table, a coffee table, and a small TV on the far wall, sitting on a rickety stand. As his eyes roamed, he found that the room was far from what he initially thought it was.

A laptop with multiple screens was open on a desk. The computer set-up was more sophisticated than the simple room alluded to. Doing a double-take of the monitor screens, he was shocked to find a live-view of the interior of the coroner's office.

Looking over his injuries, he assessed his condition. His right hand had been wrapped with a professionally applied bandage. His abdomen was sore, as were his ribs on the left side. His jaw was slightly swollen, but all teeth seemed in place.

Turning his head slightly, he spotted a light coming from what appeared to be a kitchen. The noises on the other side of the door indicated that someone was moving around. Now and then, Lefleur caught a glimpse of an older man. He smelled brewing coffee.

Reaching down to his right side, he felt for his Glock, relieved to find it still secured in his holster.

Whoever this is, apparently isn't afraid of me, or he would have disarmed me, Lefleur thought. He looked at his watch through bleary eyes and saw it was a little after 4 AM. Feeling light-headed and woozy, he lay his head back on the pillow and closed his eyes, but threw them open again when he heard someone approaching. A man set a pot of coffee on the table, placing two mugs beside it before turning to Lefleur.

For a moment, Lefleur studied the man's features. He remembered where he had seen him before. The man had been sitting at the far corner of the Dos Amigos bar where Lefleur had gone to meet the informant. He barely recalled the hit from behind. He remembered the beating and being taken away from the bar. The last image that came to mind was the interior of a car.

Lefleur looked harder at the man, squinting as he studied his eyes.

He had seen him before the bar. Even without the bushy moustache, he recognized him from the coroner's office, that first day he'd arrived.

He would never be able to forget those eyes.

"*You know, you look like him. It's in the eyes.*" Abner Wolfe's words rushed him like a river breaking free of a dam.

If this man were who Lefleur thought he was, he would be around ninety years old. But the man in front of him didn't look a day over sixty-five. He was robust and healthy, and the muscles in his arms were taut and coiled like steel cables. The hair was grey, with a touch of chestnut, and the crow's feet around his eyes were not deep-seated.

Still, he knew who he was. He remembered the way he moved and the hard-set jaw.

And his eyes.

There was no denying who this man was.

"Uncle...Ted?" Lefleur's words were weighted with disbelief. The pain in his body faded to the recesses of his mind as the realization hit him like a ton of bricks.

CHAPTER SIXTEEN

"I don't understand." Jack gaped at the man standing above him. Pushing himself upright, he ignored the throbbing in his head but paused when a wave of nausea hit him as he swung his feet to the floor. "You died back in 1972. I saw your body in the casket. How are you alive?"

"It was all faked. Nothing but a lie," Fielding said. "At the time, it was a necessary lie. Too many things had been done, and still needed doing. Things I couldn't do if certain people knew I was still alive."

"B-b-but," Jack sputtered. "You look so…young. You have to be close to eighty-five. How is this possible?"

Fielding smiled a wry smile. "I could tell you it's thanks to clean living and no red meat, but that would also be a lie. Let's just say that knowing the secrets of the Federal Government has its perks." He leaned close to Jack and whispered conspiratorially, "Maybe the 'Captain America' movie wasn't all science fiction."

"You could have told me you were out there." Jack's brows knit in a glare, irritation teasing his soul. Of all the things that could have happened today, here stood his uncle. Alive!

Fielding sighed at the plea for understanding in his nephew's eyes. His heart ached with the anger flashing in the young man's gaze. "I couldn't tell you, Jack. So, I sent you clues. Little things here and there."

Jack assimilated what Fielding said, his mind racing over the details of the years since his uncle's apparent passing. He remembered the anonymous note he'd received after closing the serial killer case in Baton Rouge, as well as another note he'd gotten after the mall bombing.

"Those notes were from you," he finally stated, his eyes wide. Fielding nodded. "So, Wolfe wasn't suffering from dementia. He WAS speaking to you. Daily!"

"Yes. We kept in touch. I've been following your career. And, frankly, I've been pretty proud of you."

"You could have told me that in person." The irritation was back.

"No, I couldn't do that, Jack." Fielding pulled the ice-filled towel from the back of his nephew's head and inspected the lump. The contusion had noticeably shrunken. "Only a few people outside the Intelligence community knew I was still out there. It allowed me to be effective."

"Effective? Effective in what?" Jack demanded. He gently ran his fingers over the lump, checking his fingers for blood.

"Jack, I will explain everything, but not here. Not now. We need to get to Cincinnati."

"Cincinnati?" Jack questioned, his confusion obvious. "What are you talking about? Why do we have to get to Cincinnati?"

"That's where the Democratic National Convention is." Fielding crossed the small room, opened a hall closet, and pulled out a fully packed bag. "There's going to be an assassination attempt on President Taylor. I don't know many of the details, just that it's going to happen."

"W-what?" Jack sputtered. He'd said it so casually, this fact. Maybe Jack had misheard...

"You heard me. This assassin is cunning and thorough. I tried to stop him once and was hospitalized for two weeks afterwards."

"Does he have an M.O.? Some kind of signature or method that he uses?" Jack asked.

"No. And that is what makes him so dangerous," Fielding said. "In one incident, he killed a dignitary's bodyguard by shoving him down a flight of stairs. He tried to make it look like an accident, going as far as to rip the toe of his shoe up to make it look like he fell over his own feet. Guy was so busted up his insides were like Jello."

"Can you identify him if you see him again?"

"Perhaps," Fielding said. His gaze wandered absently over the room. "Though I'm sure he's in disguise. If I can find him, it's imperative that I find out who hired him, or they'll do it again. It has to stop in Cincinnati. He's dangerous. Even more dangerous than I."

"Have you contacted the Secret Service? Cincinnati Police?"

"I can't. Not in my current capacity," Fielding said. "No one would believe me, or worse, they'd think I'm part of the assassination attempt." He paused for a moment. "And if you knew my history, you wouldn't blame them." He set the bag down and looked at Jack. "But *you* can contact them. You're an active officer. They'll listen to you."

"I need some answers, Uncle Ted," Jack said, his jaw set.

"Answers can wait. We need—"

"Did you kill Abner Wolfe and Booker?"

Fielding paused for a moment, his back to Jack. Shoulders sagging, he formulated his answer. "No. Abner was my friend and partner for more than fifty years. He killed Booker and relocated to Indiana a few years later. He purchased the business Booker was buried behind to ensure that his remains wouldn't be found. After my 'death,' Abner agreed to watch over you. He even sent you the brochure about the Camp Simmons Police Department hiring. After you started working for them, he saw the kind of dedicated cop you were. He liked what he saw. But when the media and your own department started beating you up, he paid closer attention to your character and endurance. He decided that, given the right clues and opportunity, you would be capable of solving the biggest murder case in American history and could redeem your reputation and honor. So, he waited until the time was right and had the concrete removed that had encased Booker's body and sent you on your way."

"But this...assassin..." Fielding took a moment to gather his words. "He knew about you as well. He knew you were my nephew and my sister was the only blood family I had left. He orchestrated the media and professional attacks on you, paying people to make false statements against you, dragging out the drama on the front pages of the paper, and leading every news cast, knowing that it would draw my attention to you. It wasn't enough to get me out of hiding, however. But when he killed Abner, I was drawn into his game. He knew that if he hit me in the only two stable connections I had, you and Abner, I wouldn't be able to refuse engaging. That's why he paid people to make false statements against you and pushed your case to the front pages. He knew Abner would take notice of you and contact you. He gambled that I would step in and help you out." Fielding forcefully pulled the zipper on the bag. "He knew what buttons to push, and I obliged him. Once I was engaged, he told me he planned on killing the President in Ohio, and there was nothing I could do to stop him."

Jack slipped his pistol from his holster and pointed at Fielding. "I'm going to have to take you in for questioning, Uncle Ted."

Fielding crossed his arms and smiled. "I figure you'd want to do that. That's why I unloaded the magazine while you were knocked out."

Jack pulled the pistol close to him and pulled the slide back a bit. He didn't see a round in the chamber. Keeping the gun trained on Fielding, he dropped the magazine and saw it was empty. He grabbed his back-up magazine and saw that it was empty as well. Fielding held out his hand and dropped the live rounds on the floor.

"I've been doing this job for a long time, son. I am rarely caught at a disadvantage. We need to get to Cincinnati and stop this guy."

"Yeah, right," Jack scoffed. "I'll just tell them I received information about an assassination attempt on the President from my uncle, who, by the way, hasn't been seen since 1972, mainly because he was dead!" He stooped down and collected the bullets from the floor. "They'll lock me up in the state mental hospital."

"Look, Jack, just tell them you received an anonymous tip and are following up on it," Fielding countered.

"I can call and–"

"No," Fielding snapped. "We have to go down there. I don't know who we can trust. There have been times, in the past, when people sworn to uphold their oaths to protect and defend the Constitution have failed...and people have died."

Jack noticed a pained expression across his uncle's face. The expression was gone as soon as it appeared, and Fielding's face hardened again. "I know there's going to be a hit, I just don't know how it's going to go down. I need to go there and get the lay of the land." Fielding put his hand on Jack's shoulder. "But I need the only person I trust in this world, and the best cop I've ever seen, to back me up. To be honest, I'm getting too old for this, and I need help."

Jack suddenly understood what his uncle was saying. Like Fielding, Jack was a hands-on type of guy and had to visualize a crime to find the best way to understand and solve it.

"Okay. I'll book us a flight," Jack said. He was already running figures in his head to see if he could afford a plane ticket, not to mention trying to figure out how he would explain it to Gretchen.

"No flights," Fielding said, his tone no-nonsense. "If I book a flight, certain people will get wind of it and try to stop me." He looked sternly at Jack. "And when I say, 'try to stop me,' I mean they will stop at nothing to keep me from landing—including blowing the plane out of the sky."

Jack swallowed as the enormity of the types of people he was dealing with slowly sank in. "I'll drive us, then," he said. "It can't be more than four hours away."

"I'll drive you home, and we can leave my car at a safe house," Fielding said.

"I have to let my office know." Jack dialed the number, shocked when his uncle yanked the phone from his hands and hung up.

"Best keep this off the radar. Nobody needs to know," Fielding said.

"I have to let my office know I'm alright. The last thing they heard was me calling out at that bar. I'm sure people are wondering where I am," Jack argued.

"We'll be back before anyone misses you," Fielding assured.

"Ha," Jack scoffed and shook his head. "I doubt anyone would miss me. Especially the chief." He told Fielding about the deal he'd made with the chief regarding the case.

Fielding listened intently before walking into the other room. He emerged a moment later, carrying a blue folder, and tossed it to Jack. He opened the file and saw the Chief's name inside.

"Here," Fielding said. "This might help you in your re-negotiations."

Scanning it, Jack's eyes widened in surprise. He looked at Fielding and shook his head. "Is this verified? Where did you get this information?" He asked, flipping through the pages. "If this got out, the Chief would be ruined; so would half a dozen other commanders."

"I have my sources, and yes, it's all verified and cross-referenced. If you want, I can show you the videos."

"No," Jack said, closing the file. "That won't be necessary." He set the dossier down and rubbed his eyes. "I just can't get over this. You've been alive all this time and never told me. I need a moment to process."

"Do you want me to drive?" Fielding asked.

"I'm fine," Jack said quietly. "I'll process it on the road. Let's go."

Jack watched the miles of Highway I-69 pass by his window. After about half an hour of silence, he spoke.

"What did you mean when you said, 'If I knew your history, I wouldn't blame you,' in regards to the assassination?"

"Do you remember what Wolfe said about the scorpions? About 'Mokroye Delo?'" Jack nodded. "The smaller the number of people who know, the better the success rate in pulling off an assassination. There are some things I don't want you to know, Jack. If I tell you, it could seriously alter your opinion of not just me, but history itself. I'm not sure I can do that to you."

"Screw what you want, Ted!" Jack snapped. "Damnit, you owe me a complete explanation, and by God, you will tell me!"

"Don't tell me what I will do, boy!" Fielding snapped back. "I am not a nice person. I have done some horrible, unforgivable things."

"Uncle Ted," Jack said, "you told me in that letter at the lawyer's office to 'make you proud.' That's what I've tried to do. You've always been my role model."

"Trust me, kid," Fielding said, staring out the window, "I am no one's role model." He drove in silence for a long while. "If I tell you, you will hate me for the rest of your life."

"I'm willing to hear you out," Jack said. "Then, I'll decide whether to hate you or not."

Fielding took a deep breath, let it out slowly, and spoke. "Alright. You want the truth, you'll get it. But I'll warn you—you will not like what I have to say."

CHAPTER SEVENTEEN
MAY 8, 1949
OUTSIDE OF AUSTIN, TEXAS

Twenty-three-year-old Theodore Michael Fielding packed his University of Texas letterman's sweater and diploma next to his Marine Corps uniform in his footlocker and closed the lid.

Ted lay back in bed, smoking a Pall Mall and thinking about the next phase in life. He'd grown up in Fredericksburg, Texas, which was fine when he was a kid, but shipping out with the Marine Corps and attending four years at the University of Texas had taught him a thing or two. There was a bigger life out there, just waiting for him to reach out and grab it, if he had the guts.

Thanks to the GI bill, he'd graduated with a degree in engineering, topping out as the senior class president. He flirted with the idea of working for one of the oil rig companies, and had even received a few offers, but decided that he wanted nothing more than to work in law enforcement. He landed a job at the Austin, Texas Police Department, and after working for them a few years, parlayed his training and degree into a federal job, working with the Treasury Department, though his sights were set on becoming a Secret Service agent.

He looked at the packed suitcase on the floor and smiled. He couldn't wait to head back to Austin and embark on the next chapter in his life.

Ted slammed back his third whiskey sour in celebration of his future. The little bar outside of Stonewall, Texas was a mere pit stop on his way to Austin, where he would rent a room and sign up for the police force. From the corner of his eye, he watched the little blond waitress swish her skirt from table to table, collecting orders and stuffing the tips in her pocket. Ted's gaze followed her toward the bar, musing to himself as she refilled her tray. He waggled a finger at her to get her attention and pointed to his glass. She smiled and nodded in his direction before whispering to the bartender, who mixed Ted's drink and set it on her tray. She hurried it over to the table, expertly setting it in front of him.

"Here ya go, handsome," she said, giving him a wink. Ted toasted her and slipped her a five-dollar bill before downing the drink.

"Keep them coming and that fiver will continue to grow."

"The name's Gloria, and I have a way of making things grow." She ran her tongue over her lips and smiled.

"Mike," Ted said, offering his middle name, "and I don't doubt it."

She leaned closer and whispered in Ted's ear while squeezing him on the thigh. He laughed and blushed slightly at her banter.

"Well, thank you, Miss Gloria," he said, smiling. "I'll consider your offer."

She walked away, throwing him a glance over her shoulder.

Ted was still smiling when he noticed the cowboy sitting two tables away. He was watching Ted intently as his gaze slid slowly over to Gloria. The man downed his beer, pushed back his seat, and walked over to Ted's table.

"Bum a cigarette?" he asked. Ted scooped the pack off the table and offered the man one. He took it and looked at the pack.

"Pall Malls?" he questioned, snapping it in half and dropping it on the table. "Shoulda figured. I only smoke Lucky Strikes." He looked at Ted's forearm, noting the Marine tattoo. "Yeah. A Marine would smoke something as pansy-ass as Pall Malls."

"You must have been Infantry," Ted said. "We always heard that the Army smoked the Lucky Strikes, because that was what the WACS smoked, partner."

The man leaned so close to Ted that he could smell the cheap bourbon on his breath. "The name's Skip Larson. You'd do well to remember that." He stood up and crossed his arms across his chest, where they rested on his ample belly. "I don't like you, but I will give you a word of advice. Gloria is my girl. So, you'd be better off moving it along to wherever you're going."

"I don't know," Ted said. "She made me a really pretty offer, and afterwards, we're gonna have breakfast."

Larson uncrossed his arms and clinched his fists. Ted pushed back his chair and stood up, the table still between them.

"Skip, stop!" Gloria yelled, crossing the room and getting between him and Ted. "How many times have I told you, I'm not your girl!"

"You ARE my girl, Gloria, and I'll prove it, even if I have to beat the snot out of this Jarhead."

"Mike, you'd better leave," Gloria said.

"Yeah, boy, step outside and wait for me. We aren't done here."

"Oh, we're done," Ted said. He tucked a five-dollar bill under his glass and pushed the door open without looking back.

Ted walked to his Chrysler, parked in the rear of the bar. He was digging for his car keys when he felt a punch to the back of his head. He dropped his keys and fell to his knees. He grabbed his head as fireworks exploded in his brain.

"What the hell did you do that for?" Ted demanded, looking up at Larson. He managed to get to his feet, stopping the kick that Larson had aimed at his midsection. Grabbing onto Larson's leg, he twisted it and threw him to the ground. "What's your problem, buddy?"

Larson scrambled to his feet and balled his fists. "You stay away from my girl, partner," he sneered. He pulled a knife from his belt and pointed it at Ted. "You stay away from her, or I'll gut ya."

"I ain't after your girl. She was the one who came onto me."

"Liar!" he yelled, slashing at Ted. Ted sidestepped the blade and grabbed him by the arm. As the two struggled over the knife, Ted felt the blade slash against his stomach, cutting off the tail of his plaid shirt and drawing blood. When Larson brought the knife up to stab him in the neck, Ted spun around, grabbing him by the throat and twisting his hand so that the knife blade was facing Larson's stomach. Ted dropped his two-hundred and thirty-pound frame down on top of Larson, forcing him to the ground. He held him down until the man stopped struggling. Rolling off him, Ted pushed him onto his back.

The knife had impaled itself into Larson's chest. Blood pooled from the wound, soaking the man's shirt. Ted winced in pain, grasping his stomach as he checked Larson's pulse.

He was dead.

Staggering to his feet, Ted saw that he was covered in his and Larson's blood. He pulled the knife out of Larson's chest and limped to his car. He found his car keys lying in the gravel outside the driver's door. His head snapped up as voices drifted from the bar. Panicked, Ted fumbled and dropped the keys again.

"Damn it! Come on, come on, come on."

He dropped to the ground, the sharp rocks cutting into his knees and palms as he searched for the keys. Finding them, he pushed them into the lock, and just as he saw the door to the bar push open. Two people stepped out, and his heart sank when he realized one of them was Gloria. He figured the other was the bartender. Ted slid into the front seat, ducking down out of sight. Gloria and the man spotted Larson and rushed toward him.

Gloria's scream pierced the air just as Ted started the car. He kept his headlights off as he sped out of the parking lot, spinning gravel.

Ted squeezed the gash on his stomach to try to stop the bleeding, but the loss of blood was making him light-headed. His eyelids drooping, he barely felt the car swerve into the ditch, stopping abruptly against a culvert and sending the knife flying onto the floorboard.

The need to escape was overwhelming. Ted tried to open the door, but his strength ebbed away, along with his consciousness.

He didn't know how long he'd been out by the time a pair of strong hands pulled him from the front seat of his car and placed him on a soft surface. He raised his head, his eyes swimming in tears as a flashlight shined in his face and down his body. He surveyed his surroundings through blurred vision and realized he was inside another car. He watched the large figure of a man return to his car and climb inside. The man backed Ted's car out of the ditch and pulled it past the car where Ted lay. A few moments later, he returned and got into the front seat.

"You'll be fine, son," the man assured. "I'll see that you get patched up."

Ted lulled in and out of consciousness as the car traveled a short distance and pulled to a stop. The door nearest his feet opened, and the man helped him walk to a large house, lit up from inside. The stranger laid Ted on a cushioned couch and removed his shirt, wadding it and throwing it in the corner.

"Bird!" the man bellowed. "Bring me some towels and a sewing kit. We got a hurt man here!"

A couple of moments passed before a woman ran into the room, arms full of towels, a pitcher of water, and a bottle of isopropyl alcohol.

"Doesn't look too bad, but he's gonna need to be stitched up." The man threw a thumb over his shoulder. "Grab the whiskey from the bar. He's gonna need a couple of shots."

Bird walked to the bar and removed a bottle of whiskey, uncorking it as she stepped to the side of the couch. Ted blearily saw her cringe as the man cleaned the blood from the wound.

"Here," the man said, "take a swig or two of this." He held the liquor bottle to Ted's lips. Ted swallowed the liquor, feeling it burn all the way down. This was much better stuff than what he'd been drinking at that bar. Once he'd taken a second swallow, the man took the bottle away.

"I'm not gonna tell ya this isn't gonna hurt, because it's gonna hurt like hell," the man said. "Bird, hold his shoulders."

He poured the medicinal alcohol directly on the wound. Ted screamed and tried to double over, but Bird's hands held him fast. The alcohol was equivalent to a blow torch being jammed into his abdomen. Bird pressed his shoulders down while the man threaded a needle. Catching his breath, Ted lay back, relieved when the fire began to subside. Just when his breathing had returned to normal, the man jammed the needle into Ted's torn flesh, holding the lacerated skin together as he quickly stitched. Once the wound was closed, the man wrapped a bandage around Ted's stomach and back, securing it with a pin. Soaked with sweat, Ted's exhausted muscles slowly contracted. He felt himself start to drift into sleep.

"You just rest here," the man soothed. "Bird and I will pick up your car and park it in the barn."

"Th-thank you, sir, for your hospitality," Ted mumbled. He tried to sit up, but failed. "I-I have to leave. I have to get away..."

"Son, don't worry about anything right now." The man patted his shoulder. "You need to rest. Whatever happens, we can deal with it in the morning."

Wearily, Ted slumped back on the couch, too weak to do anything but nod.

"You got a name, son?" the man asked.

"T-Ted, sir," he said, his eyes sliding shut. "Ted Fielding."

"All right, Ted. Get some rest."

"I can't thank you enough, Mister..."

"Johnson, son," the man said. "Lyndon Johnson."

Ted awoke to find himself in a large bed. He tried to sit up, but the pain in his stomach stopped him. He lay back down, trying to remember what had happened to put him in such pain. Searching through his whiskey addled brain, a memory became so clear that he gasped out loud.

He had been cut in a bar fight–and a man was dead.

Panic ran through Ted's mind. He didn't remember where he was or how he'd gotten here, but he knew his rescuer would turn him over to the police if he found out that he'd killed someone.

Despair welled in Ted's chest, spilling out in rivers of tears down his cheeks. His future, and everything he'd worked so hard for the past six years, was over.

Pain seared through him as he fumbled for a cigarette from off the nightstand. He struck a match, touched it to the tip, and inhaled deeply. As he smoked, the nicotine calmed his nerves and helped solidify his thoughts.

"I've got to get out of here." Ted's voice broke through the silence in the room. He pulled himself up, fighting the pain and nausea as he swung his legs over the side of the bed. Taking a moment to catch his breath, he slowly stood, pressing a hand to his stomach.

That's when he stopped and looked around the room. It was a small room, with trophies displayed along the walls and shelves. When he spotted the painted portrait of a man in uniform, something his host had said came rushing back to him.

He recognized the man in the portrait. He remembered the man helping him from his car and doctoring him. And he recalled who the man had said that he was: Lyndon Johnson...United States Senator.

"Oh my...God," Ted breathed. He knew that he was finished. A man in Senator Johnson's position, once he'd heard what Ted had done, would turn him over to the authorities in a heartbeat.

Clad in his boxer shorts, Ted slowly opened the bedroom door and listened to the hushed voices coming from downstairs. Stepping closer to the railing, but staying out of sight from any onlookers below, Ted peered over the banister.

Lyndon Johnson was talking with a uniformed sheriff. Ted strained to listen, but realized it wasn't necessary. Johnson made no attempt to speak in hushed tones. His voice carried as though he'd spoken into a microphone.

"So, someone killed Skip Larson, eh?" Johnson asked, his brow raised. "Sheriff McClaren, I knew Larson's daddy. He was a drunk son of a bitch, and his boy was always a pantywaist pain in the ass," Johnson said. He gripped the sheriff by the arm in a friendly gesture. "But I'm sorry to hear he's dead."

"A waitress by the name of Gloria said she'd waited on a young man who'd told her his name was Mike. Said he'd ordered several drinks and flirted with her," the sheriff said. "She said that Larson was kinda sweet on her, although she never returned the affections. Anyway, Larson had gotten jealous with the guy flirting with her, and the two men almost went to blows in the bar. Mike decided to leave, and Larson went outside and confronted him. That's when he was stabbed."

"Any witnesses?" Johnson asked.

The sheriff nodded. "Gloria and the bartender found Larson in the parking lot. They said they saw a dark sedan, possibly a Chrysler, pull out of the lot right before they found Larson's body." He shifted on his feet and frowned. It looks like the killer took the knife, but before he died, Larson ripped off a part of his shirt. The blood was tested, and it's a different blood-type than Larson's, so it looks like the killer was injured in the fight." He held up a paper bag. "And we have this," He reached inside with a handkerchief and withdrew a shot glass, holding it out to Johnson. "We may be able to get some fingerprints from it."

Johnson took the handkerchief and glass and held it up to the light, glancing up when his wife stepped into the room. "Bird," he called to her, "would you mind pouring Sheriff McClaren some of your famous lemonade?"

Sheriff John McClaren bowed slightly at the sight of the Senator's wife and turned to face her.

From his hiding place, Ted's brows shot up in surprise as he questioned whether he could trust his own eyesight. The moment Sheriff McClaren turned toward the Senator's wife,

Johnson quickly wiped the glass clean, eliminating any chance of recovering fingerprints.

"That won't be necessary, Mrs. Johnson. I appreciate it, though," Sheriff McClaren said. He looked back at Lyndon, who wrapped the handkerchief back around the shot glass and handed it back to the law officer.

"Well, I hope you find something out," Johnson said. "I may not have liked Skip Larson, but nobody deserves to be stabbed down like a hog."

"And you're sure that you didn't hear or see anything last night?" McClaren asked. "We found a rut cut into the drainage canal by the culvert, like someone might have run off the road."

"If the car's not there, the killer must have managed to get it out and get down the road," Johnson said. Placing his hand on the sheriff's shoulder, he walked toward the front door. "Probably halfway to Houston by now."

"When we find this guy, we should be able to match the torn, bloody shirt, and maybe even the knife, if he hasn't tossed it somewhere," McClaren mused.

"If there's anything I can do to help, you know where to find me. I'm either here or in the Senate," Johnson said, holding the door open for the Sheriff.

"I appreciate your time, Senator," McClaren said, affixing his Stetson back on his head. "If you hear anything, you let me know."

The two men shook hands, and Johnson closed the door after him. Before he could duck out of sight, Johnson glanced up and locked eyes with Ted.

"Get back in that bed, boy. You'll rip open your stitches!" Johnson bellowed. "I'll be up there in a minute."

Seeing no need to argue, Ted shuffled back into the bedroom, crawling back under the covers and biting back the pain. He had just settled into bed when Johnson walked into the room, carrying a bag, which he set on the floor. He settled his large frame on the foot of the bed.

"Mike? You told me your name was Ted."

"Mike's my middle name," Ted answered.

Johnson nodded. "What happened?" he asked without preamble.

Ted ran down what he remembered about the night before, his account of a near-perfect match with Gloria's testimony to the sheriff. When he came to the part about Lawson hitting him in the back of the head, Johnson checked Ted's scalp and saw a lump with a bit of blood.

"Sounds like a clear-cut case of self-defense, if ya ask me," Johnson said, after Ted had finished telling his side.

"Maybe so. But it destroys my chances of going to work for the Austin Police, the Treasury Department, or any federal office," Ted said. He lay back with his arm across his eyes, but quickly removed his arm and looked Johnson in the eye.

"Why did you wipe my fingerprints off the shot glass?"

A sly smile crept across Johnson's face. "Oh. You saw that, eh?"

"Yeah," Ted said, thinking. "If they don't have my prints or a good description of who I am, then they have no way of finding me."

"Well," Johnson began, "they have part of your shirt with your blood on it."

"Yeah, but without anyone to match it to, I'm in the clear," Ted said excitedly. He then swallowed deeply. "But, you're a senator. You're required to turn me over to the police, aren't you?"

Johnson laughed a deep, throaty laugh. "Son, you have no idea what kind of shit storm you've fallen into, do you?" He picked up the bag. Reaching inside, he pulled out Ted's torn shirt and the blood-encrusted knife. "This is the only evidence they have against you. This vanishes, and you go on with your life."

Ted perked up when he heard Johnson's words.

"You'd—you'd get rid of this stuff? You'd keep my secret?" Ted asked hopefully.

Once again, Johnson laughed. But this time, the tone was much more menacing. "Hell no, son." He tucked the shirt and knife back inside the bag. "I'm going to keep this."

"But...why?"

"You naive little piece of shit," Johnson said. "Leverage."

Ted swallowed, realization slowly coming to him.

"I see from your tattoo that you were in the Marine Corp. Okinawa?"

"Guadalcanal and Iwo Jima," Ted whispered.

"Killed many Japs?"

"Had to, or they would have killed me."

"I was in World War Two. Won a Silver Star," Johnson proudly stated.

"I remember the newspaper stories when you ran for the senate," Ted said. "I voted for you."

Johnson ignored Ted's attempt at appeasing him. "Did you have a problem killing the enemy?"

"No. It was my job, and I followed my orders."

Johnson stood up and walked over to the oil painting of himself in his U.S. Naval Reserve uniform. "Good, good. I need a man who isn't afraid to kill when the time comes. Someone good at following orders."

"Senator...I'm not a killer. I'm just a guy—"

"No, son. You are a killer. You have killed and you will kill again, if I deem it necessary," Johnson said. He held the bag in front of him. "Or I will turn your little pansy ass over to the Sheriff so fast your head will spin."

Ted sat back on the bed, defeated.

"So, this is how it will work," Johnson began. "Have you ever heard of the term, 'Mokroye Delo?'"

Ted shook his head.

"It's an old Russian term, from the 19th century. It means 'Wet Dealings', or 'Wet Works'," Johnson said. "It's a euphemism—a polite way to say 'spilling blood', like in a murder, or an assassination. The Cossacks were very effective when it came to their 'wet works'." Johnson leaned closer to Fielding. "And so am I."

"What does that have to do with me?" Ted asked.

"It's very simple. When there are some 'wet dealings' that I need done, I call you and you do it. Understand?" Johnson raised a brow. "You decide that you don't like the arrangements and renege on the deal, then I anonymously release what's in this bag to the Sheriff's office with your name, and your life is over."

Ted found himself nodding in agreement.

"And, in return, I will pull some strings and get you hired on to the Austin PD," Johnson said. "And after a couple, three years, I will sponsor your application to the Treasury Department. How does that sound?"

Ted perked up when he heard the conditions and nodded more vigorously.

"Ya see, son, in a few years, I plan on running for president. I'll need a good man to be in my administration. A man who will follow my orders, regardless of what they are, when I need something special done." Johnson leaned in and extended his hand to Ted. "Can I trust you? Do I have your word on it?"

Ted paused for just a second, then shook Johnson's hand. "Yes, sir, Senator. You have my trust and my word."

Johnson jerked him forward so hard that Ted cried out against the pain in his stomach. The older man leaned close to his ear. "I never trust a man until I have his pecker in my pocket."

CHAPTER EIGHTEEN
OCTOBER 19, 1951

It was five after eleven when rookie Austin Police Officer Ted Fielding ended his second shift duties and parked his cruiser at the main police station on First Street Northeast.

Johnson had been true to his word. He'd kept Fielding's secret, pulled some strings, and seen to it that the police department hired Fielding. All the while, the bloody shirt and knife remained in his possession to keep his young recruit in line. Johnson had even set Fielding up with his sister, Josefa. They'd dated a few times, and Fielding felt himself falling for her. But that dream was shattered one evening when an old street cop pulled him to the side.

"You have any idea who that Josefa woman is, son?" Senior Patrolman Davis Westmoreland asked.

"Yeah. She's Senator Lyndon Johnson's sister. Why do you ask?"

"Look, I don't know you, but you seem like a good kid, so I'll just shoot straight from the hip: senator's sister or not, she's a whore," Westmoreland said. "I busted her twice for prostitution."

The revelation shook Fielding. He broke off any further contact with Josefa, deciding that his career was more important than his future with her. He was certain that Johnson knew his sister was a prostitute and wondered if the Senator had set him up for a fall.

Fielding cleaned out the front seat of his cruiser and checked the back seat to ensure nothing had been left behind from his prisoner transport earlier this evening. Carrying his duty bag, he walked into the squad room and turned in his patrol trip sheet before heading to the dressing room to change.

"Fielding!" Desk Sergeant Manny Ruiz yelled. "Ya got a phone call."

Setting his bag down, Fielding walked to the desk and picked up the receiver. "Officer Fielding."

"How ya doing, son?" Lyndon Johnson's voice boomed from the receiver.

"I'm doing well, sir," Fielding answered. He was puzzled that the Texas Senator was calling him at such a late hour. "What can I do for you?"

"I have a job for ya. Something personal," Johnson said. "I'm going to call you when you get home. I don't want to go into it on this phone."

Fielding gulped. His throat was dry, and he felt a cold sweat break out on his neck. "Well... I..." he stammered. "I mean, I was going out for a drink..."

"You are heading home, boy, where you will wait for my call," Johnson said, menace in his voice. "You want a drink, then get a goddamn drink at home." Johnson hung up, leaving the young man stunned.

Fielding hustled out of his uniform and left the building, throwing his car in gear and speeding out of the parking lot. He pulled into the driveway of his small apartment, and his heart skipped a beat as his phone's shrill ring sounded from inside. Fumbling for his house key, he jammed it into the keyhole, pushing the door open with his shoulder and racing for the phone. He snatched it off the cradle mid-ring.

"I'm here," he said, his breath catching in his throat. The line was quiet for a long while. "Hello?"

Johnson finally spoke, "Let me tell you something, son." He paused, and Fielding heard the clink of ice cubes in a glass and assumed that Johnson was taking a drink. "When I tell you that I have a job for you, your only answer is, 'Yes, sir. Where and When?' Is that clear?"

Fielding took a deep breath, steadying his nerves. "Yes, sir. Where and when?"

"That's more like it," Johnson said. "Did you know that Sheriff McClaren stopped by today, talking to me about that killing a couple of years back? Of course, I still didn't know any more than what the papers said, so there was nothing for him to bite onto. But just so ya know, he's still fishing."

"I appreciate you taking care of me, Senator," Fielding said around the lump in his throat.

"I know you do, son. You damn well better." Johnson took another swig of his drink, not bothering with manners. "Now, to business. Ya ever heard of a man named John Kinser?"

"No, sir. Should I know him?" Fielding asked.

"Owns a miniature golf course in Austin– off Bayberry Street."

"Ok. I know the place."

"That sombitch thought he could blackmail me," Johnson said.

"Blackmail? How did he do that?"

"Look, son, I know you and Josie are kinda seeing each other, but you have to understand that she sees a lot of guys. One of 'em is that bastard, Kinsor," Johnson said. "He thought he could use her–lifestyle–against me to extort money. He said he would go to the press about Josie, unless I paid him to be quiet."

"So, what are you going to do?" Fielding asked.

"Nobody blackmails me! Nobody!" Johnson snapped. "That's where you come in, son."

"Do you want me to arrest him?" Fielding asked, trying to keep up.

"Arrest him? Hell no. I want you to kill him!" Johnson laughed. "That little shit needs to be taught a lesson."

"K-kill him?" Fielding sputtered. His blood turned to ice.

"That's right. Do you have a problem with that?"

"Well, I-I mean, I'm not sure if I can do that."

Johnson's breath deepened and became heavy. "Son, you swore to me that you would do whatever I needed done. I took you at your word. Now, you either do this, or I swear to God I will have your ass arrested first thing, by your own people in the morning for old Skip's murder. You decide. Just be careful. Never know who will be knocking at your door!"

The phone clicked in his ear, and Fielding realized Johnson had hung up on him. He put his hand to his forehead, wiping the perspiration.

Knock. Knock. Knock.

He jumped, his heart leaping to his throat as his vision blurred. His breath came in gasps as he worked to calm himself. When a second set of knocks echoed throughout the small hallway, he stepped toward the door, pausing long enough to pull his revolver from his duty bag. He steeled himself as he grabbed the doorknob. Holding the pistol behind his back, he pulled the door open, fully expecting to see uniformed officers, or at least a plainclothes detective, standing in the doorway.

Instead, a young man in a delivery outfit was holding a package.

"T. Fielding?" he asked, reading from a scrap of paper.

It took all he had to nod in acknowledgement. The boy handed him a clipboard. Eyeing him, Fielding tucked the revolver in the front of his pants, ignoring the delivery boy's shock, and scribbled his name on the paper.

"Uhh...I was told to be here at exactly seven-ten PM, sir," the boy said in a trembling voice.

Fishing in his pocket, Fielding pulled out a couple of crumpled-up dollar bills and stuffed them in the boy's hand before closing the door. He carried the box to the couch, pulled the pistol out, and placed it back in his bag, and sat down.

The phone rang. Fielding's head snapped up, his heart betraying him all over again as it pounded fear through his veins. Forcing his hand to move, he picked up the receiver and listened.

"That could have easily been Sheriff McClaren," Johnson said. "Now, open the box."

Fielding obeyed. An envelope partially concealed something beneath it. With slow movements, he picked up the envelope, his eyes falling to the small caliber handgun. Swallowing hard, his fingers trembled as he opened the envelope and pulled out a folded sheet of paper and a key. Tucked deeper inside the envelope was a wad of hundred-dollar bills.

"The paper lists the hours the golf course is open and when Kinser will be alone," Johnson explained. "You have two days. Catch him when he's alone, pop him behind the ear, then ransack the place. Take some money and a couple of items to make it look like a robbery." He paused, waiting for Fielding to acknowledge him. "Ya hear me?"

"Yes. I hear you."

"Good. Now, you switch shifts and start work in the morning, right? Make sure you're the first car on the scene, so if you messed anything up, you can fix it before the detectives get there."

"What do I do with the gun and the note?" Fielding asked.

"Mail them back to me," Johnson said. "And keep the cash. Think of it as a bonus."

The line went dead.

Fielding sat for a long time looking at the gun and cash. He cradled his head in his hand and fought back the bile roiling up from his stomach.

The sun was just cresting the tops of the buildings when Fielding received the call from dispatch. He pulled into the mini-golf course parking lot. A woman, visibly shaken, was standing outside the front door, hugging herself.

"What's going on, ma'am?" Fielding asked, looking into the front of the business.

"Mr. Kinser," the woman said, the words catching in her throat. "He's lying in the back. He's dead. And a man is lying there with a gun!"

"Stay here while I check this out," Fielding said, his voice urgent. He stepped through the front door, just like he had the night before. Scanning the interior, he looked for any scrap of evidence that might have been left behind. Instead, he saw the man he'd knocked unconscious starting to come around. He took the gun from his hand and placed handcuffs on his wrists, walking him outside and placing him in his car. Kinser was lying face down, the blood had run from the three bullet wounds in the back of his head and pooled beneath him, congealing. His right arm was also blood-covered.

A little bit after ten o'clock the night before, Fielding had used the key Johnson had provided him and slipped into the business unnoticed. Dressed all in black and wearing a pair of work gloves, he'd moved silently through the business, keeping his eyes fixed on the light coming from an open door in the rear of the building. Kinser had been working at his desk, counting the cash and adding the day's take on an adding machine. Creeping up behind him, Fielding had drawn the revolver and noticed his shaking hand. He'd taken a deep breath and squeezed the trigger, just as Kinser turned in his chair toward him. Kinser had seen the pistol and thrown his arm up, trying to block the shot. He'd groaned loudly and tried to rise, but Fielding had pushed him down, spinning the chair he was sitting in so that Kinser was facing away from him. He'd pushed the barrel of the pistol against Kinser's head and fired three quick shots. Kinser had weakly moaned and slipped out of the chair, collapsing onto the floor. Fielding had then ransacked the office, grabbed the cash from the table, and fled out the back door.

But then, he'd froze and hid behind the door, a figure, armed with a pistol, had stepped into the office and looked down at Kinser. Thinking quickly, Fielding had stepped out from the door and struck the intruder behind the ear, knocking him unconscious. When he fell, Fielding had grabbed the pistol from the man's hand and traded it for the pistol he'd used on Kinser before stuffing the cash he'd taken into the man's pocket.

Running the two blocks to where he'd parked his car, Fielding had stopped and managed to pull the mask from his face before vomiting into a trash can. His eyes bleary with tears from nausea and shame, he'd picked up the trash can and brought it with him, making certain that he didn't leave anything that would tie him to the scene.

He'd steadied his shaking hands and slipped the key into the ignition, being careful to drive as normally as he could. He'd stopped at a dumpster a few blocks away and tossed the trash can into it.

He'd made it home without incident, though his heart and mind were in shambles, and had thrown the black clothes and mask into the back of his closet. When he could calm himself, he dialed Johnson's number and mumbled, "It's done, but there was a problem." Fielding had told Johnson about the intruder and what he had done. Johnson was quiet for a long moment.

"Don't worry about him. He's expendable," Johnson had quietly said. "Send his gun back to me and make sure you're there to arrest him in the morning." He'd hung up the phone before Fielding had a chance to speak.

Fielding had wiped the sweat from his face and set the receiver back in the cradle. He'd picked up the box that the gun had come in and wrapped his shirt in it, stuffing it inside. Sealing it, he'd set it by the door before falling out on his bed, too full of adrenaline to sleep.

Now that he was back on the scene, his survival instincts were kicking in. After arresting the man, he found a license with the name "Malcolm Wallace." Fielding walked the perimeter of the room, making certain he hadn't left anything to tie him to the murder. He found a small trash can in the storeroom and brought it to the office, replacing the one he'd taken.

When he was satisfied, he strode out of the business, passing the woman on his way out. He walked to his squad car and picked up the microphone.

"Unit 815 to Headquarters."

"815, go ahead."

"I'm gonna need a homicide detective out here. Mr. Kinser is dead. I have a suspect in custody."

When the detectives pulled up, Fielding passed on what he had observed when he'd entered the business. The detective dismissed him to transport the suspect to the detective unit in District One. After he dropped Wallace off, Fielding stopped by the post office and sent a sealed package back to Lyndon Johnson.

CHAPTER NINETEEN
OCTOBER 18, 1956

"You want what?" Lyndon Johnson asked, spilling his bourbon on his shirt as he rose from his chair.

"I want to work for the Secret Service," Fielding said. "I've been working with Austin PD now for five years, all the while taking care of your ever-increasing 'problems.'"

"But I need you here, in Austin," Johnson said, dabbing the wet spot on his shirt with a washcloth. "What makes you want to do something like that?"

"I told you when we first began our—arrangement—that I wanted to go Federal. Austin Police was just a steppingstone."

Johnson thought back on the day he'd taken Fielding in. "Well...come to think of it, you working for the Secret Service could be beneficial to me," Johnson said, rubbing his sizable jaw. "I plan on running for president in '60, so having you on my White House staff might work out just fine." Johnson set the glass down and placed his hands on Fielding's shoulders. "Mighty fine idea, son. Mighty fine indeed."

Ted knew with the Senator's recommendation he could apply for a position with the Treasury Department and spend sufficient time working the job before switching to the White House detail. This meant getting as far away from Texas as possible and escaping the pressure of constantly being under Johnson's thumb. He knew he might encounter him while in Washington, D.C, but the way the presidential election was shaping up, Johnson didn't have the clout or the votes to land him in the White House.

While Ted was toying with the idea of escape, Johnson squeezed his shoulders, and pain shot through them.

"Don't think this is gonna relieve you of your responsibility to me," Johnson said. "I can keep my eye on you just as much in Washington, D.C. as in Austin." He twisted his knuckle into Fielding's brachial nerves. "I still own you, boy. Don't forget that."

"So," Police Chief Carl Shuptrine began, "you're moving onto bigger and better things?"

After Fielding sailed through the hiring process with the Treasury Department, he submitted his resignation to the Chief. Shuptrine, who had taken over the year before, had instituted some much-needed updates to the department, including portable radios for the special units and patrol, and female officers in support positions. When he heard Fielding was leaving, he wanted to personally discuss the matter with him.

"Yes, sir," Fielding said, accepting the seat offered. "I appreciate my time here. I've learned so much. I'm sure it will help me succeed with the Treasury Department."

"I did some asking around on your behalf," Shuptrine said. "I heard that you sailed through the testing and placed in the top five. There's just one thing, though. I didn't realize you were friends with Senator Johnson."

A bead of cold sweat ran down Fielding's back. "Well, I wouldn't exactly call us 'friends,' sir, more like...a mentor, I guess."

Fielding held back his true feelings, knowing that Shuptrine wouldn't pry, especially since Johnson was involved. Although Fielding felt that Shuptrine wasn't able to prove anything against the senator, Shuptrine wasn't a fool. He knew that Johnson was as crooked as a dog's hind leg.

"Well, good luck, son," Shuptrine said, standing and offering his hand. "If you ever want to come back, there will always be a place for you here. And with your experiences, we can probably squeeze you into a detective slot, or a crime processing tech."

Fielding rose and shook the Chief's hand. "Thank you, sir. I appreciate the offer, and I'll keep it in mind."

Fielding walked out of the office, stopping by the desk sergeant long enough to place his badge and service revolver on the desktop before heading out the door.

His next stop would be Washington, D.C.

CHAPTER TWENTY
JUNE 15, 1959

"Fielding!" The unit chief in charge of the Counterfeiting and Forgery Division of the Treasury Department bellowed. "My office—and bring your report!"

Fielding gathered his paperwork together and headed for the chief's office. He wasn't dreading the meeting. He was looking forward to it. After six months of work, he'd presented the case file on one of the biggest counterfeiting rings in the Northeast, and he was ready to shut them down. His information was solid: checked and re-checked with confidential informants and enough evidence to ensure a conviction. Compiling the overwhelming information on the ring of thieves, he passed the information on to his supervisor, requested a meeting with the unit chief about the case, and proceeded with prosecution. His supervisor took a day to read over the information and speak with other agents who had assisted Fielding. When he was satisfied that everything was in order, he met with the chief, setting up an appointment for him to meet with Fielding.

Fielding entered the office, his eyes going to another man who was in with the chief.

"Agent Fielding," the Unit Chief began, "this is Assistant Federal Prosecutor Randall Smart." Fielding reached out and shook the man's hand. "Now, I understand you have a case you'd like us to look over?"

JULY 6, 1959

Charles Joseph Whitman looked out of the transport window as it touched down on the airfield at Guantanamo Bay, Cuba. The loading door opened, and he hoisted the duffle bag on his shoulder as he hustled out of the plane. Saluting the commanding officer, he received his assignment and went off to find his quarters. He unloaded his duffle and made himself comfortable in his new home.

He was sure that his father was angry with him. The last time he saw him, the man had beaten and thrown him in the swimming pool, nearly drowning him, because he'd come home drunk after a night out with his friends. Once he'd sobered up and cleared his head, he'd gone to the local enlistment office and joined the Marines. Two and a half months later, after finishing boot camp, he was sitting at his first posting and learning what it meant to be a Marine.

A year after Whitman arrived in Cuba, Ted Fielding stepped out of the Ninth Judicial District courthouse, trying to keep his face from bursting into a stupid grin. He hurried down the steps, where he was met by the unit chief and his supervisor.

"Guilty on all counts!" Fielding said, his Texas drawl slipping in on "counts."

His bosses shook his hand and took him out for the best dinner of his career. Fielding felt good enough that evening that he decided this was the time to request a transfer to the Secret Service White House detail.

"Funny you should mention that," the Unit Chief said, "Vice President-Elect Johnson made some inquiries about your availability. I told him you were wrapping up a major case, but once that was completed, you'd be free to come to work for him at the White House."

Fielding took a long swallow of the Whiskey Sour and wiped his mouth.

Ted, like many in the country, had been surprised that John Kennedy had selected Johnson as his running mate. The reason was obvious: not only could Johnson deliver the South to Kennedy, he could also deliver all the big Texas oil money to the campaign.

And Johnson would show the Washington deadheads that he had the power to influence and win a presidential election.

Ted hadn't heard from Lyndon in almost a year and hoped he was done with him. But, like the proverbial bad penny, Johnson kept showing up in Fielding's life.

CHAPTER TWENTY-ONE
APRIL 8, 1960

Henry Marshall looked at the ever-growing pile of reports on his desk and ran his fingers through his thinning hair. Twenty-four years as the Director of the Agriculture Adjustment Agency in Robertson County, Texas, and Marshall had never seen voter fraud and corruption on the scale he was currently investigating.

Billie Sol Estes was not a man unknown to Marshall. His name had surfaced when the fraud case had come to light. Estes had kept himself under the radar until Marshall received several citizen complaints accusing him of illegal purchases from farmers who felt pressured to sell to him because of his political connections. Many of the farmers came forward, providing evidence that Estes and his attorney, John Dennison, had committed voter fraud on a huge scale. The case was complicated enough with these two players, both of whom had known reputations in and around Robertson County. Still, it became even more problematic when the political ties were discovered, and the trail led to the current sitting senator in Texas, and presidential candidate, Lyndon Baines Johnson.

Marshall asked Dennison and Estes to come in for a casual meeting to see if they would cooperate with the investigation. Both agreed to come in, but neither admitted to any of the facts Marshall laid out for them. After they left, Marshall wasn't as confident in the case as before they arrived.

That was two days ago.

"Are we sure about this?" Marshall asked his chief clerk.

"Yes, sir," Glenn Hazlett answered. "Mr. Dennison is listed as the attorney on file for Senator Johnson."

"Just because Dennison represents Estes and Johnson doesn't mean they know the other's dealings. Hell, the first thing Dennison did when I interviewed him was announce that there was an attorney-client privilege argument and said that he can't discuss issues regarding one client with another.

Before we can implicate Johnson, we need to have solid proof that links the three together. That's how we frame a conspiracy."

"But don't we also have to consider who benefits from the voter fraud?" Hazlett asked. "We have sworn testimony that Estes was behind rigging the elections so that Johnson could win his senate seat in '48 and again in '52. You and I both know that Lyndon Johnson is a crooked son of a bitch."

"Sir." The department secretary stood at the door, waiting for Marshall to motion her in. "Here's a letter that just came in from a special courier."

Marshall took the letter and opened it, slipping on a pair of glasses. Hazlett stood silently as he read it. Marshall slid the glasses off and chewed on the earpiece. "Looks like this case has lit a fire under someone's ass." He handed the Clerk the letter.

After reading it, Hazlett felt the blood drain from his face. "You're being transferred to the Washington, DC office? Did you request this?"

"Hell, no, I never requested it," Marshall said. "I drafted a letter to the head of the Department of Agriculture, detailing the information we compiled on the case, and asked for instructions on how to proceed. Apparently, their answer is to remove me from my post here, 'promote me,' and get me out of the way."

"But if you didn't request the transfer, who did? Who recommended the order?"

Marshall dragged his Rolodex to him and began flipping through the cards. "I need to make a phone call," he said, waving a hand of dismissal

A torturous twenty minutes later, Marshall stepped out of his office. Hazlett and other employees gathered in the small room.

"The transfer is valid and irrevocable," Marshall said. He turned to Hazlett. "I want copies of everything we have on Estes and Denning. I'm bringing them with me and will coordinate the investigation from Washington. This isn't over. Not by a long shot."

Marshall turned to go back to his office, but Hazlett stopped him. "Who issued the transfer order, Chief?"

Marshall looked over Hazlett's shoulder, not speaking until he was confident no one could hear.

"Cliff Carter. The same Cliff Carter who has ties to Billie Sol Estes." Marshall narrowed his eyes. "The same Cliff Carter who is the right-hand man to Senator Lyndon Johnson."

CHAPTER TWENTY-TWO
JANUARY 19, 1961

The day before John F. Kennedy was sworn in as the 35th president with Lyndon Johnson as his Vice President, Ted Fielding showed up at the White House front door and met with his new supervisor, Roy Kellerman.

"How do you know the Vice President?" Kellerman asked.

"Oh, I worked with the Austin Police. We came to know each other while I was in Texas," Fielding answered.

"Well, however you know him, he specifically asked for you to be on his Security detail." Kellerman glanced at Fielding. "It's my call, but I want your input. Are there any issues between you two that I need to know about?"

"Oh, no, sir," Fielding lied. *Besides the fact that he has proof I've killed two people, no problems at all!* "I would be happy to serve on the Vice President's detail."

"Good," Kellerman said. "There will be times when the President will travel abroad in a particularly hazardous situation. During these times, I may need to pull you to augment the Presidential staff, but for the most part, you will guard the Vice President."

"That sounds great, sir." Fielding offered a false smile. "I promise to give you my best."

"That's all I ask," Kellerman said. "The Vice President wants to see you. He's waiting on you in the Eisenhower building, so you'd better hurry."

Fielding hurried through the White House toward the building located near the West Wing. Johnson was in a secondary office at the opposite end of the hallway, where Richard Nixon, the current Vice President for one more day, had his office. Johnson was leaning against his desk, reading through a stack of papers, when Fielding walked to the door frame and knocked. Johnson motioned him in.

"So, how ya making out?" Johnson asked. "Finding your way around this place alright?"

"Yes, sir," Fielding said. "Mr. Kellerman seems like he's a good man."

"Learn all you can from him. He knows his job well." Johnson walked behind the desk to the overstuffed chair and sat down heavily. "You probably know that I was less than satisfied with how the election came out."

"Yes, sir, I do."

"Did you know that in 1954, I was elected the youngest Speaker of the House in Senate history?" Johnson asked. He lit a cigarette and drew in deeply. "I was tough, but fair, especially with the new members." He reached for a drink he'd poured before Fielding had come in.

Fielding glanced at his watch. It wasn't even nine AM yet, and Johnson was already nursing a drink. Wisely keeping his thoughts to himself, he worked to focus on Johnson's words.

"When Kennedy started running for president, I had to call him on the carpet for missing votes. But I wasn't hard on him. I gave him and his people the best committee assignments and helped him along in his career, and even after all of that, they still complained about me to the Ethics Committee. When I found out about it, I met with Kennedy and told him in no uncertain terms that they were going to have to cut the crap or there would be some serious consequences." Johnson rolled the glass between his hands. "I think he resented me for that."

He drained the glass and stood up. Walking to the credenza, he took the top off the Scotch bottle and poured himself another drink. "And then, during the campaign, Bobby made such a big deal about the heart attack I had five years ago. He force-fed it to the media, and they bought it, even though they wouldn't touch the story about Kennedy's Addison's disease. They kept it quiet, but those of us in the Senate knew what was happening." Johnson sipped the Scotch. "Hell, I only took the vice president slot so I could run for president against that pansy-ass Kennedy in 1964."

"You-you're running for president again?" Fielding stammered. "I didn't know that."

"Son, do you know what a 'dynasty' is?" Johnson asked.

"I have an idea," Fielding said. "Like the Ming Dynasty. It's a ruling class that runs a country for years, centuries, sometimes."

"Exactly," Johnson said. "I firmly believe that if Kennedy finishes eight years in office, Bobby will run in '68. It would be a tough campaign, but if John does a decent job, Bobby would be a shoo-in. And if Bobby wins over the populace the way his brother did, Ted would be in the saddle when he's done. Now, it's anyone's guess whether or not the country will want to extend the Kennedy name as president. Now, we're talking about twenty-four years of the Kennedys holding the presidency. Any way you slice it, that's how you define a dynasty."

"Do you think the country would allow that sort of thing to go on?"

"Son, I don't know. But I do know this: one way or the other, I will not live to see the presidency. And if I know my Kennedys, I will not be vice president in four years." Johnson steepled his fingers in front of him. "And Kennedy won't be president long either. If I have my say, he's a one-termer." He leaned close to Fielding. "But there's something I want you to know, son. I will plow through anything or anyone that gets in my way."

Johnson's voice held the same razor-sharp tone as when he'd told Fielding what he'd wanted done with John Kinser.

Fielding swallowed hard. He couldn't be asking him to do the unthinkable, could he? Was Johnson that much of a monster?

He shifted on his feet when he found Johnson staring at him. Realizing the man was waiting for his answer, he forced the words past his lips. "Yes, sir. I understand."

"Good," Johnson said, dismissing Fielding with a wave of his hand.

Fielding walked out of the office, mulling the statement in his mind. He had a sick feeling that he was about to be asked to handle another of Johnson's "problems."

He prayed that the "problem" wouldn't be President Kennedy.

FEBRUARY 20, 1961

Private First-Class Charles Whitman walked into the command office at Guantanamo Bay Base and was handed a letter. It had an official US Government seal in the corner. He opened it, quickly read it, and smacked the paper with the back of his hand.

"Hey, Sergeant?" Whitman called. The staff sergeant poked his head out of his office.

"What do you want, Private?"

"I just got my Top-Secret Security Clearance," Whitman said. "I'm in line for a promotion."

"Whitman," the Sergeant said, "you are one hell of a sniper, but you won't be commanding men without proper training." He stood up and walked to Whitman. "Have you ever heard of NESEP?"

"No, Sergeant, I haven't."

"It's the Naval Enlisted Science Education Program. It's a test you take to enter Officer Candidate School. Are you interested?"

Whitman smiled and nodded. "You bet, Sergeant."

CHAPTER TWENTY-THREE
APRIL 18, 1961

"What do you mean, 'they found out?'" President John Kennedy demanded. He bit the end off a cigar and spat it into a trash can. Allen Dulles, Director of the Central Intelligence Agency, handed him a report. Kennedy scanned it and crumbled it up, slamming it to the desktop. "Goddamn it, Allen, you said your people were reliable."

Johnson sat on the couch in the center of the room, sipping a bourbon and smoking a cigarette. He'd decided being a fly on the wall was the best strategy. Across the room, Colonel Howard Burris, Chief Air Force aide to Johnson, and Arthur Schlesinger, Special Assistant to the President, stood quietly.

Kennedy hadn't listened to Dulles when he'd warned him about the invasion. He'd been too distracted with his own problems to be interested in what was being said.

"With all due respect, Mr. President, the operation would have been successful if you had followed President Eisenhower's plan," Dulles said. "Deputy Director Bissell was confident that Operation Zapata would have overthrown that bearded bastard, Castro. If we'd moved on to Trinidad like we'd planned..."

"We discussed that, Mr. Secretary," Kennedy said. "You know Trinidad didn't have landing fields big enough to land the B-26s, and if they were present, they would implicate the United States as assisting the rebels. An uprising by home-grown guerrillas wasn't exactly the image we wanted to produce, was it?"

"They were ready for us on Playa Larga," Dulles said. "When the troops hit the beach, they were hit with spotlights. After a firefight broke out, Castro himself showed up. The '*USS Houston*' was damaged and intentionally beached, and we lost the '*Rio Escondido*.'" Dulles said. "And Osvaldo Ramerez, the local resistance leader, was captured. Word is that he was executed immediately." He looked down at his feet. "We lost twenty of our people. We aren't certain how many rebels were lost."

Kennedy turned his back on Dulles and stared out the window. He took a long drag on his cigar and slowly blew out a cloud of smoke.

"First, the Russians beat us into space last week, and now this. I am getting tired of these other countries slapping us in the face." He looked over his shoulder at Dulles. "Get everyone out of there. I will not let this situation define my administration. Do you have any idea how much of a public embarrassment this is for me and your organization? If I knew I wouldn't be crucified in the press, I would splinter your agency into a thousand pieces and throw it to the winds." He turned to face Dulles. "I think I need to reevaluate whether my administration can afford to keep the CIA in its current state, and you, Allen, in your current position." He turned his back on the man, a sure sign of dismissal. "Arthur, I need you to stay."

Dulles inclined his head toward the President and turned to leave the Oval Office. He looked at Johnson, seeking some form of camaraderie and support, but Johnson merely shrugged. Dulles scowled at him as he left.

Kennedy sat down and noticed Johnson still on the couch, nursing his drink. "You've been uncharacteristically quiet, Lyndon."

"Just considering options, Mr. President."

"I need to know that we show a united front on this," Kennedy said. "We cannot waver in the eyes of the public."

Johnson rose from the couch and extended his hand to Kennedy. "Mr. President, I assure you, you have my unwavering support."

Kennedy shook his hand, and Johnson walked out, leaving the President alone with his thoughts.

Johnson walked into his office and loosened his tie, dialing the phone. While he waited, he poured himself a glass of the good Scotch he kept for himself, not that swill that Kennedy served. "Allen, we need to talk."

"Lyndon," Dulles said, "I won't stand for the President disbanding us. He has to be stopped."

"That's what we need to talk about."

"Come in," Johnson said as Fielding stepped into his office. "Close the door."

Fielding obeyed and walked toward Johnson. "Yes, sir?"

"I don't have to tell you that the President is fit to be tied," Johnson said. "This whole Cuban operation has ticked him off worse than a bee in a bull's ear." He paced his office, puffing away on a cigarette and shaking his head. "I warned him about backing those rebels."

"I don't know what to say, sir."

"Ever hear of an investigator named Henry Marshall? Works with the Agriculture Department."

"No. Can't say that I have."

"Well, a few months ago, I got word that that son of a bitch had started investigating me for voter fraud."

Fielding wasn't surprised. It had long been rumored that Johnson had fixed several elections by stuffing ballot boxes and intimidating voters to keep them away from the polls and guarantee he would win the elections. Knowing that someone had finally caught up with the crooked bastard almost brought a smile to Ted's lips.

Almost.

"I need you to keep an eye on him for me. Find out whatever dirt you can dig up from the IRS, the FBI, or even within his own office," Johnson said, twisting the pile of papers in his hand. "I haven't worked this hard and given up so much to have some chicken-choking, backwater Ag agent take it all away." He leaned closer to Fielding. "If the time comes, I will need your 'special' services again."

Fielding waited for that shoe to fall. He figured Johnson hadn't just called him in to inform him of the investigation without an ultimate solution in mind. He found himself nodding in agreement.

"Understood, sir. I'll see what I can find out."

It took about a couple of weeks of digging for Fielding to find the information Marshall had amassed. His best resource was a cute redhead who worked as a secretary in the agriculture office. She became way too talkative after Ted took her out on a few dates and promised her the moon. A few drinks, a few steak dinners, and a little pillow talk after he took her back to her place helped loosen her tongue.

"Old Man Marshall has his agents down in Texas working overtime, doing interviews and getting affidavits signed," the redhead said. "He's looking to bring a case against the Vice President! Can you imagine? I mean, Lyndon Johnson is the second most powerful person in the free world, and Marshall believes that he can bring him down? Either that man has more courage than the rest of the government, or he's a damn fool."

"Does he have a timeline that he's looking to do this?" Fielding asked.

"He told the agents in a staff meeting he's looking to file an indictment by the middle of June on Billie Sol Estes, who was a close associate of the vice president. I mean, I voted for President Kennedy and Vice President Johnson. I believe in them." She sighed and shook her head. "I would just hate to see something happen to mess up President Kennedy's administration."

"Is there any way you can get me a copy of that information?" Fielding asked. He leaned in closer to her and took her hand. "I think it would only be fair if Vice President Johnson knew what was going on with the case against him. Don't you agree?"

"I don't know," she said, squeezing Fielding's hand. "I could get into trouble."

"Think of the good you can do," Fielding urged, playing on her patriotic spirit. "You're right. The nation needs to be strong, and any kind of scandal this early in President Kennedy's administration could doom it. Since I am sworn to protect the President and Vice President, I need to do what I can to head off any kind of threat against them. I'm sure you understand."

She looked into Fielding's eyes and could see the depth of his dedication to his job.

"All right," she agreed. "Meet me here tomorrow night at six. I'll have the paperwork then."

Lyndon looked over the file as Fielding stood quietly in front of his desk. He flipped page after page, his glasses perched on the end of his nose, his lips moving as he read through the report.

Billie Sol Estes had sicced John Dennison of Marshall; he had even had Clifton Crawford Carter, Johnson's Chief Political Advisor, offer him a job in the Washington office, but Marshall wouldn't budge.

"I can admire a man dedicated to his duty, but he has gone too far," Johnson mused aloud. "A single-minded man like that can only be a problem for me."

He finished the report and closed the file folder, setting it down on his desk and removing his glasses. He rubbed the bridge of his nose and leaned back, chewing on the earpiece of his glasses. He looked up at Fielding.

"Leave me," he said. "I'll get back with you. I have some thinking to do."

Fielding backed out of the office. He steeled himself for Johnson's call back, certain of the outcome.

CHAPTER TWENTY-FOUR
MAY 5, 1961

Just like everyone else in the world, Ted Fielding's eyes were riveted to the television set in the Secret Service office, in the West Wing of the White House. On the small screen was the image of Cape Canaveral, Florida, where the Mercury-Redstone 3 rocket stood erect on the launch gantry. At the top of the rocket, sat "Freedom 7," the Mercury capsule, with its sole occupant, Naval Aviator Alan Shepard.

After three days of delays, the inaugural flight of the Mercury Program, NASA's first attempt to send a human astronaut into space, was ready to launch. All the hopes and dreams of a United States space program, designed to compete against the Soviet Union and its aggressive space program, rode along with Shepard in that small capsule.

The countdown drew to 'One,' and the powerful rocket engines propelled the spacecraft forward, breaking gravity and introducing America to what the media began calling the "Space age."

"This is one of those things that you'll never forget," Fielding told the other agents. "It's one of those things that, years from now, someone will ask you, 'Where were you when man first stepped into the Final Frontier?'"

Fielding was walking down the hall toward the Oval Office when he saw Johnson step out and shake President Kennedy's hand. He paused and nodded. "Mr. President."

"Ted," Kennedy acknowledged.

Johnson enclosed Fielding's hand in his and pulled him close. "I want you to take care of the issue with the Agriculture Department," he said bluntly.

Fielding felt Johnson's grip tighten.

"I need it done as soon as possible," Johnson said. "The President is planning a trip to Europe and the Soviet Union at the end of the month. I want Marshall dealt with before he returns."

CHAPTER TWENTY-FIVE
JUNE 3, 1961

Clint Peoples surveyed the scene surrounding Henry Marshall's death. The sheriff, Howard Stegall, had ruled it a suicide. Peoples hadn't known the man other than by reputation, but from what he did know, he'd been driven, dedicated to his job, and didn't seem like the type to take his own life.

As he walked around the scene, he tried to piece it together. There had been no photographs taken, no blood samples collected, and no fingerprints lifted from the rifle or Marshall's truck, on orders of the Robertsons County Sheriff, Stegall. Stegall had even gone so far as to have inmates from the local jail wash and wax Marshall's truck, to "Spare the family the trauma of the clean-up."

Marshall's wife had found him next to his old pickup truck, which was parked on the farm. He'd been shot five times with his own rifle, which lay near his body.

Shot five times. Never in his twenty-two years with the Texas Rangers had Peoples ever seen a person shoot themselves five times while committing suicide.

"In my opinion, sir," Peoples said to Colonel Homer Garrison, the Director of Texas Public Safety, "it would have been utterly impossible for Mr. Marshall to take his own life."

"I agree, Clint, but it's the sheriff's ruling," Garrison said. "We can't just step into another jurisdiction without being invited in by him."

"Colonel," Peoples said, resting his hands on his gun-belt, "even the man's wife and brother don't believe he did it himself. Hell, the damn *funeral director doesn't even believe it*. The family is ready to offer a reward to find out who killed this man, and the undertaker, who has seen more death than most folks, said that he believed it was murder. He even brought it to the county judge's attention to try and get him to change the rendering on the death certificate, but the judge refused, saying, 'It stays as a suicide, because that's what Sheriff Stegall said it was.'"

"Look, Clint, I'm not going to tell you that you can't look into it. I mean, you can do some poking around, just don't cross paths with the Sheriff, ok? We have to maintain a working relationship with them."

"I won't, Colonel," Peoples said. "If I find out anything, I'll make sure the Sheriff is the first to know."

After Peoples left, he stopped at a local filling station a couple of miles from the Marshall farm.

"Howdy," he said to the attendant. "Can you fill it up? I've got a long drive back to Austin."

The attendant pulled the pump from its holder and stuck it into the gas tank. Noticing the Ranger badge clipped to Peoples' belt, he asked, "You here looking into that Marshall killin'?"

"Just nosing around a bit. Why? You know something about it?"

"Well, the day he died, a stranger came through. He asked where the Marshall place was, and I gave him directions."

"Really? Remember what he looked like?" Peoples asked, pulling out a notepad and writing the description provided. "You think if I sent an artist by here, you could give him enough details for a sketch?"

The attendant scratched the scruffy beard on his chin and nodded. "I'm pretty sure I could."

Peoples pulled a business card and a five-dollar bill out of his wallet. "Thank you, sir. We'll be in touch with ya." He slipped his six-foot-two frame into the front seat and pulled out of the parking lot, pointing the front end toward Austin.

Fielding stepped off the Douglas DC-8 and onto the tarmac at Washington-Virginia airport, also known as "Bailey's Crossroads."

He was not happy that he'd had to bypass the President's trip to Vienna and travel down to Texas to alleviate Johnson of another of his self-generated "problems." Kennedy was scheduled to meet with Khruschev, and Fielding would have loved to witness that historic moment.

He walked to his car, tossed his overnight bag into the front seat, and slid inside. Sitting behind the wheel, he gripped it firmly and re-ran the incident at the Marshall farm over in his mind.

The man was bigger than he'd expected and put up more of a fight. Fielding couldn't believe he'd had to shoot him five times before he died. The only saving grace was that Sheriff Stegall owed Lyndon his election and was more than willing to help Fielding out with the cover-up, even though he never learned Fielding's name or laid eyes on him. Once Fielding left, Stegall cleaned the scene of any incriminating evidence and gave Fielding time to get away.

Fielding's eyes shot open.

"Dammit!" he shouted at the windshield.

He remembered the gas station, where he stopped and asked for directions to Marshall's farm. The clerk had gotten a good look at him, even with the sunglasses and ball cap. If the man saw him on TV with Johnson, he might be able to identify him. He had to let Lyndon know about this.

More fixing needed to be done.

JUNE 30, 1961

"Mr. Schlesinger is here to see you, sir," Evelyn Lincoln said, poking her head into the Oval Office. Kennedy was reviewing the latest intelligence reports on the Soviet Union's treatment of Francis Gary Powers, a veteran American pilot with the CIA's U-2 espionage surveillance program, who was shot down over the Soviet Union on a surveillance flight in May of 1960. He'd been put on trial and had publicly apologized for his and his country's actions. He was sentenced to ten years for espionage and imprisoned for the past thirteen months in Vladimir Central Prison, one hundred and fifty miles east of Moscow.

Negotiations for his release had begun, but it was slow going due to the Soviets' reluctance to give up a valuable intelligence source.

Kennedy set the papers aside and greeted Schlessinger. The men shook hands, and Schlessinger handed the President a folder.

"Mr. President, here is the memo you asked me to draft, regarding the current operations of the CIA and CAD and my recommendations."

Kennedy opened the folder and began to read. He glanced up and motioned for Schlessinger to have a seat. After reading the sixteen-page document, he opened the box on his desk where he kept his cigars and offered one to Schlessinger, who declined. He lit the tobacco and walked to the window, a cloud of smoke encircling his head.

"Arthur," he began, "once I'm re-elected, I'm going to take a long, hard look at your recommendations. The CIA has gotten out of hand. It's just a matter of time before it turns on its own, like a rabid dog." He crossed his hands behind his back, feeling the stiffness of the brace. The brace had been a lifesaver after his war injury, keeping his back straight and taking the strain off his neck and shoulders. "And, when that happens, none of us will be safe from their wrath."

AUGUST 1, 1961

"Evelyn," Kennedy stepped into the outer office and found her at her desk. "Find the Vice President and have him come to my office."

Kenny O'Donnell and Bobby Kennedy were already waiting in the Oval Office.

Evelyn made a couple of phone calls and tracked Johnson down at the Senate Office Building. A little while later, he walked into the Oval Office and found Kennedy on the phone. He nodded to O'Donnell and the Attorney General.

"I'll get back with you," Kennedy said, hanging up. He looked at Johnson. "Who the hell is Billie Sol Estes?"

The back of Johnson's shirt became sticky as he broke out into a cold sweat. He lit a cigarette, hoping to calm his nerves. "Billie is an associate of mine, from Texas," he answered. "Why do you ask?"

"Because, apparently, your 'associate' threatened Wilson Tucker, a Deputy Director with the Agriculture Department, telling him that he would embarrass me if an investigation he's involved in isn't discontinued," Kennedy said. "Tucker told me that Estes may have tried to bribe as many as three agents to squash this case."

Kennedy walked up to Johnson and stood nose to nose with him. "I want to know how deeply you are involved with Estes. Find out if his threat has any legs, or by God, I will see to it that you are thrown to the wolves, Lyndon! I didn't bust my ass to achieve this office just for you to backdoor me out of it!" Kennedy sat down in his rocking chair. "Now, be straight with me."

Johnson took a deep breath and explained his relationship with Estes, leaving out the part involving Marshall. O'Donnell and Bobby listened silently while the younger Kennedy occasionally asked a clarifying question. After Johnson finished explaining, he returned to his office. Seething, he snatched the phone from the desk and made a call.

"Set it in motion," he barked into the phone. "I don't care how long it takes, or what it costs. That son of a bitch is gonna pay."

SEPTEMBER 15, 1961
09:30 AM

Private First-Class Charles Whitman walked away from the Hogg Auditorium, his newly purchased engineering books under his arm. He wore his khaki uniform, which drew a few stares from passing students. Since the wall had gone up last month, separating East and West Germany, some of the students of drafting age were afraid that a war was going to escalate in Europe and that they were going to be forced to fight the Communists on their home soil.

Whitman wasn't worried about the communists in Europe. He knew from the Top-Secret Clearance briefings that the real threat from the communists was coming from Southeast Asia. Particularly from Vietnam.

He stopped on the patio outside the student union and pulled up a seat, spreading out his books to examine them. He thumbed through them, trying to wrap his head around the idea that he was a college student and that his goal of being a commander was now within reach.

He gathered his books and strode off toward the Battle Oaks, a set of Texas live oaks on the campus of the University of Texas, in Austin, that had survived the Texas War for Independence. He paused and looked back toward the bell tower, located in the center of the campus. Whitman shielded his eyes against the pounding Texas sun and squinted.

"One of these days, I need to go up to the top and check it out," he said to himself.

SEPTEMBER 15, 1961
10:30 PM

Thirteen hours away, in Vietnam, Ted Fielding checked the suite where the Vice President was sleeping. All was quiet. He decided to sit for a while outside of Johnson's room, smoking a cigarette and letting the coolness of the night sweep over him.

It had been a long day, moving into night. Fifteen hours before, Air Force Two had touched down in Saigon. The Vice President and his military aide, Colonel Howard Busser, had met with the Vietnamese President, Ngo Dinh Diem, in a closed-door session, discussing the possibility that the Prime Minister would petition President Kennedy to add sixteen thousand more U.S. troops to the advisors in country who were there assisting the South Vietnamese.

"Mr. President," Johnson said through an interpreter, "the United States people are sympathetic to the plight of your country. As I'm sure you know, our own country fought a civil war a hundred years ago. The result was a unified country and a prosperous economy."

"From a military standpoint," Colonel Burris said, "it makes sense to have a democracy in this part of the world. And we all agree that the Red Chinese are supplying the North Vietnamese with weapons and support, just as they did in North Korea, so that they can spread the doctrine of communism throughout the hemisphere. We cannot allow that."

"And, you feel that if I personally appeal to President Kennedy, he may provide us with troops and equipment to help us in our fight?" Dinh Diem asked.

"I don't see how he can refuse," Johnson said.

Fielding stood quietly in the corner, his eyes darting around the room, watching the interpreter and the servants flitting about the room, providing refreshments for the diplomatic group to help stave off the thick humidity which caused their suits to stick to them.

After the meeting, Dinh Diem allowed the Vice President's party time to freshen up before taking them on a tour of Hanoi and showing off its natural beauty and ornately constructed temples that dotted the landscape.

Hours later, the group returned to the hotel and prepared for a state dinner. Fielding assisted Johnson in preparing while he spoke with Burris.

"The President needs to approve this request," Johnson said. He slipped on his black coat with tails and adjusted the cuffs of his silk shirt. "I have a lot invested in our involvement here."

"I just got off the phone with Allen Dulles," Burris said. "He agrees that his people need to be in on advising President Dinh Diem. He also agreed that, if Kennedy doesn't accept the petition, he will still send operatives to Vietnam, working behind the scenes, providing aid and assistance to Dinh Diem."

"Dulles has no faith in Kennedy having the backbone to step into this conflict," Johnson said.

"Well, you saw how Kennedy took him to task for the Bay of Pigs fiasco and even threatened to dismantle the CIA," Burris said.

"I spoke with Dulles right after the meeting. He has plans in the works to make sure that his agency survives the current administration." Tightening his silk bow tie, Johnson checked himself in the mirror. "Even if the current administrator does not."

SEPTEMBER 18, 1961

"I'm sorry, Lyndon," Kennedy said. "I can't see this administration justifying sending thousands of American soldiers to South Vietnam to help in a local conflict."

"But, Mr. President, South Vietnam is the only hope we have to establish a democracy in Southeast Asia," Johnson argued. "President Dinh Diem personally appealed to me to bring his plight to you, in hopes that you will extend the Christian hand of compassion to aid his struggling people."

"Lyndon," Kennedy began, settling in behind the Resolute desk, "Eisenhower made the decision to step into the Vietnam conflict and send in advisors. I continued his policy, out of respect for his military genius and presidential status. But I do not see how immersing ourselves in another conflict, like we did in Korea, will benefit the nation." He leaned back and touched his fingers to his lips. "The military complex and the private sector are too intertwined in this. I can see how some people can and will profit from a war in Vietnam, at the cost of American lives."

Johnson felt his face flush, as if Kennedy was aware of his wife's investments in Bell Aircraft. Johnson knew that Bell had been developing the HU-1A helicopter, which would be the state-of-the-art military helicopter and deployed into the jungles of Vietnam. Lady Bird was set to make millions with her investment, and Johnson knew that, ultimately, he would retire from politics and be set for life on just the profits alone from the stock.

"Please relay my apologies to President Dinh Diem," Kennedy said. "I'll tell you that by the '64 election, we will have all troops out of Vietnam and will look twice before involving the United States in a civil war not of our making."

Johnson nodded. "Yes, Mr. President." Leaving the Oval Office, he stormed back to his office, pulling a cigarette from its pack and having it halfway smoked by the time he reached his desk. He grabbed the phone from the cradle and dialed Allen Dulles. "Yeah, Allen. It was just like you said. Kennedy refused to listen to Dinh Diem."

"Are we still a 'go' on the plan I discussed with Burris?" Dulles asked.

"Yes. Send in your own advisors," Johnson said. "And then we need to bring up the other option you and I discussed after the Bay of Pigs."

"Just give me a timeline," Dulles said. "One of my operatives is currently in the Soviet Union. It will take some time to get him back to the US."

"Before the end of '63," Johnson said, hanging up the phone.

CHAPTER TWENTY-SIX
OCTOBER 12, 1961
JOHNSON RANCH, STONEWALL, TEXAS

"What was that?" Fielding asked his partner, Abner Wolfe. The two men, along with four other agents, had been assigned to Johnson as he returned to the ranch to recuperate from life in Washington.

Fielding had met Wolfe during one of Kennedy's overseas trips. They had shared a room and struck up a friendship, working closely together on the front lines to defend the President. Knowing that Fielding was assigned to Johnson, Wolfe requested that his primary assignment be with the Vice President's detail so they could work as partners.

The partners were patrolling the perimeter in an older pickup truck when they heard the shot.

Their first fear was an assassination attempt, but the men knew that the Vice President was secured in a bunker built under the main house of the ranch and was unassailable to gunfire.

"I think it came from the tree line," Wolfe said. He turned the truck in that direction and punched the accelerator. As they approached a break in the trees, Fielding spotted three men loading a deer in the back of a jeep. When they spotted the truck, they rushed to the jeep and jumped inside, intent on making a quick getaway.

"Come on, Charlie!" one of the men yelled to a man who stood still as the truck approached. Snapped back to reality, the man grabbed the door and jumped in, just as the driver threw it in gear and sped out, throwing mud on the windshield of the agents' truck.

Wolfe swerved to avoid the mud flow, sliding sideways into a tree. When it came to a jarring stop, Fielding was tossed into Wolfe. He pushed off him and shoved the door open, running after the jeep. He got close enough to see the license plate and repeated it several times before he could write it down. Abandoning the chase, Fielding returned to help the agents assess the damage.

Thankfully, they were able to free the truck from the tree and get it going again. As they drove back to the ranch house, Fielding called the local police.

"Three white men, young, clean-cut—they looked like college students," he said.

The officer who took the report came back with information on the license plate. "It belongs to a student living on campus at U of A, in Austin."

"You have a name?" Fielding asked.

"Yeah," the officer said. "The jeep is registered to a Charles J. Whitman."

Whitman pulled the knife down the deer's carcass, cutting across its belly and opening the cavity. He cut away the internal organs and tossed them on a pile of newspapers spread out on the floor of the Goodall-Wooten dorm room bathroom. The deer hung from the shower head, which creaked under the weight, threatening to break free from the wall.

He thought he heard a knock on his dorm room door, but with the bathroom door closed, he wasn't sure. He stopped cutting and listened.

Knock, knock, knock.

There was no mistaking the sound that time.

"Who is it?"

"Hey, Charlie," came the answer. He recognized it as Devin Hunter, the floor supervisor for the dorm.

"What do you want, Devin? I'm...just getting out of the shower."

There was a pause, and some muffled conversation.

"Uh, ya need to open up," Hunter persisted. "There are some...the campus cops are here and need to talk to you."

"Damn," Whitman muttered. He looked down at the bloody mess around him. As panic seized him, he ran a towel under the water, trying to wipe away as much of the blood as he could while peeling off the soiled clothes.

"Hey, Charlie. You really need to open the door," Hunter urged.

"Give me a minute. I said I was in the shower!" Whitman snapped. He had just dunked his head in the sink when he heard a key in the door. He pulled the shower door closed just as Hunter, followed by two uniformed officers and two men in plain clothes, entered his room. "Hey! I've got rights, you know. You can't just barge into my room without my approval. I'll file a complaint with the dean's off—"

"Sit down and shut up, Marine!" a plainclothes man snapped. Whitman reacted just as he was trained to: he sat down and shut his mouth. Looking closely at the plainclothes officer, his eyes widened.

"You recognize me, don't you?" Fielding asked. "You're lucky I didn't shoot you." He pulled out his ID case and held it out in front of him. Wolfe moved past him and looked around the room. "I'm Agent Ted Fielding, and this is my partner, Abner Wolfe, with the United States Secret Service."

Whitman examined the badge and swallowed hard.

"Do you have any idea whose ranch you were poaching that deer from?" Fielding asked. Whitman slowly shook his head. "That ranch belongs to Lyndon Johnson, the Vice President of the United States." Fielding leaned close enough so that their noses almost touched. "You are in a lot of trouble, Private."

"In here," Wolfe called from the bathroom. "In the shower."

Fielding held Whitman's gaze for a long moment before looking past him into the bathroom. The fresh blood from the deer carcass was smeared on the sides of the tub and walls.

"Who else was involved?" Fielding asked. To his credit, Whitman identified the other two students involved but took full responsibility on himself. "You're here in Officer Candidate Training, I see. I was a Marine myself, while Wolfe over there was a Gunnery Sergeant."

Whitman looked at Wolfe and nodded. "Gunny," he said quietly.

Sheriff Hugo Klaerner from Gillespie County, where the ranch was located. nodded to his deputy, who stepped forward and pulled out a pair of handcuffs. "You're under arrest, son, for poaching and trespassing."

"We'll transport him to the jail and book him, if ya'll want to follow us back," Klaerner said. "Then, we'll pick up the other kids."

"Much obliged, Sheriff," Fielding said.

Klaerner took Whitman by the arm and walked toward the door. "I'll have my deputy take the carcass with us." He said, nodding toward the younger officer. The deputy slowly shook his head and went into the shower to cut down the deer.

"What about all of this mess?" Hunter asked. "What am I supposed to do with it?"

"Hell, clean it up or make a stew. I really don't give a damn," Klaerner irritably replied.

"Hey, Sheriff, mind if I transport Whitman?" Fielding asked.

"Don't matter to me, just as long as we get him there in one piece."

Neither Fielding nor Whitman spoke for the first mile. Fielding sensed that Whitman wanted to talk but was afraid to open his mouth.

"So, you're a Marine?" Fielding asked, breaking the silence.

"Yes, sir," Whitman said. "PFC, sir."

"What was your MOS?"

"Two-thirty-one."

"I was one-ninety-three. I was a Lance Corporal."

They spoke about the Marines for a while and then about engineering. Whitman chewed the fingernails on his shackled hands.

"Is Vice President Johnson mad?" he asked.

"More disappointed than anything," Fielding said. He sighed. "You're not a bad guy, Charlie. You just made bad choices."

They arrived at the jail half an hour later. Whitman was booked, his photo was taken, and then he was fingerprinted.

"Will this affect my officer training?" he asked.

"Don't rightly know. I guess that's between the Corps and the University, son," Sheriff Klaerner said. He looked at Fielding, who gave him a look of disappointment.

Fielding and Wolfe drove back to the ranch in silence. When they arrived, Johnson was still up in his study. Wolfe headed to his room and bed. Fielding was tasked with reporting to the Vice President.

"How'd it go?" Johnson asked. He pulled out a stool and straddled it.

"We got him. He's been booked," Fielding said. He sat down heavily in a cushy leather chair.

"Problem, Ted?" Johnson asked. He poured two whiskeys and handed one to Fielding. He sipped it, surprised that Johnson had given him a drink from the good stock.

"Whitman," Fielding said, thinking. "He seems like a good kid. He took full responsibility for the incident and asked us to cut the other guys some slack. I told him that I would run it by you, but I wouldn't make any promises." Fielding carefully watched the Vice President, trying to anticipate his response. "Plus, he's a fellow Marine."

"Is he a good shot?

"I don't know, but he did drop that deer with one shot."

Johnson tapped his finger against his glass, then drained it. "I'll call Sheriff Klaerner and see what they can do about the charges, but someone has to pay."

"I understand, sir," Fielding said, rising from the chair.

Johnson picked up the phone and made a call, holding a "just-one-minute" finger up for Fielding. After a couple of minutes, he hung up. "Go down to the jail and bail Whitman out. Bring him back here. The other two kids are being released without charges."

Fielding paid the one-hundred-dollar fine, and Whitman met him in front of the jail.

"Vice President Johnson would like to meet you," Fielding said.

Whitman shrugged, but there was no hiding his trembling as he climbed into the car. "Is he mad at me?"

"No. Just curious," Fielding said. They drove in silence until they reached the ranch. The agents guarding the gate waved them through, and Fielding parked the car and escorted Whitman to the study, where Johnson sat behind his desk. In the corner stood a man he didn't recognize. He was looking at a pocket watch.

"Come in, come in," he said, rising and offering his hand. Whitman reached out and shook it. Johnson motioned to Fielding. "You can go. I'll let you know when we're done here." Fielding nodded and closed the door after him.

As he walked down the hall, a sinking feeling settled deep in his gut about Whitman's situation. He knew this feeling well. It was the same one he'd had when Johnson had offered him the deal to keep him out of trouble a few years back.

And the feeling soured his stomach.

CHAPTER TWENTY-SEVEN
DECEMBER 22, 1961

Christmas was quickly approaching the White House, though President Kennedy wasn't there to see it. At least, not in the weeks before Christmas. The President took a trip to Venezuela in the middle of the month, and then, a couple of days before Christmas, took another trip to meet with the English Prime Minister in Bermuda. Fielding was invited to go, since he was a single man who didn't have to worry about leaving a wife and family behind. Fielding had gladly accepted and had just been assigned to the inner circle of protection when he received a phone call from Johnson.

"When will you be returning?" Johnson asked.

"We should be back on the twenty-second."

"I have an—assignment—for you when you return. And this one is highly personal."

Upon his return, Fielding went right from the plane to Johnson's office. The Vice President was highly agitated, and as soon as Fielding walked in, Johnson slammed the door behind him. There was another man in the room, sipping a drink and glancing at his pocket watch. Fielding recognized him from when he'd brought that kid, Whitman, into his office for his private conversation.

Johnson motioned toward the man. "This is Doctor Howard Booker. He's a Special Advisor from the Intelligence community."

Fielding nodded in acknowledgement.

"Josefa needs to go," Johnson said.

Fielding felt the words like a smack in the face. "Y-your...sister? Why? What has she done?" He was hesitant to speak in front of the newcomer.

"Don't mind Booker. He's on my team," Johnson said. "She's trying to blackmail me, dammit. Just like that bastard, Kinser." He pointed his finger at Fielding. "She may be my sister, but she's a whore and a liability. I need her removed, and I want you on a plane tonight to take care of it."

"Sir, I—"

"I don't care if the two of you had a fling. She's gonna be the death of me, politically, and I can't allow her to be." Johnson's eyes narrowed when Fielding shook his head in disbelief. In a flash, he'd grabbed him by the collar and yanked him forward until they were face to face. "By God, boy. You will do this, or I swear I'll have you thrown behind bars and buried for that murder you committed. What's a little more blood on your hands?"

Fielding slowly pried Johnson's hands from his jacket and took a deep breath, struggling to keep his temper in check. "What I was going to say, sir, is that I need to get a fresh change of clothes. Then I can be on the next flight to Austin."

Johnson straightened Fielding's coat, smoothing out the lapels. A snake-like smile crept across his features. "Well, you are a cold-hearted bastard, aren't you?" Slapping Fielding on the back, Johnson walked to his desk and picked up a piece of paper. "Stop by the Agency office and see an agent named Carson. He has something for you that will make it easier."

He walked to the door and grabbed the knob. "Get it done before Christmas. I don't want you to have to miss Christmas morning at the White House. It is quite the extravaganza."

Fielding knocked on Josefa's door and waited. He was holding a single white rose, wrapped in sheer plastic. She opened the door, her face revealing her surprise.

"Oh. Ted." Her gaze travelled along his body. "I didn't expect to see you again."

"I was just passing through and thought I would stop and say 'Merry Christmas,'" Fielding said.

She held the door open and moved aside. When Ted passed the threshold, she noticed the flower behind his back.

"Is that for me?" she asked.

His gloved hands escaped her attention. "Yes."

When her back was turned, Ted removed a strange-looking pistol from the inside of his coat. Designed by the CIA, the pistol's job was to fire a frozen dart containing a poison made of shellfish. Upon contact with flesh, the dart would enter, leaving behind only a pin-prick-sized hole. Once the poison entered the bloodstream, it would immediately travel to the heart and shut it down.

The CIA agent who gave it to Ted called it a "heart attack" gun.

Aiming at the base of Josefa's neck, Ted fired the weapon. She immediately slapped at her neck, as if she had been stung by a bee. Spinning around, she looked at Ted, confusion in her eyes.

Then she saw the pistol.

"Ted...why?" she asked. Then she cursed. "God damn Lyndon!"

She walked toward him and grabbed his arm, but the effects of the poison hit her.

Josefa winced at the pain in her chest and clutched it. She slipped to the floor, struggling to breathe as she grasped at Fielding's clothes. When he pushed her off, she collapsed onto the floor and reached for him again.

Uneasy about relying on the effects of the poison, Fielding pulled a pillow from the couch, knelt over Josefa, and pushed the pillow down over her face. She tried to shove it away, but as her lungs shut down, so did her ability to fight back.

Fielding held the pillow in place a few minutes after all movement stopped and slowly rose. He placed the pillow back on the couch, making sure to put the side he'd smothered her with against the couch cushion.

Checking that he'd left nothing behind, Ted pulled out a handkerchief and opened the door, pausing long enough to collect the rose, and quietly closed the door behind him.

Fielding lugged his suitcase back to his room in the East Wing of the White House. Since he was single, he resided in the Executive Mansion along with the other single agents. Because the housing was limited, he shared his room with Abner Wolfe.

He set the bag down by his bed and glanced at his friend. Wolfe was sitting at his desk, reading through some paperwork.

"Where have you been?" Wolfe asked.

"The Vice President sent me on an errand, back in Texas." Fielding yawned. "I have to go check in with him."

Johnson was on the phone when Fielding walked into the Vice President's residence on Christmas Day.

"—and, there are no clues as to the cause of death?" Johnson asked, motioning for him to have a seat. "I see. Well, please let me know what you find in the autopsy and if there's anything I can do to help. Yes, yes. It is a blow to me and my family. We will work on the funeral arrangements as soon as the body is released. Thank you for calling."

He hung up and walked over to the credenza and poured himself a drink, even though it was nine-thirty in the morning. Turning to Fielding, he offered a toast.

"Merry Christmas, Ted. It looks like the makin's of a Happy New Year."

CHAPTER TWENTY-EIGHT
FEBRUARY 9, 1962

Charles Whitman scratched his head as he tried to make sense of the chapter on stress levels on a suspension bridge. Even though he had a fairly good understanding of mathematics, the level of knowledge that was needed for bridge design was beyond his grasp. He hadn't realized the Mechanical Engineering course would be so challenging.

He leaned back in his seat, stretching his back. Allowing his gaze to wander the Texas Student Union, he looked to see if there was anyone he recognized. His eyes lit up when he noticed a fellow student heading toward him.

Whitman had a few friends, though fewer since his arrest for poaching that deer. The other two students who'd been poaching with him were released without charges, but it still reflected on their college transcripts. Francis Shuck Jr. was the only friend who'd stuck by his side. Shuck was a fellow engineering student who'd taken a shine to Whitman. He'd helped him through some of the rough spots in class, but knew enough not to give him too much help. If Charlie wanted to be any type of leader, he would have to learn to stand or fall on his own.

Grabbing his shoulders tightly, Shuck asked, "Have you heard anything from the Marine Corps?"

"No," Charlie said on a laugh as he spun his chair to face him. "Not a word. The way I figure it, the best-case scenario is that they'll overlook it, and I'll continue with my studies."

"And what's the worst-case scenario?" Shuck asked, crossing his arms over his chest.

"Worst case is that they'll pull my scholarship and put me back on active duty," Charlie said. "The die's already been cast," he said, his gaze dropping to the floor. "There's nothing I can do about it."

Kathleen Francis Leissner had seen Charlie in her Economics class but had never worked up the courage to speak with him.

He always seemed to be with a group of guys, making him appear unapproachable. Plus, he was two years her senior. Something must have changed recently, though, because lately Charlie was rarely seen with anyone.

Kathleen wasn't an overly outgoing person. In fact, she was downright shy, but her determination overrode her overt shyness.

She counted it quite fortuitous when she found Charlie sitting alone in the student union. Shuck was getting a cup of coffee when he saw her come in. He'd met her a few days back, while hanging with a couple of friends, and Kathleen, or "Kathy" as she preferred to be called, had mentioned that she thought Charlie was cute and wouldn't mind getting to know him.

Kathy found an empty seat at the table where Charlie was sitting and settled herself in. Charlie, who'd been reading, leaned back in his chair with his hands behind his head and his eyes closed. He'd remained quiet and unmoving for so long that Kathy wondered if he'd fallen asleep. She let out a sigh, defeated that he hadn't noticed her, and stood up. She had decided to leave and forget striking up a conversation, but Schuck took notice. Walking across the union hall, he bumped into Kathy, causing her to drop one of the books she was carrying, and slapped the desktop. The sharp 'crack' pulled Whitman from his reveling with a start. Arms flailing, he pitched backward, his balance shot, and crashed onto the floor.

"Oh, my!" Kathy exclaimed. She rushed to Whitman's side and reached down to help him up. "Are you okay?"

Whitman lay on his back, staring up at the stucco ceiling tiles. It took him a moment before he noticed the prettiest eyes he'd ever seen. The girl stood over him, hand outstretched. Behind her stood Shuck.

"Are you okay?" Kathy asked again. "I'm so sorry. I didn't mean to startle you."

"Yes," Whitman said finally. "Just caught me off guard."

She and Shuck helped Charlie up, and he settled back in his chair. "You're in my econ class, aren't you?" he asked.

"Yes," Kathy said, her cheeks flaming red. "I'm surprised you recognized me."

"How could I not? You're the prettiest girl on campus."

"Charlie," Shuck said, with a grin, "this is Kathy Leissner."

Charlie stood up clumsily and shook her hand. "Charlie Whitman. Glad to meet you."

Kathy smiled shyly. "You're a Marine, aren't you?"

"Yes, ma'am."

"Do Marines drink coffee?"

"Yes, ma'am, we do."

Kathy smiled. "So do education majors."

APRIL 4, 1962

The early part of 1962 was relatively quiet, where the Kennedy Administration was concerned. Fielding had been assigned to more protection details with the President than with the Vice President, which was just fine with him.

After Kennedy had questioned Johnson about his connection to Billie Sol Estes, the relationship between the two men had soured. Though they kept the dispute out of the public eye, behind closed doors, Johnson voiced the theory that Kennedy would boot him from the '64 ticket.

The idea of him losing to Kennedy a second time caused the legendary Johnson's temper to flare. Fielding had seen it several times in the years past and knew what Johnson was capable of. And today wasn't any better.

Fielding was once again in Texas.

A man by the name of George Krutilek sat in his 1961 Plymouth with the windows rolled up and a garden hose pushed through a vent window. The car was parked in his enclosed garage.

Krutilek was an old enemy of Johnson. Just last month, he'd decided to approach the Texas Attorney General's office to give testimony before an empaneled grand jury about the depth of corruption Johnson was involved in from 1948 to the present.

Krutilek had confided in Sheriff Stegall about his plan to speak to the grand jury. Stegall, who owed his career to Johnson, continued his allegiance to the Vice President and made him aware of Krutilek's plans.

Fielding was sent to take care of the problem.

Fielding had entered Krutilek's house and waited for him to come home. Once he arrived, Fielding came up behind him and covered his face with a chloroform-soaked rag. Krutilek pitched forward, striking his head on the coffee table, before passing out. Fielding put him in the front seat of the car, attached the garden hose to the exhaust pipe, before running it through the vent window, and turned the car on. The carbon monoxide took less than an hour to build up to lethal levels. Fielding took the time to write out a suicide note on Krutilek's typewriter, blaming money problems and fear that he had made a mistake telling the Attorney General he would testify against Johnson and that any testimony would be a lie.

Fielding flew back to Washington later that day, assuring Johnson that his problem had been dealt with.

CHAPTER TWENTY-NINE
MAY 20, 1962

"*Happy birthday to you...*" Marilyn Monroe began. Her breathlessness added to her sensuality. Attired in a bejeweled dress, beige to the point of looking nude, she stood in the spotlight in the center of Madison Square Garden.

She had been introduced by Peter Lawford, the President of the United States' brother-in-law, who was initially perplexed that she hadn't immediately appeared on stage. Buying time, Lawford had continued his praise for the star as Monroe finally emerged from backstage in the middle of his intro. The crowd erupted in applause as Monroe, wrapped in a mink wrap, strode onto the stage, dominating it as she walked to the podium next to Lawford. Without missing a beat, Lawford leaned into the microphone. "Mr. President, the rather *late* Marilyn Monroe."

After allowing Lawford to remove her wrap, Monroe flicked the microphone, checking its volume. Shading her eyes from the blinding light, she peered through the darkness and saw John Kennedy sitting in the audience. Exhaling deeply into the microphone, she caressed it with her fingers in a suggestive manner.

"*...happy birthday to you.*" She dragged out the words, manipulating her voice for full effect. "*...happy birthday, Missster President, happy birthday to you.*" She raised her arms and then broke out into a rendition of the Bob Hope standard, "Thanks for the memories," changing the words to aim at Kennedy specifically. After the verse, she implored the crowd by shouting, "Everybody!" and led them in a verse of "Happy Birthday."

A large cake was rolled out to center stage, and Kennedy himself emerged from behind the curtain.

"I can retire from politics, now that I've had 'Happy Birthday' sung to me in such a sweet manner," he said.

Lyndon Johnson, along with Fielding, who'd been assigned to Johnson's detail for the night, clapped along with the crowd. Johnson glanced across the table at Jackie, whose smile was fixed on her face. As he watched her, he noticed the subtle twitch in her jaw muscles as she joined the others in applause.

"Could you believe that show last night? I couldn't believe that dress. She looked practically naked," Johnson said to Fielding. "And I thought Jackie was going to pull a muscle in her face, trying to hold that plastic smile of hers. You know he and Bobby both are screwing her, right?"

The revelation wasn't news to Fielding. He'd spoken with other agents on the White House detail who had personally escorted Monroe through the rarely used basement door where she would meet with Kennedy. Most of the time, it was when Jackie was gone on a trip, although there were a few instances when she had come in right under the First Lady's nose. She'd even met with Bobby at the White House, and the two brothers had taken turns with her.

"I heard the President had a bad back from the war," Fielding said. "Apparently, it's not as bad as we were led to believe." He looked conspiratorially at Johnson. "You know, if information were leaked to the press about their liaisons, it might be enough to force him to resign."

"Bullshit, son," Johnson said. "The press in this country loves him. They probably wouldn't believe it unless they had photos and eyewitnesses, and even then, they STILL might not believe their own eyes. No paper would print the story." He poured himself a drink and pointed the glass at Fielding. "Hell, back in '56, that cold-hearted bastard was out on a yacht in the middle of the Mediterranean Sea with some little side piece of tail, while that sweet young wife of his was delivering their stillborn son. Apparently, he was 'so devastated' that he was hesitant to get back to his heartbroken wife."

Fielding opened his mouth to make a statement, but Johnson waved him off. "No. The best way to bring those blue-blooded sons-a-bitches to their knees is to hurt them.

Take away what they value." Johnson smiled his cobra smile. "Money, property, women. You take away those things, and they will collapse like a house of cards."

Fielding shook his head. He knew what Johnson was getting at.

"Might take some time," Fielding said. "She's a major player right now."

"She's a druggie," Johnson said. "And if my sources in Hollywood are correct, she's having career problems. Shouldn't take much to push her over the edge."

Fielding began plotting out the best way to make her death seem like an accident, but stopped himself mid-thought.

"My God. I'm actually contemplating how to kill Marilyn Monroe!"

MAY 6, 1962

Whitman and Shuck were browsing in the university bookstore. Charlie bought an engineering textbook, and the two walked outside in the bright spring sunshine.

"How are you and Kathy getting along?" Shuck asked.

"Oh, man. She's great," Charlie said. "I really owe you one for fixing us up."

"Well, maybe she'll keep you out of trouble." Shuck elbowed Charlie in the ribs.

Whitman glanced up at the tower, which dominated the school's skyline. "Ever been up there?"

"Nah," Shuck said. "Never really thought about it."

Whitman pointed up to the top, just under the clock face. "See those waterspouts between the pillars?"

"Yeah."

"Those are like gunports. Get someone who's a good shot with a rifle, like a trained sniper, and, man, he could hold off an entire army up there before they could get to him."

Shuck, the son of a Houston oilman, had never served in the military. He looked at Whitman like he'd grown a second head. "Man, Charlie, they teach you Marines some weird ways of thinking."

"Come on," Whitman said. "Let's go up to the top. I want to check it out."

"I don't know," Shuck said. "I don't really like heights."

"Tell you what," Whitman said, placing his hand on Shuck's shoulder. "You come up with me, and I'll buy you lunch. Besides, I need to know that you'll be there when I need you."

"All right," Shuck said, "but I'm picking the restaurant."

"Deal." Whitman wrapped his arm around Shuck's shoulder, and the two students cut across the plaza, heading for the tower.

JUNE 1, 1962

"I see the Dallas News has chimed in on this." John Kennedy said to his Chief of Staff, Kenny O'Donnell.

Just a few days before, O'Donnell had brought to the President's attention the suspicious death of Henry Marshall and how it led to the office of the Vice President.

"They're going to follow the trail from Marshall to Billie Sol Estes, directly to Lyndon, Jack," O'Donnell said. "Marshall died under suspicious conditions, even though the Sheriff and undertaker ruled it a suicide. There are rumblings that Marshall had begun an investigation of Estes and that Marshall was working on bringing a criminal case against Lyndon. Estes is using the same attorney that Lyndon used when he was investigated for bribery, so there is, at least, a connection there."

"Bobby spoke with J. Edger, and they're opening an investigation, using the full resources of the FBI," Kennedy said. He shook his head. "God damn that Johnson! I knew he was going to be a problem, but dammit, I needed him to carry the south." Kennedy eased himself into his rocking chair, his back throbbing. "If there's anything concrete, they can pin on Lyndon, tell Bobby not to hold back. I can always find a replacement Vice President."

"So, Bobby is getting the FBI involved in the Marshall case, eh?" Johnson asked Fielding. "We're good, right?"

Fielding nodded. "Yeah. There won't be anything to come back to you directly. I covered my tracks." He didn't feel that it was prudent to mention the gas station attendant. He figured that if he kept in the shadows and out of the public eye, no one would ever tie him to that gas station.

And if the clerk did, Fielding was becoming well-versed in removing problems.

CHAPTER THIRTY
AUGUST 4, 1962

Fielding knocked on the bungalow door and glanced around as he waited for an answer.

Eunice Murray opened the door just a crack. "Yes. Can I help you?"

Fielding held his credentials up and removed his sunglasses. "Ma'am, I'm Agent Ted Fielding with the US Secret Service. I've been sent here by the President's office to make sure the perimeter is secure," he lied.

The truth was that Fielding had been sent on orders from the Vice President to inflict damage on Kennedy. Johnson had given him free rein to do as he saw fit with the Monroe issue.

"Oh," Murray said, eyeing him suspiciously. "No agent has ever done that before."

"New protocol, ma'am," Fielding said. "The communist threat is on the rise, and we need to ensure that the President's safety is protected."

"Do you mean—does the President think—" She stepped outside the door, glancing behind her. Lowering her voice to a whisper, she leaned closer to him. "Miss Monroe, is a communist?"

"No, no," Fielding said with a chuckle. "But if the communists find out that the President is visiting Miss Monroe, they could use the information to try to harm him." He leaned in closer. "National Security. You understand."

"Oh, yes. Yes, I do," Murray said, holding the door open for him. "But please be quiet. Miss Monroe is sleeping in the back bedroom."

"I promise," Fielding said.

He walked around the interior of the small residence, checking the windows and doors. He had just stepped onto the patio when he heard a yawn behind him. Turning, his eyes widened in shock to find Marilyn standing in the middle of the living room. She was in a full stretch and was naked as the day she was born. Glancing at Ted, she smiled, unashamed of her nakedness.

Even though she was beautiful to behold, Ted was more distracted by her face. She looked tired and haggard, her hollow eyes surrounded by dark circles. Her hair looked like it hadn't been washed in a week, yet she still emanated charm and innocence.

"Hi," she said, her voice silky. "Anything I can do for you?"

Fielding stood in stunned silence, his mind racing about what she could do for him. After a prolonged, awkward silence, he realized he was speaking. "Oh, n-n-no, ma'am," he sputtered. "I'm with the, uh—" his mind went blank as she bent over to retrieve a magazine on the table. "I'm with the President's security detail. I just...need to...check the perimeter..." His eyes wandered. "...to make sure everything is secure...before he visits."

"Owww," Marilyn squealed. "Jack's coming to see me?"

"Yes, ma'am," Fielding lied. "He'll be here around eight o'clock. If it's alright with you, I need to check your room to ensure that it's secure."

"Oh, Jack is coming tonight!" Marilyn said. "Oh, yes. Let me get my robe." She scurried back to her room, and Fielding heard a rustle of clothes. Marilyn emerged, cinching the belt on a satin robe around her waist. "It's been weeks since I've seen Jack," she said sadly. "I miss him so." She slipped her arm through Fielding's and pulled him close. "Did you know, when he was a senator, he promised to leave that stick-in-the-mud Jackie and marry me once he was president?" she whispered. Her eyes grew hard. "Then that rat Bobby messed everything up." She released him and sat down at her dressing table. Picking up a brush, she passed it through the blond locks.

Fielding stood behind her for a moment, reading the profound sadness in her eyes before moving on to check out her room. He swallowed hard, his mind trying to wrap itself around what he intended to do that night.

When he stepped into Marilyn's room, he stopped short. The room was a mess. On the floor, pages from a script were spread out. He picked one up and read the title, "What a way to go!" The bedclothes were in a state of disarray, with the blankets lying halfway on the floor. On the nightstand next to the bed was a framed photo of Joe DiMaggio, several pill bottles, and a partially empty vodka bottle. He paused long enough to pick up the bottles and read the prescriptions.

Barbiturates and Nembutal.

He pulled out a notebook and jotted down the names of the medications, as well as Marilyn's alcoholic preferences.

Stepping to the window, he opened it and peered out at the backyard. A high privacy fence surrounded the rear of the property. Most of the fence was concealed by large shrubs that had been equally placed along the perimeter. Ted noticed a gap in the shrubbery, where the gate was located.

Closing the window, he strode out of the room and headed toward the backyard. He checked the gate and found that the lock was rusted. When he pushed on it, the lock broke in his hand. He pulled the door closed and headed back to the house. Marilyn was standing in the kitchen, sipping a cup of coffee Eunice had poured for her.

"Is everything okay?" she asked.

"Yes, ma'am. Everything is just fine," he assured. "I'll advise the President that the location is secure." He nodded to Murray and Monroe. "Thank you, ladies, for your cooperation." He started to leave, but turned back to Marilyn, taking her hand. "It is a pleasure to have met you, Miss Monroe."

Fielding checked his watch. It was half past midnight. He pushed the gate open on the perimeter fence and crossed the yard, approaching the bungalow. The light in Marilyn's room was on. He looked in the window and saw her lying across the bed, naked. She was holding the phone receiver in one hand, as if making a call. The other handheld a vodka bottle. The pill bottles were tipped over, and the pills had spilled onto the bed.

"Oh, Jack," she mumbled. Her voice was slurred and thick-tongued. "Y-you promised."

Fielding pulled on the window, which he'd left unlocked. It opened smoothly and quietly. He climbed into the room, pausing long enough to ensure he hadn't disturbed Monroe. Stepping to the bed, he stared at her. She was lying on her back, one leg bent, the other straight. She'd fallen asleep, or maybe even passed out. Her breathing was slow and labored.

Fielding took a corner of the sheet and pulled it over her, concealing her body. One leg was still exposed. He reached into his pocket and pulled out a syringe. It was filled with a mixture of Phenobarbital, Nembutal, and alcohol. The quantities would be lethal, post-injection.

"God forgive me," Fielding said softly. Anger then flared in his mind. "Goddamn you, Lyndon."

Fielding took Marilyn's left foot in his hand. He caressed it tenderly, steeling himself for what he had to do. Massaging her toes, he separated the big toe from the second one and plunged the needle between them, injecting the lethal concoction into her bloodstream. Removing the needle, he pulled a handkerchief from his pocket and held it against the injection site, applying pressure so that it wouldn't bleed or bruise. The chemical cocktail would take a few minutes before it traveled the length of her body, depressing her respiratory system and slowing her heart until it stopped.

A few minutes passed. Fielding removed the handkerchief and laid his fingers against the pulse in Marilyn's neck. He felt the beat slow down, until it abruptly stopped. He stifled a gasp when he realized she was gone. Using his handkerchief, he removed the bottle from her hand and placed it on the nightstand. He took her hand once more and held it, taking several deep breaths to calm himself.

Climbing back out of the window, he pulled it closed behind him.

He didn't expect the sobs to come. They started deep in his chest and rose to his throat. He leaned against the outside wall, tears saturating his eyes and running down his cheeks.

He struggled to maintain his composure as emotions threatened to erupt from his throat like lava from a volcano. His body shook with grief, the enormity of what he'd done punching him full in the chest. Ted had killed others with his own hands, but the twinge of guilt about what he was doing was much more visceral this time. To remove someone so vibrant, so well loved and adored by the world, drove him to his knees in despair.

He wasn't sure how much time had passed when the last gasp in his chest calmed and he was able to find composure. His legs trembled as he stood and wiped his eyes with his shirt sleeve before glancing back inside.

Marilyn lay motionless on the bed just as he had left her.

He slipped across the yard, opening the gate and closing it behind him. When he turned, he stopped short as his heart leapt into his throat.

Abner Wolfe was standing just outside the gate.

"We need to talk, Ted."

Ted poured cream into his coffee while Wolfe sipped his black. They'd stopped at an all-night diner a few blocks from Monroe's bungalow. Except for the fry cook and waitress, they were the only patrons.

"You were sent here on Johnson's orders, weren't you?" Wolfe asked, keeping his voice low.

"Why do you ask?" Ted was unwilling to commit to an answer.

"I was sent to my first job four years ago," Wolfe said. "Took out a state auditor who had the goods on Lyndon. Made it look like a suicide." Wolfe took a sip of his coffee and looked at the table. "I was in a car wreck and killed a family of three," he said quietly. "I was a drunk minor, and Lyndon made it go away. Paid off the family and kept me out of jail." He looked Ted in the eye. "That bastard owns me."

Fielding was speechless and a bit relieved. Finally, there was someone he could unload his guilt onto who understood the weight of carrying out Johnson's orders.

"What did Johnson have against Monroe?" Wolfe asked after a long moment of silence. Fielding's eyebrows rose sharply, shocked that Wolfe knew who his victim had been. "Hey, I'm not a fool. I checked out the address as soon as I saw you stop by this afternoon."

"Why were you following me?" Fielding snapped. His voice was loud enough to attract attention from the other night owls in the diner.

"Why do you think, Ted? I was on orders from the boss," Wolfe said. "And, keep your voice down, for Pete's sake!" He leaned across the table. "After the foul-up with the gas station attendant in Texas, Johnson wanted me to make sure that you didn't mess things up again."

"Look, I may have spoken with the attendant for a few minutes, but—"

"I had to go back and kill him, Ted," Wolfe stated flatly. "Lyndon couldn't leave any loose ends, especially after that Texas Ranger, Clint People, started poking his nose into the case. Look, you got sloppy. I would expect you to do the same thing. It's called 'teamwork.' We need to be able to watch each other's backs."

Fielding felt his temper flare, but it slowly ebbed. Wolfe was right. They were in the same boat, and they needed each other.

"Kennedy humiliated him in front of Bobby and Kenny O'Donnell. Dressed him down for that Agriculture Scandal," Fielding explained. "Johnson knew about the relationships John and Robert Kennedy had with Marilyn. It was his way of sending them a very subtle message that he could get them where they live, and he knows their secrets." He sipped his coffee. "Bobby forced her to have an abortion, and she was going to go to the press about them anyway. By having her...removed, it forced Kennedy to owe Johnson a favor."

"You killed her," Wolfe said.

"Yes," Fielding confirmed. "It was the hardest thing I've ever had to do." He stirred his coffee absently. "I held her hand. I didn't want her to meet her end alone."

"Mighty decent of you," Wolfe said. "Have you met that guy, Doctor Booker?"

Fielding thought for a second. "Briefly. He was in the meeting Johnson had with that Whitman kid, and I saw him again when he briefed me about his sister. Why do you ask?"

"I don't know. There's just something about him that I don't trust. I'm not even sure what a 'Special Advisor' is. But I heard he may be involved in some of that mind control stuff the CIA started back in the fifties."

Ted had heard of the CIA's experimental mind-altering project called "MKUltra," which started while he was attending U of A, in the 50s. The organization sought out members of the military and college students to act as guinea pigs to test it, but from all he had heard of the project, it was dangerous. And even though they offered him a fat paycheck to participate in it, Ted steered clear of it.

"He's probably caught up in the same situation we're in," Fielding said. "Just keep your distance until we know more about him. Have you tried the injections?" He asked. Johnson had offered him the opportunity to augment his physical abilities and possibly even his lifespan by accepting experimental injections over a span of two years. Other than some minor side effects, the shots hadn't caused him any long-lasting problems.

Fielding never really faced the hypocrisy of taking one experimental drug over the other offered in college. He just guessed Johnson was a better salesman than the CIA.

"No," Wolfe said. "I told Johnson that I don't do any type of drugs, especially not something as questionable as the ones he offered. And you're a fool for allowing them to shoot that stuff in you."

"Maybe," Fielding said. "But what's done is done. Anyway, they're supposed to extend your life expectancy by a good ten to twenty years."

They sat quietly, stirring their coffee for a few minutes.

"So," Wolfe said, "how did Johnson get to you?"

Fielding told Wolfe the tale of his fight in the bar and the aftermath. When he was finished, Wolfe reached across the table and shook Ted's hand.

"It's a pleasure to meet someone whose life is more messed up than mine."

CHAPTER THIRTY-ONE
CURRENT DAY

"You killed Marilyn Monroe?" Jack Lefleur stared incredulously at his uncle. Fielding nodded, his expression grim. Stopping at a gas station in Van Wert, Ohio, about two and a half hours from Cincinnati, Lefleur pulled up to the gas pump, wasting no time in jumping out of the car. Grabbing the nozzle, he shoved it into the gas tank and leaned heavily against the car, trying to keep himself from falling over under the weight of his uncle's confessions.

It was his own fault. He'd told him he wanted to know the truth, and Fielding had seemed more than happy to unburden himself to Jack. His story was so fantastic that it was almost impossible to believe. Some of it he would have to verify when he returned to the office, but Jack was sure that there were parts he would never be able to confirm. If Ted were anything like the man he portrayed himself to be, there would be no evidence of his crimes and nothing to tie him to them.

He felt his phone vibrate and pulled it from his pocket. It was Reubans.

"Jack," she said breathlessly. "Where the hell have you been? Your department has an all-points bulletin for you."

He looked through his phone's history and saw that he'd received about a dozen calls from Peterson, as well as dispatch and others. He'd been so engrossed in Fielding's story that he hadn't even felt the phone vibrating over and over.

"I've been—tied up," Jack said. He looked over his shoulder as Fielding came out of the station carrying two cups of coffee. "What's going on?"

"They went to that bar you went to and found several people beaten nearly to death. Witnesses said that you and another guy beat them and left the bar. The detectives have been looking for you, but no one knew where you'd gone off to. And then my safe was broken into, and the evidence stored in there was stolen. I—"

"Your safe was broken into?" Jack asked. He paced away from the car, glancing at Fielding.

"Yes. Everything you and I went over. It's all gone. Fortunately, I still have the digital photos saved on the hard dr–" Reubans stopped mid-sentence. Jack could hear her typing furiously on her computer keyboard. "Dammit! Someone installed a worm virus. It's going through the photos on the hard drive and wiping them out. Jack, what the hell is going on?"

"I can't tell you," Jack said. "But I'll get the evidence back. Look, Lara, some serious things are going on that I can't discuss right now. Just know that what I'm working on ties directly into our investigation, but it's deeper and more complex than we realized. Lives are at stake, and I'm trying to save them."

Reubans was quiet for a long moment. "Okay, Jack. I don't know why I should, but I trust you. Just—be careful."

"I will." Jack hung up.

Back in the driver's seat, he looked at Fielding. "You broke into Reuban's safe and took our evidence we recovered from Booker, didn't you?"

Fielding sipped his coffee and looked Jack in the eye. "I sure did." His Texas drawl was thick. "You two got close to finding out the truth, Jack. Really close. I'll tell you everything you want to know, but it's for you to know. You can't let anyone else know what I'm telling you here. If the truth were ever made public, the entire world—everything you know and love—will be destroyed, faith in our system of government will be shattered, and the country itself will be shaken to its foundation."

"Why? Because you killed Marilyn Monroe and some other low-level dignitaries?" Jack asked.

"It goes deeper than that, Jack. Way deeper," Fielding said. "Let's go. We need to get to Cinci."

Jack pulled out of the parking lot and turned on US-33, heading for the I-75 interchange.

"Now, where were we?" Fielding asked.

CHAPTER THIRTY-TWO
AUGUST 17, 1962
NEEDVILLE, TEXAS

"I now pronounce you, man and wife," Father Leduc said, sealing the traditional Catholic ceremony between Charles Whitman and Kathleen Francis Leissner.

Patrick Whitman, honored to have the title of "best man," smiled next to his brother. Charles kissed Kathy and turned toward his family, who'd driven from Florida to Kathy's hometown of Needville to see them tie the knot.

Charles's parents had been honored when he and Kathy chose to marry on their twenty-second wedding anniversary. Charles Senior was surprisingly cordial toward his son and his new bride. He even kissed Kathy and welcomed her into the family.

Friends of the bride and groom drank and danced at the small reception while the newlyweds accepted handshakes, kisses, and gifts from the guests.

"He's such a handsome boy," Francis Leissner said, hooking her arm in Margaret Whitman's.

"Looks like you raised a good boy," Raymond Leissner told Charles Senior. "Kathy's mom and I both think he'll make her a good husband."

"If he can keep his head about him," Charles Senior said. "Sometimes that boy flies off on a tangent and makes some poor decisions—like joining up with the Marines. He joined without my permission, you know."

"Well," Ray said, "he looks like he has some powerfully influential friends." He pointed to an envelope that appeared to be filled with cash. The envelope was from the Vice President's office. He plucked it off the table and pulled out the card. Quickly, he counted the cash. A soft whistle escaped through his teeth. "Holy Moley! That's five hundred dollars."

Charlie walked over to Ray and took the card from his hand. He read the note and smiled, then passed the note to Kathy.

"To Charles and Kathleen:

Congratulations on your marriage. Please allow me to host a small party at my ranch, in your honor, at a time convenient to you. Please accept this gift as a token of my good wishes. Your Friend, Lyndon B. Johnson."

CHAPTER THIRTY-THREE
OCTOBER 16, 1962
JOHNSON RANCH, STONEWALL, TEXAS

Charlie Whitman sipped a beer and smiled at his wife of less than two months. Although they'd received the note from Vice President Johnson inviting them to his ranch, he was still shocked when a member of Vice President Johnson's office called them at their small, off-campus apartment and asked them to come to the ranch that weekend to celebrate their wedding.

"Charlie," Johnson said, "your wife tells me that you were an accomplished pianist at just twelve years old. Is that right?"

"Yes, sir, Mr. Vice President."

"Well, would you be so kind as to grace us with a song?"

"It's been a while since I've played in public," Charlie said meekly.

"Well, son, we're all just friends here." Johnson put his hand on Charlie's shoulder and ushered him toward the piano. Charlie took a seat and flexed his fingers, then began to play selections from Chopin and Bach. After he finished, the room burst into applause. Accepting it, he went to the bar, grabbed a beer, and downed it. He watched Johnson speak privately with an aide and then leave the room.

"Hey, Charlie," Shuck called to him. "Are you going to Vietnam to kill 'Charlie?'" he laughed. "Would that be considered suicide?"

"The Marine Corps can kiss my patriotic ass!" Charlie responded. Kathy, always the level-headed one, patted her husband's arm to calm him and pulled him down to whisper in his ear. Charlie laughed at the private joke and kissed his wife on the cheek.

In the corner of the room, another man, not part of the party, laughed at Charlie's statement. Charlie stepped away from the group and offered the man a beer. "I take it you don't like the Marines either?"

The man accepted the beer and took a swig. "I didn't like the power they thought that they had over me."

"No longer active?"

"The Marines are just the military arm of the totalitarian regime currently in power. After what that bastard Kennedy did in Cuba, I'm surprised he hasn't been brought before a world court."

"You sound like a communist," Charlie said. He didn't try to hide the disgust in his voice. "If you hate the President so much, why are you even here?"

"I'm a Marxist," the man said. "And I was invited." He walked off, sipping his beer.

Grabbing a nearby waiter, Charlie asked if he knew who the man was.

"He said his name was Alek something." The waiter's eyes lit with recognition. "Hidell! That was it. But the Vice President called him 'Lee.'"

Fielding stood next to Wolfe and sipped a ginger ale while lighting another cigarette. While surveying the room, he'd noted the conversation between Whitman and the man who'd identified himself as 'Hidell.' After the two had separated, Fielding scanned the dignitaries from Washington and Texas. Some, he knew by their reputations, while others had attached themselves to the Vice President in hopes of rising to the top of the heap.

He wandered around the room, catching bits and pieces of conversations.

"I can't believe Kennedy intervened in a situation that was strictly a state's matter. Sticking his nose into that University of Mississippi fiasco," John Connally, candidate for Governor of Texas, said. "I mean, I don't care if that Negra' boy—what was his name?"

"Meredith. James Meredith," Congressman Ray Roberts supplied.

"Yeah, Meredith. I don't care if he was a soldier; he still violated Mississippi state law by trying to enroll as a student."

"Well, I agree with you that Kennedy shouldn't have sent in federal troops, but if he plans on getting the Negro vote in '64, it may have been a wise thing to do, politically speaking."

Fielding felt a nudge and turned to see Wolfe. Wolfe inclined his head toward the bar.

"Looks like Booker made it," Wolfe said. "Have you found anything out about that guy?"

"He's an active-duty Captain in the Marines," Fielding said. "He has a medical degree and a secondary degree in psychology. He believes in using hypnosis to treat his patients."

Wolfe looked at Fielding in amazement. "How the hell do you know all of this?"

"I asked him," Fielding said with a shrug. "He is very forthcoming."

"I wonder why Lyndon keeps him as a Special Adviser."

"I don't know." Fielding pointed to Booker with his glass. "But it looks as if he has designs on Whitman."

Both agents watched Booker. He was in deep conversation with Whitman. Booker looked at his watch and indicated the time. Whitman nodded, and the two headed out of the room together.

"I've got a bad feeling about this," Fielding said. They sipped their drinks, each startled when Lyndon burst into the room. He looked around and, after seeing a couple of his aides, motioned them over. The men conversed in hushed whispers and then went into Johnson's study. Fielding grabbed Wolfe by the arm. "Something's up."

They followed them to the study, and Fielding knocked. Johnson pulled the door open. After considering their intrusion, he motioned them inside.

"The President is on the line, sir," one of the aides said, handing the phone to Johnson. He snatched it from his hand.

"What's the situation, Mr. President?"

Fielding and Wolfe stood with their backs to the door. Johnson chain-smoked one cigarette after another as he wrote down notes and muttered something about Cuba and missiles. He hung up and looked at his aides.

"We have to get back to Washington tonight," he said. "Two days ago, one of our intelligence agencies took surveillance photos that show Soviet intercontinental missile launchers located in Cuba." He shook his head. "Goddamn Cubans are gonna try and pay us back for that goddamn Bay of Pigs disaster."

The flight back to Washington on Air Force Two was a flurry of activity. Johnson spent most of it on the phone in his office while Fielding was on the other line, coordinating with the security details for the First and Second families should something escalate with the Cubans. When they touched down, they made their way to the White House. Kennedy was in the Oval Office.

"You know, this goes back a year ago, to Vienna, when Khruschev snubbed Kennedy," Johnson said. "That Russian bastard has started a pissing contest and is showing Jack that he has the biggest dick."

OCTOBER 22, 1962

"We have the bunkers stocked and ready," Hazelwood said, addressing the assembled agents in a briefing room in the East Wing. "The President and Vice President have been advised that we have approximately four minutes to relocate them to the emergency shelters in the event of a threatened or impending nuclear strike." He pulled Fielding to the side and lowered his voice. "The President and Vice President have not seen eye to eye on the blockade idea. I understand that the discussion between the two during the last cabinet meeting got pretty heated."

"What were they disagreeing about?" Fielding asked.

"Well, Lyndon supports the military option, while the President believes he can resolve the situation with diplomacy," Hazelwood explained. "Some back-door negotiations are going on with the Russians that might prove fruitful. But, for us, that's neither here nor there. Our job is to protect the President and Vice President, whatever the solution—even if it's a nuclear one."

Hazelwood stepped to his desk and picked up a pile of file folders. He handed them out to the agents. "These are your specific assignments. The President is giving a speech tonight to the American people to explain what's going on in Cuba."

Kennedy's speech was straightforward, and he didn't sugarcoat the details. He put all strategic U.S. forces on alert and ordered the Navy to issue a quarantine of the area surrounding Cuba.

"It shall be the policy of this nation to regard any nuclear missile launched from Cuba against any nation in the Western Hemisphere as an attack by the Soviet Union on the United States, requiring a full retaliatory response upon the Soviet Union.

To halt this offensive buildup, a strict quarantine on all offensive military equipment under shipment to Cuba is being initiated. All ships of any kind bound for Cuba, from whatever nation or port, will, if found to contain cargoes of offensive weapons, be turned back. This quarantine will be extended, if needed, to other types of cargo and carriers. We are not, at this time, however, denying the necessities of life as the Soviets attempted to do in their Berlin blockade of 1948."

"He's calling Khruschev's bluff," Fielding said. He and the other agents had gathered around the small television set in the briefing room and were glued to the President's speech.

"It's about to get a whole lot more interesting," Wolfe said.

OCTOBER 24, 1962

"They've turned back!" A voice announced over the speaker in the Oval Office. The commander of the "*U.S.S. Joseph P. Kennedy*" had intercepted a Lebanese tanker, which was believed to have offensive missiles onboard. When challenged, it turned away and refused to violate the blockade.

Kennedy looked across the table at Lyndon, who was rubbing his jaw in irritation. The behind-the-scenes negotiations had forestalled a confrontation, which is what Kennedy had wanted all along, in opposition to Johnson's warlike stance.

"We have a little bit of breathing room," Kennedy said. "Let's push our advantage. Get Khruschev on the phone. We need to see what we can do to end this."

Johnson rose from the table and excused himself. He knew that he was no longer needed or wanted in the process.

CHAPTER THIRTY-FOUR
DECEMBER 25, 1962

Fielding sipped his Scotch on the rocks and picked up hors d'oeuvres from the serving plate passed around by the White House waiters.

He watched several people dancing "The Twist," by Chubby Checker, but, having never learning to dance, he remained a spectator. Plus, he hadn't brought a date, so there was that.

"It was nice of the President to throw this party for us," Fielding told Wolfe. Unlike Fielding, Wolfe had brought a date. She leaned against the bar, in deep conversation with the bartender.

"Yeah," Wolfe said. Glancing at Rhonda, he frowned when he noticed how tightly her dress was pulled across her backside. "We've had a tough year, with all the rioting in Mississippi and those damn Cubans acting up." He took a swig of the bourbon in his glass. "We're lucky to be alive, my friend."

The booze and food flowed, as did the conversation and war stories the agents exchanged. While they discussed their exploits, Fielding stood quietly in the back of the crowd, taking in their tales but not feeling compelled to participate in the revelries.

Though still mostly alone, he felt better this Christmas. Last year's spirit had been destroyed when Johnson ordered him to eliminate the Vice President's sister on Christmas Eve. Fielding had returned home and spent the next week secluded and drunk. He hadn't even attended the department's New Year's Eve party. He'd emerged from his alcoholic fog and sworn to himself that he wouldn't allow Johnson to use him again...until the next time.

Fielding listened to the other agent's stories and laughed when it was appropriate, showing the right amount of concern and attention.

It was difficult for him to participate. Many of the stories he had to contribute highlighted his executions of his boss's enemies.

Snatching a shrimp puff off a tray, he re-joined Wolfe.

"I see you aren't in the middle of the brag-fest there," he said. He could tell that Wolfe had a substantial lead on him in getting drunk.

"No," Wolfe slurred. "Let 'em one-up each other." He pointed his glass at Fielding. "They have no idea what we've had to do to preserve this administration and presidency."

Fielding looked at him and shook his head. "I'm not proud of what I had to do, Abner," he said. "I only did what I did because I had no choice."

"You're a coward," Wolfe said. Before Fielding could respond, he smiled. "I'm a coward, too." He lifted his glass and toasted his comrade. "Here's to cowards! Men without enough guts to say no. Hey, it takes a lot of guts to be a coward."

Fielding pushed Wolfe's hand down. "I won't drink to that, Abner. I'll admit I'm a coward, but I won't drink to it."

"Suit yourself, Ted," Wolfe said, draining his glass. "Whatever gets you through the night." He glanced over his shoulder at Rhonda, who was sipping her drink and motioning him over. "I know what's gonna get me through THIS night."

Fielding raised his glass in a toast to Wolfe and turned his attention toward the center of the room. All heads had turned to focus on one man. Fielding stepped up to the front of the crowd and saw Booker holding sway over the crowd.

"I would like a volunteer, if you please," Booker said. A slightly tipsy blonde in a low-cut dress came forward and raised her hand.

"I volunteer."

"Why, thank you, Miss...Miss?"

"It's Missus Clayton. Betty Clayton," the blonde answered. Fielding looked over at Christopher "Clay" Clayton, one of the uniformed agents, and saw the embarrassment on his face.

"Well, Missus Clayton, do you have a watch?" Booker asked. Betty checked her wrists and shook her head. "That's fine," Booker said, reaching into his vest pocket and pulling out a pocket watch. "I have one." He let the watch dangle from its chain in front of Betty. "Do you like my watch, Missus Clayton?"

Betty giggled and nodded.

"It is rather heavy, though." Booker held the watch chain, and the watch began swinging back and forth. "See how heavy it is? It's so heavy that it swings from side to side. Can you see it?" Betty nodded while her eyes followed the swinging watch. "That's it. Just follow it with your eyes." Betty stayed focused on the watch, her eyes in synchronization with the steady swinging. "Your eyes are getting as heavy as the watch. Heavy...heavy... So heavy that you can't keep them open." Betty's eyelids drooped lazily until they finally closed.

Booker snapped his fingers on both sides of her head, seeing if he could get a reaction. When he received none, he continued. "Now, Betty, tell me, can you hear me?" Betty nodded robotically. "Good. I'd like you to obey whatever I say. Do you understand?" Again, she nodded. "Betty, please raise your right arm and place it on your head." She complied without hesitation. "Good. Now, quack like a duck." She quacked long and loud, inciting laughter from the crowd.

Fielding laughed. Glancing beside him, he noticed Wolfe approaching, his arm around Rhonda's waist. Wolfe nodded toward Clayton, who was nervously laughing along with the others.

"He's gonna get it when she wakes up," Wolfe said. "And it sure gives me an idea of what Booker may have been doing with that kid, Whitman."

Betty continued for another thirty seconds before Booker stopped her. He had her count to three, then snapped his fingers. She woke up and looked around the room, confused by all the laughter. Quickly, Clayton took her by the arm and moved her to the far corner of the room. They whispered to each other while Betty's face turned red with embarrassment.

She fled the room, taking time to grab her coat and purse while giving Booker a death glare. Booker raised his glass and laughed at the fleeing woman with Clayton in tow.

Wolfe, watching the encounter, finished his drink. "That man is dangerous."

CHAPTER THIRTY-FIVE
FEBRUARY 3, 1963

Charlie speared a piece of pot roast and a potato and shoved them into his mouth, chasing them down with a swallow of milk.

"Dinner is great, Kathy." He grabbed her from behind and pulled her down into his lap, kissing her on the cheek.

"Thank you, sweetheart," Kathy said, hugging his neck.

Charlie was happy. He'd given up his friendships with the students he'd gotten into trouble with early on in his collegiate career. Known to be a practical joker around his dorm, Charlie had straightened up and begun to take his studies and life more seriously. Most of it had to do with the calming effect that Kathy had on him, but he had to give some credit to the relationship he'd formed with Vice President Johnson and his advisor, Harold Booker. Booker had helped him with his social anxiety and concentration by introducing him to hypnosis. Booker would hang his watch in front of him, letting it sway back and forth in front of his eyes. Charlie never remembered anything during the sessions, but the peace he felt and the clarity of his thinking were enough. It calmed him, making him more even-tempered with Kathy and reducing the violent outbursts that unexpectedly overtook him. It also alleviated the stress caused by the lack of communication between him and the Marine Corps. After his arrest for poaching, he had expected to hear from the Corps one way or the other on his future at UT. It had angered him that no one took the time to call or write him, letting him know if he was facing punishment for the arrest. With no word, he'd been left in limbo and without resolution. This was something that Charlie had found difficult to deal with. Doctor Booker had helped him accept things as they were and to put aside the anxiety, freeing him to concentrate more on the things he could handle, rather than things out of his control. Charlie had been leery of the hypnosis at first, but when Booker had told him that he'd used the techniques dozens of times on other patients, he'd calmed down and accepted the treatments.

Booker had called it "Project MK Ultra."

As Charlie and Kathy ate their dinner and discussed their day, there was a knock on the door.

"Oh, that's probably Mary Hutchens, the lady next door. She borrowed the fry skillet and said she would bring it back by after dinner," Kathy explained.

Waving her back to her seat, Charlie opened the door and was shocked to see a Marine Corps Lieutenant, in dress greens, his cover low on his eyes.

"I'm looking for Private-First Class Charles A. Whitman. Would that be you?"

Whitman immediately snapped to attention and presented the officer with a salute. "Sir, yes, sir!"

"As you were, Private," the officer said. "I'm Second Lieutenant Kirkwood Taylor, Second Marine Expeditionary Force, Marine Special Operations Command."

Whitman stepped to the side. "Please, come in, sir."

Taylor slipped his cover off and tucked it under his arm. "Thank you." He walked into the living room and saw Kathy emerge from the kitchen.

"Is that Mary—oh. I'm sorry," Kathy said, her expression displaying her confusion.

"Ma'am," the Lieutenant acknowledged her with a nod. He reached into his coat pocket and produced a folded set of papers. "Private Whitman, you are ordered to report for active duty at Camp Lejeune, North Carolina, on thirteen February, where you will be promoted to Lance Corporal and assigned to my unit." He handed the papers to Whitman, who unfolded them and scanned the pages. Kathy stood at his arm, reading the papers as well.

"B-but, I'm in NESEP? I'm on track for OCS," Whitman sputtered. "You can't just—"

"Can't just what, Private?" Taylor snapped. "You are the property of the United States Marine Corps. That means it doesn't matter what you want or whether you think it's fair or not. You follow orders." He smacked the papers in Whitman's hand. "And these are your orders. As for your NESEP, you're lucky you aren't up for an Article 933, 'Conduct Unbecoming of an Officer or a Gentleman,' after that stunt you pulled in your dorm room. You have ten days to report, Lance Corporal."

When Whitman realized that he had referred to him by his new rank, a momentary thrill excited him. But then understanding dawned. He would be stationed in North Carolina, not in Austin, with Kathy. And apparently, she sensed it as well.

"Charlie," Kathy said, fear in her voice, "what about us?"

"I need to call Mr. Johnson."

CHAPTER THIRTY-SIX
JUNE 26, 1963

Ted Fielding watched as President Kennedy waved to the thousands of West Germans who had gathered to see him as he made his way off the stage in front of the Schöneberg City Hall, near the Brandenburg Gate, in Berlin.

"Two thousand years ago," Kennedy had said in his speech, "the proudest boast was 'Civis Romanus sum'. Today, in the world of freedom, the proudest boast is 'Ich bin ein Berliner'..."

But Fielding did not have the chance to hear the speech. Instead, he was with the Berlin Polizei in a back room of their police station. The man handcuffed to the chair in the center of the room had tried to get onto the stage where the President and German Chancellor were sitting as Kennedy was preparing for his speech. Fielding and Wolfe had intercepted the man and discovered a large knife tucked into his waistband. After subduing him, they passed him off to the German authorities for interrogation.

Lyndon Johnson sipped a scotch and lit another cigarette. He watched the speech Kennedy had given in Berlin and paced his office. Booker entered without knocking.

"What is it?" Johnson snapped.

"You wanted me to keep tabs on Lee?" Booker asked.

"Yes, I did. What is he up to now?"

"He's still in New Orleans, working for a coffee company, greasing machines," Booker said. "He's also opened an office for the 'Fair Play for Cuba' Committee and is recruiting people to pass out leaflets. New Orleans Police are closely monitoring his activities."

"Good," Johnson said. "The more the locals get to know him and his politics, the easier it's gonna be to explain him away when the time comes." He motioned toward the television. "And, as long as Kennedy is making these grand overtures to the Germans and these other Communist Bloc nations and ignoring Cuba, this plays right into Lee's mindset. How about the rest of the folks? Are we on the same page? No one is losing their nerve, are they?"

"No, sir," Booker assured. "Dulles told me that his people are standing by, waiting on the word to be given."

"What about our Marine?"

"Settling in at Camp Lejeune. So far, he's keeping out of trouble," Booker said. "I need to make regular visits with him, if you want the programming to hold well past the event."

"Do whatever you have to do," Johnson said. "Charlie is the only loose cannon. We need to make sure we remain in control of him."

"Do we have a set time and place?"

"I've already spoken with the President. He agreed with me that Texas will be crucial in the '64 election. With all the infighting amongst the different factions in the Party, his going to Texas in a show of support and unity is the only way to get them all on the same page and beat whoever the Republicans will run against him," Johnson said. "So, we're going to Texas the third week of November, around the twenty-first and twenty-second."

CHAPTER THIRTY-SEVEN
CURRENT DAY

Lefleur parked in the garage across the street from the main Homicide and Criminology building on Linn Street in Downtown Cincinnati. With the Democratic Convention in town, the parking lots and streets were filled with visitors and delegates, some wearing "KELLY/WELLS: A BRIGHTER FUTURE" hats and t-shirts, while others wore the color of their respective party. The businesses responded to the influx of people by doubling their fees for their lots. Lefleur scanned his debit card through the reader and grimaced at the amount charged to his account.

He was out of his car and walking toward the building by the time he noticed that Fielding wasn't going with him. "Where are you going?"

"The President is staying at the Hancock Arms during the convention," Fielding said. "I'm gonna take a look around inside."

Without another word, Fielding headed south toward Fifth Street.

Lefleur walked to the front door and approached the sergeant sitting at the desk. Presenting his credentials, he identified himself. His ID still listed him as a lieutenant, and he didn't feel that this was the best time to correct his rank.

"What can we do for you, Lieutenant?"

"I need to talk to the shift supervisor in charge of homicides," Lefleur said.

"Detective Byrnes is in her office," the sergeant replied. "Take the elevator to the sixth floor. I'll let her know you're on your way up."

When Lefleur stepped off the elevator, Byrnes was waiting for him, along with a man in a suit he immediately recognized.

"Lieutenant Lefleur? Sergeant Dannie Byrnes and this is…"

"Secret Service Agent Clarence Pierson," Lefleur said, reaching out and shaking both of their hands. "We're...old friends."

"Did you find out who your John Doe was?" Pierson asked.

"Yes. And it opened a whole new set of questions and mysteries," he said. "Which is why I'm here." He told them everything he could about the assassination attempt.

"Where did you get this information, Jack?" Pierson asked.

"I'm...not at liberty to say, Clarence," Lefleur said. "But I trust my source and believe that it's credible. The attempt may be at the Hancock Arms."

"I was telling Clarence that a security guard died at the Hancock Arms," Byrnes said.

"How did the guard die?" Lefleur asked.

"He fell down a flight of stairs. Hit his head and busted up his insides."

Something clicked with Lefleur.

"Was the toe of his shoe all scuffed, like he caught it on the stairs?" Lefleur asked.

"Yes, it was," Byrnes said.

Lefleur scratched his chin. "Anything seem, I don't know, out of the ordinary with this 'accident'?"

"The other security guard said something. I didn't think much of it." Byrnes shrugged. "I was informed that the guard was very particular about how he responded to his radio traffic. The other guard informed us that when Bailey died, his traffic wasn't the same. He used different wording, or his response was different. Why? Is that significant?"

"The assassin," Lefleur said, "he's done this sort of thing before—killed a man like this and tried to make it look like an accident."

"Our investigation determined that it was an accident. But Bailey left behind a note."

"What kind of note?"

Byrnes walked to her desk and found the copy of the note under some reports. She handed it to him. "There are blood stains on it, so it's hard to make heads or tails of it."

Lefleur read over the words. Without context, they made no sense to him, either. "What can you tell me about this guy? What did you say his name was, 'Bailey'?"

Fielding approached the revolving door at the Hancock Arms and nodded to the doorman as he entered the main level of the hotel, instantly being transported back to the 1930s. He placed his aged hand on the art deco styling on the handrails of the Grand Staircase as he ascended to the lobby. He noted the plainclothes officers standing at the top of the stairs, but wasn't sure if they were hotel security or Secret Service. They nodded to him.

Fielding paused for a moment, pretending to read the captions on the celebrity photos posted on the pillars as he surveyed the lobby. The main check-in desk was busy with incoming guests. The bellmen hustled the luggage carts into the elevators, transporting the guests and their bags to their rooms. Fielding walked the length of the lobby to the display case, which documented some of the hotel's history. He was reading about the Roosevelt Room and its history when one of the maintenance men walked through the lobby. He stopped reading and looked at the man, his memory seeking out the man's face. Fielding knew he'd seen him before.

Roger McLean. The assassin. The man who had previously tried to kill him.

Fielding turned to follow him, but the man disappeared behind the check-in desk, into an inner office. Fielding stopped at the desk. "Hi. Can you tell me who that man is who just walked through here? He looked familiar, like a guy I used to work with. He was a good fellow."

"I'm not sure," the desk clerk said. "I think his name is Jack or something."

"Zack," one of the other clerks said, motioning over his shoulder in the direction the man had gone. "His name is Zack. Would you like me to try and get him for you?"

"No, that's not necessary. I'll see Zack later," Fielding said. "Seems like you have a lot of security here today. Some big mucky muck staying here for the convention?"

"I'm not at liberty to say, sir," the front desk clerk replied. He turned his attention to another set of guests checking in.

Fielding figured the President would be staying in the Roosevelt Suite, located on the twenty-second floor. He walked toward the elevator, but two of the plainclothesmen stopped him before he could board it.

"Hold on, please. The elevator is occupied."

Fielding could see the outline of the pistols on their hips and knew he was dealing with the Secret Service. The President was on the move.

"All of them?"

"Just for a few minutes, sir. Sorry for the delay."

Fielding waited, knowing there were more agents between him and the Roosevelt Suite. And with Zack still on the premises, he knew he still had a chance to save the President.

He walked back to the front desk. "Hi. Can I get a room?"

"Well, sir. We are all booked up for the convention," the clerk said. "Might I recommend..."

Fielding set five one-hundred-dollar bills and his Secret Service ID, showing him as a senior supervisor, on the counter and slid them toward the clerk. The young man cast a puzzled look at Fielding, who set another hundred on top of the pile. "You were saying?"

The clerk placed a clipboard over the money, and when he picked it up, the money was no longer there. He entered several commands into the computer and glanced around, making sure that no one was watching. He slipped the money into his pocket and nodded. "Ah. It appears that we have an opening on the sixteenth floor."

"That will be just fine," Fielding said with a smile.

CHAPTER THIRTY-EIGHT
OCTOBER 12, 1963

"What do you mean 'Whitman's been arrested'?" Johnson demanded. "Last reports I heard, he was an exceptional Marine."

"He was arrested for gambling and other charges," Booker said. "His court-martial is set for the end of the month. He's looking at ninety days' hard labor."

"He's the key to this whole thing," Johnson said. He lit a cigarette and paced the floor. "People are all in place, and you need to give him another treatment before he carries out the mission."

"I'm well aware of that, Mr. Vice President," Booker said, "but isn't there some way we can do it without him?"

"What's the problem, son? Getting cold feet?" Johnson asked.

"No, sir," Booker said. "It's just that Whitman is a good man, inside. The drugs and hypnosis have changed him. Of all the test subjects I've used in Project MKUltra, Whitman has been the most responsive. He's fundamentally changed. And...I regret doing to him what I've done."

"You regret?" Johnson snapped. He stepped close to Booker, towering over him and pushing his finger into the man's chest. "Let me tell you something, you little piss ant. You don't get to regret your decision. You do your damn job and do it well, or the next time you feel regret, I'll make damn sure it's the last time." Johnson walked to his desk and sat down heavily. "You need to fix this thing with Whitman. I don't care what you do, but I need him in Dallas."

"I'll—do what I can, sir," Booker said. He left the Vice President's office, and with the strength of desperation, a plan began to formulate in his mind.

NOVEMBER 1, 1963

Whitman carried his bundle of clothes and toiletries to his cell in the brig at Camp Lejeune. The guard gave the cell a final once-over, and when he was satisfied that it was clean, he stepped out and held the door open for Whitman. Whitman wore an orange jumpsuit with a large "P" on the back, signifying that he was a prisoner. Stripped of his corporal rank, he was back down to a Private First Class.

"Once you're settled in, there is a captain who's requested to come in and do some kind of psych evaluation," the sergeant said. "You'll be in solitary confinement for the first month. But I'll warn you right now, Marine, you step out of line, break any rule, or just tick me off, I see to it that your ass spends the entire ninety days of your sentence in that cell, and not in the general population!" The sergeant handed him a small pile of mail. "Here. These came for you while you were going through your Court Martial."

"I understand, Sergeant," Whitman said, taking the mail. Setting his pile down, Whitman made his bunk, then sat down and looked around his cell. It was an eight-by-ten concrete block with a bunk, a toilet, and a sink. There was no window, but a small shelf was built into the wall, where he could place his personal items. He stacked his clothing and set his toiletries next to the sink. Reclining on the bunk, he flipped through the letters, pleased to find that they were from his wife.

After his arrest for usury, gambling, having a firearm on base, and threatening another Marine over a thirty-dollar loan, Whitman had been held in seclusion until his court-martial and was not allowed any contact with anyone except his court-appointed attorney. While in his cell, Whitman started a diary of his life as a Marine.

"I have learned to hate the Marine Corps and its stifling rules," Whitman wrote. "The inefficiencies in the command structure and the way they use Marines as their personal pawns sickens me. I don't think I can be part of an organization that abuses its people like the Corps does. As soon as I'm able, I'm appealing to Vice President Johnson to facilitate my discharge."

"Whitman!" the sergeant bellowed. "There's a Captain Booker here to interview you."

Whitman put his notebook away and stood to face the door as it opened. Booker entered, followed by another Marine. Whitman snapped a salute to Booker and did a double-take when he saw the Marine with him.

He could have been his twin brother. The height and weight were right, as were the facial features.

"We don't have much time," Booker said, looking back at the closed door. "Get out of that jumpsuit and put on Corporal Dennison's uniform."

The Marine, whom Booker identified as "Dennison," was already stripping out of his utility uniform. Whitman handed him the jumpsuit as he pulled on the green uniform.

"Listen carefully," Booker said to Dennison. Whitman could see by the look in the man's eyes that Booker had used hypnosis on him. "You are no longer Greg Dennison. You are Charles Whitman. You know your history and why you are here?" Dennison nodded robotically. "You are to write in this journal daily, documenting every act that you do and any thoughts that you have, as Charles Whitman. Do you understand?"

Dennison nodded and adjusted the jumpsuit. "How long will I be here, Captain?"

"You have ninety days to serve, Private Whitman," Booker said. "The first month, you'll spend in solitary, then they will move you to the general population."

"Thank you, Captain," Dennison said, saluting Booker. He looked at Whitman, who was wearing the corporal stripes. "Corporal."

Booker knocked on the door to get the sergeant's attention. When the door opened, Whitman held his breath and stepped out of the cell, keeping his head slightly down.

"Thank you, Sergeant," Booker said. The sergeant saluted him and nodded to Whitman. Both men stepped out of the brig and climbed into the car.

Booker glanced at Whitman. "Dennison will be here until the twenty-fifth. Then, I'll switch you out."

"Understood," Whitman said. "Will I meet the others on the team?"

"You've already met the most important one at your wedding party," Booker said.

CHAPTER THIRTY-NINE
PRESENT DAY

President Alexander Kelly handed the pile of papers back to his campaign manager, Martin Bristor. "The platform isn't inclusive enough," he said. "The Environmental Lobby is going to feel left out if we don't toughen up the language on climate change."

"I thought we offered them an olive branch when we talked about the Kyoto Accords," Bristor countered. "What more should we offer them?"

"I don't care," Kelly said. "Just throw something in there to appease them. Tell them we'll ensure the coal industry shuts down their mines, and if they don't, we'll bankrupt them. It's worked before!"

Bristor nodded and jotted down a few notes. Walking to the phone, he called the Chairman of the Democratic National Committee. After a brief conversation, he left.

Kelly glanced at his watch. It was five-thirty. "What time am I supposed to be there?"

"Twenty-one hundred hours, sir." Brett Sullivan, Chief of White House Security, double-checked his watch. "We will leave here at twenty-thirty hours."

The U.S. Bank Arena on Broadway was only three blocks away from The Hancock Arms, but there were numerous places within that three-block area where an attack could be launched against the President, especially with the current political climate in the country, namely, in Cincinnati. After the scandal involving the President and the White House erupted, several prominent lawmakers from the opposing party, as well as members of his own party, called for President Kelly and Vice President Wells to step down. Protesters had gathered outside the arena, some peacefully chanting, while others were more aggressive. Cincinnati Police had reported fifteen arrests in the past two days, and the Secret Service had reported a dramatic increase in unverifiable threats against the life of the Chief Executive.

To ensure security, Air Force Two, carrying the Vice-President, would not land at the Cincinnati/North Kentucky International Airport until twenty-thirty hours. The motorcade would transport Wells directly to the Arena, where he and the President would be presented, as Wells accepted the Democratic nomination. Once the convention was over, the President would fly out first, and the Vice President would be housed at the Netherland Hilton overnight, set to return to Washington in the morning.

Sullivan personally inspected the Hancock Arms and the Roosevelt Room, ensuring the rooms would be a safe house for the President and a place to fall back to, in case a threat should arise. The room was situated in the center of the floor, so that no one from either the north or south stairwells could open the door and immediately launch an attack. The floors above and below had been inspected and cleared. Agents had been assigned to prevent anyone who tried to exit the elevator or stairwells from entering onto the floor. They would also be searching all the employees who came onto the floor to perform their duties.

Sullivan was never a man fully at ease, but with the security measures he'd set in place, he felt cautiously optimistic that the President was protected.

"When will we meet with Mrs. Kelly?" the President asked.

"The First Lady will leave at twenty-hundred hours and meet you at the Arena," Sullivan replied.

"Good," Kelly said. He loosened his tie and sat down on the bed. "Call Carol and have her come over. I need...a massage. And, if she's unavailable...call Adam."

Sullivan had seen the leer on Kelly's face before and knew what he really meant when he said he needed "a massage."

"Yes, sir," he said. He pulled out his cell phone and scrolled through his contacts, stopping in the "Cs." He punched the number and stepped into the bathroom for a moment of privacy.

Sullivan's duty was to keep the President healthy, safe, and happy. Unfortunately, one aspect of keeping the President happy was to keep his mistress on stand-by and out of sight until the President decided he needed "a massage." He spoke briefly and tersely before hanging up. "Carol is en route."

"Make sure you let your people know that she's on her way," Kelly said. "I'm going to take a shower."

"Yes, sir," Sullivan said. He was stepping into the hallway to advise his team of the impending visit when his phone rang.

Lefleur listened as Pierson informed Sullivan about the information he'd provided.

"We don't know when or where the attempt will be, but it might be best to keep the President in his room as long as possible," Pierson said. "How secure do you feel there?"

"This floor and the one above and below are one hundred percent secure," Sullivan said. "I'd bet my life on it."

"Let's hope it doesn't come to that, Mack," Pierson said. "I'm coming over and bringing Lieutenant Lefleur and Detective Byrnes to see if we can help out."

"Have they been vetted?" Sullivan asked. He felt the irritation rising in his neck. "I'm not sure what else they can bring to the table here."

"Mack, you know me," Pierson said. "Of course, they've been vetted. I trust them."

"All right," Sullivan begrudgingly agreed. "Call me from the front desk when you arrive."

Zack, whose real name was Roger McLean, stood in room twenty-sixteen. Two floors above, the President was preparing for his speech. One floor above the room McLean had prepared. He reached into the pocket of his work overalls and pulled out a set of car keys with a remote attached. Pointing it at the ceiling, he clicked the button and held it down for four seconds. The effect was immediate.

Fielding stood on the landing of the twenty-first floor, directly below the door which led to the twenty-second floor. A strip of tape was taped across the door and the railing of the stairwell leading to the twenty-third floor. In bold letters, it screamed: CAUTION—DO NOT ENTER. He glanced up to the corner of the landing and spotted a video camera staring down at him. Knowing the Secret Service the way he did, he knew that the wireless camera had been placed there by agents to monitor anyone approaching the door from the stairwell.

Turning back, Fielding was walking back down the stairs when the door on the twenty-first floor swung open. A Secret Service agent held it open.

"Excuse me, sir. Can I help you?"

"I was walking the stairs," Fielding said. "Whenever I stay here, I walk the stairs to the top floor and come back down again to get in my aerobic exercise." He pointed up the stairs. "I see they're closed off today, so I'm headed back down. Is there a problem?"

"Are you a guest here, then?"

"I just said I was, son," Fielding said. He reached into his coat and pulled out his room key, holding it in the agent's face. "Room sixteen ten."

"Can you show me some ID?" the agent asked.

"No," Fielding snapped. "Can you? What are you, hotel security?"

The agent produced his ID case and showed his badge. "Secret Service."

Fielding's eyes went large as he stared at the badge. "Oh. I'm s-sorry, young man," he stammered. His hands shook as he reached into his coat pocket and produced his wallet. "D-didn't mean any disrespect, sir."

The agent scanned his wallet. In one worn plastic sleeve was a Florida driver's license bearing the name "Theodore Nick," from Crestview, Florida. Directly across from the Florida license was a business card, which read, "Nick's Aeronautics."

"What sort of company do you have?" the agent asked.

"We do crop dusting in northern Florida and West Alabama," Fielding said, the pre-established cover running off his tongue like honey. "I own a fleet of Cessna Ag-wagons, two M-18

Dromaders, and a Rockwell Thrush Commander. Actually, I flew the Commander here to meet with the Ohio Secretary of Agriculture to discuss the newest forms of aerial-applied chemicals and delivery systems. Did you know that when you dust fifty acres of low or medium tillage farming system with 4-D or Clarity applications, the pre-tilled farm or fallow fields will..."

"I'm sure your job is very interesting, sir," the agent said, "but please, be more careful. This is s secure area."

"I'm sorry, son," Fielding said. "I sure didn't mean to trespass."

The agent handed him back his wallet and escorted him through the stairwell door, toward the elevator. "I'll see to it that you get back to your floor."

He touched the button, summoning the elevator. When the door chimed, an ear-piercing alarm cut through the quietness of the hallway.

"WHAT'S THAT?" Fielding yelled.

"SOUNDS LIKE A FIRE ALARM," the agent yelled back.

The elevator door opened, and he pushed Fielding in and pressed the button to the sixteenth floor. Before the door closed, Fielding saw the guard walk to room twenty-one sixteen while keying his microphone.

In room twenty-sixteen, McLean stood on a step ladder and pointed the remote at the ceiling. After holding down the button for two seconds, the sensor he'd placed in the smoke alarm clicked into place, and the alarm sounded. He slowly packed up the step ladder and awaited the repair call.

Fielding arrived at the lobby just as Lefleur, Byrnes, and Pierson stepped from the Grand Staircase. Catching Lefleur's eye, he motioned him toward the men's room.

"I'm going to use the restroom," Lefleur said to Pierson. "Call Sullivan and let him know we're coming up." He stepped into the restroom and found Fielding standing at the sink.

"Something's up," Fielding said. "I can't be sure, but I believe the assassin is here. He may be an employee. The smoke alarm started wailing on the twenty-first floor when it shouldn't have been."

"The President is on the twenty-second," Lefleur said, alarmed.

"The room on twenty-one is directly underneath the Roosevelt Suite," Fielding said. "Just be—"

"Wait," Lefleur said. "What did you just say?"

"I said that the smoke alarm is sounding on the twenty-first floor."

"And the room on twenty-one is directly underneath the Roosevelt Suite."

"Does that mean something?" Fielding questioned.

Lefleur pulled out a copy of the note Bailey had scribbled.

UMBEN...ROSLELLT...SUTE.

"First impression," Lefleur said, handing the note to Fielding. Fielding studied the scribbling.

"Under Roosevelt Suite," Fielding said. "What is this?"

"I'll explain later," Lefleur said. "Use your Secret Service ID and see if you can find out where this supposed assassin is right now." He headed out of the bathroom and rejoined Pierson and Byrnes. "We need to get to the Roosevelt Suite right away!"

While the trio made their way to the elevators, Fielding approached the check-in desk and withdrew the Secret Service ID with Wolfe's name on it. "I need to know where McLean...I mean, Zack, is—NOW"

A different clerk than the one who had checked Fielding in examined his ID and looked at Fielding. His eyes wandered to the computer screen and to a typed list that was taped to its corner. The list of Secret Service agents on duty on the presidential detail. He scanned the names, looking under the "Ws." When he didn't see the name "Wolfe," he reached for the phone.

"I'm not on the presidential detail," Fielding said, reading the clerk's face. "I'm working at the US Bank Arena. We've received information on an attempt on the President's life." He leaned closer to the clerk, his voice taking on a guttural tone. "Do you want history to judge you as the man who could have stopped the assassination of the President, but instead, you hesitated...and the President died?"

"N-no, sir," the clerk sputtered.

"Then tell me where Zack is. NOW!"

The clerk fumbled with the phone receiver and called the back office. "Front desk to base. Where is Maintenance Unit 3 located?"

"M-3 is on twenty-one, on a fire alarm. He's been there for six minutes."

Fielding raced to the elevator, praying he wasn't too late.

CHAPTER FORTY
PRESENT DAY

Six minutes earlier, McLean stepped off the maintenance elevator on the twenty-first floor. He immediately heard the ear-piercing scream of the alarm and smiled to himself. He emerged from the service hallway and saw the Secret Service agent standing outside of twenty-one sixteen. He was yelling something, but McLean held his hands to his ears and mimed that he couldn't hear him. The agent checked the maintenance cart, searching for weapons. He then patted McLean down and had him empty his pockets. McLean pulled out his wallet with ID and the set of car keys with the remote attached. Satisfied, the agent stepped aside so he could unlock the room door and enter the room. McLean slammed the door behind him before the agent could follow.

Quickly setting up the step ladder, he removed a telescopic rod from the maintenance cart and ascended the ladder. He popped the smoke detector from its base and removed the modified siren he'd installed, before pulling the battery and silencing the alarm. Replacing the battery, the alarm remained silent as McLean re-attached it to the ceiling. He folded up the ladder and placed it on the cart. Once it was secure, he walked around the room, spotting the small Xs he'd drawn on the ceiling. With four hard jabs, he punched the telescopic rod through the Xs, puncturing the finger-thick canisters of Sarin gas situated under the carpet. He closed the rod by pushing it against the floor, being careful not to touch it, and tossed it onto the cart before stepping out of the room.

"That should do it," McLean said to the agent. He pulled the door closed and walked to the service corridor. Once inside, he called for the elevator and checked his watch. He had been there for seven minutes. He estimated that the gas would disperse into the President's suite within two minutes, giving him a minute to execute his escape plan. But hedging his bets had worked for him in the past. He reached into the maintenance cart and found a can of WD-40.

The elevator dinged, the doors slid open, and McLean found himself face to face with Fielding.

"Hello, McLean," Fielding said. "Nice try."

Before Fielding saw it coming, McLean sprayed him in the face with the WD-40. Fielding screamed and grabbed his eyes, just as McLean grabbed him and kneed him in the stomach. He threw Fielding out of the elevator and hit the button, sending the elevator up.

Lefleur showed Byrnes the note from Bailey. "I think this says, 'Under Roosevelt's Suite.'" Byrnes took the paper from him and read it again.

"It could," he said, passing the note to Pierson. "What? You got an epiphany while in the john?"

"You could say that," Lefleur said. "If there is an assassination attempt, it may be imminent."

Lefleur, Pierson, and Byrnes stepped off the elevator on twenty-two and met Sullivan.

"Everything appears secure," Sullivan said. "I just checked on the President, and he's fine."

"Get in touch with your people on twenty-one," Lefleur instructed. He showed Sullivan the note. "This was written by a security officer who died under questionable circumstances a few weeks ago. I think he was trying to tell whoever found him to check under Roosevelt's Suite."

Sullivan was a pragmatic man with an open mind. After glancing at the note, he touched his lapel mic. "Team One leader to Team Three."

There was a long pause before the agent responded.

"Team Two to Team One leader, we have an issue here!" the agent cried out. The tension in his voice was palpable.

"What's going on, Team Two?" Sullivan asked.

"We have a guest in custody who tried to penetrate the perimeter," the agent said. "He's making statements that the President's life is in immediate danger." The agent released the mic and came back a few seconds later. "He has an S.S.

ID, identifying him as "Abner Wolfe," but he has a Florida driver's license with the name "Theodore Nick."'

Lefleur's stomach dropped when he heard the name. "Ask him if anyone else has been on the floor."

"Has anyone else been on the floor?" Sullivan asked.

"Just the maintenance man. He reset a smoke alarm that was going off."

Lefleur grabbed Sullivan by the arm. "What room?"

Sullivan asked the question. "Room twenty-one sixteen."

Lefleur looked at the Roosevelt Suite and the number.

Twenty-two Sixteen.

"Under Roosevelt's Suite," Pierson said. "Get that door open. NOW!"

Sullivan slid the key card into the lock and pushed the door open. The stench was overwhelming.

The President lay on the bathroom floor, gasping for breath. Though the door was partially closed, the panic on his face was visible to all. His mistress was stretched out on the floor, lying in a pool of her own vomit and waste.

She was dead.

An agent who had responded to the commotion lay sprawled midway into the main room, the pass key still in his hand. His last breath remained fixated on his face in a silent scream.

Sullivan turned to Lefleur and shoved him into Pierson and Byrnes, pushing them out of the room before shutting the door. He grabbed a towel from the bathroom and tied it around his face. Fighting the nausea rising in his throat, he hauled the President off the floor and threw him over his shoulder. President Kelly vomited down Sullivan's back, defecating on the front of the agent's suit. Sulliven pulled the door open, and both men stumbled into the hallway.

Seeing Sullivan convulse, Pierson covered his mouth and ripped the microphone and transmitter from the man. "Team One to Med One. Medical Emergency. What floor are you on?" Pierson demanded. He knew that the President had his personal physician traveling with him, but wasn't sure where the doctor would have been in the hotel. A brief pause, then the radio cracked. "We are on twenty-three. Coming down now."

"Negative!" Pierson said. "We've been compromised. We're coming to you. Call 911 and get an ambulance heading this way."

Lefleur looked down the hall and spotted a storage closet. He gave the door a hard kick, splintering the frame as the door flew open. Grabbing a sheet, he and Byrnes wrapped the President up. He was semi-conscious and pale. "I've got him. Byrnes, get Sullivan. Clarence, tell your people to shut down the hotel. The assassin has to still be here."

Lefleur carried Kelly to the elevator, followed by Byrnes, Sullivan, and Pierson, who was coordinating the hotel's shutdown.

"Shut off all elevators going down. Lock them off on the top floors as soon as we get off on twenty-three. EMS should be responding. Full security protocol. That means everyone is searched and checked before being escorted up here."

Fielding stood with his hands on his head, his eyes still stinging from the WD-40. Pierson's radio traffic and excitable tone were loud enough to be heard over the agent's radio earpiece. "Team One to Team Two. Escort your prisoner to twenty-three."

The guard acknowledged, then pointed his pistol at Fielding. "Move to the elevator, old man. And don't try and give me any of your crap about crop-dusting." Fielding stepped into the elevator, facing the back, as the agent closed the door. The agent inserted the override key and pressed the button for the 23rd floor before turning toward Fielding. Before he fully faced him, Fielding lowered his right arm fast and forcefully, striking the agent in the brachial nerve complex on the right side of his neck. The nerve strike drove the agent to his knees, and he instantly lost consciousness. Fielding snatched the pistol from his hand and yanked his radio free before turning the key in the override and stopping the ascending elevator between floors. He pressed the button for the 24th floor, and, when the door opened, he shoved the agent's limp body into the service hallway, then closed the door as he thought of where he should go.

He thought about his confrontation with McLean. In the past, he'd avoided the dragnet by way of the roof. But Fielding knew that the snipers located there would limit his escape route.

Unless McLean bet on them shutting down the elevators and sending them to the top floor. Once there, he would have a way to escape internally.

McLean wasn't going to let the time get away from him. He knew once they found the President dead, they would shut down the hotel and elevators to try and contain the situation and catch the assassin.

He exited the thirtieth-floor service elevator and found the door that led to the hotel's top floors, where the elevator motors were housed. He used the duplicate key he'd made from Bailey's key and entered the stairway, ending up on the top floor of the hotel. Once in the room, McLean opened the laundry chute and saw that his rope was still secured in place. He cut the cord holding the rope and watched it free-fall down the three-hundred-thirty-foot chute to the laundry room in the basement. He tied a repelling harness onto a spare piece of rope and looped the main rope through it. Stepping into the chute, he slipped inside and began slowly repelling down to the bottom.

Fielding took the elevator to the twenty-seventh floor and exited into the service hallway. The hallway was roughly twenty-five feet long and housed two staff elevators that allowed the staff to keep out of the prying eyes of hotel guests. On the walls hung fuse boxes and fire extinguishers, as well as emergency shut-offs for the water and power in each room. Fielding knew none of this would help McLean escape.

Except for one access panel, labeled "Laundry."

Fielding had read the hotel's history. It was built back in the 1930s, and, to expedite hauling dirty laundry from the upper floors to the basement laundry room, the laundry was tossed down the chute, where it fell thirty floors.

Fielding put his ear to the door and listened intently. He heard scraping on the inside of the chute, and a light, steady knocking against its side. Withdrawing a Swiss army knife from his pocket, he pried open the thin, metal door and peered inside the chute. A rope hung down the center of the opening, taut, as if weighed down by a person. He looked down the hole, but it was too dark to tell if there was anyone on the rope. But what his eyes couldn't see, his ears could hear. Someone was descending the rope, grunting as they occasionally struck the side and bounced off.

Fielding pulled out his cell phone and dialed Lefleur's number. When Jack answered, he was breathless.

"Ted, where are you?"

"Listen, Jack." Fielding pulled his head out of the chute and struck it on the side, knocking the phone from his hand and sending it tumbling down the chute. "Damnit!"

McLean jerked his head up at the noise. His action was rewarded by Fielding's phone striking him in the face. Screaming, he fell back, letting go of the rope. The descending harness went slack, and he free fell two floors before grabbing the rope and slowing his fall. The sudden stop ripped the skin from his palms, even beneath the protection of his leather gloves.

McLean wiped blood from his face, gingerly fingering the open gash between his eyes. Dizzily shaking off the blow, he continued down the rope.

Fielding leaned into the hole as far as he could see and pursed his lips. When he heard McLean scream, he allowed himself a small smile. He thought about crawling down the rope after him, but didn't think he had the strength to descend twenty-seven floors and then engage the assassin in a physical altercation. He grabbed the rope and was about to cut it when he discovered the thick, nylon core running through the center. There was no chance his knife could cut through.

Backing out of the hole, Fielding turned back in the elevator. He scanned the buttons and pressed the one marked "B" for "Basement." Knowing he'd found a way to pursue, he stepped out of the elevator again and grabbed a fire extinguisher from its bracket, dropping it down the laundry chute. A satisfying grunt met his ears.

Fielding didn't even try to hide the smile this time.

Jumping back into the elevator, he turned the key to the non-stop mode. The doors closed, and he rode the elevator to the lower bowels of the hotel.

Lefleur stood in the doorway of the doctor's room and watched him work on President Kelly.

"Some sort of neurotoxin," the doctor was saying. "It's a nerve gas, working on his mucus membrane and digestive system."

"Can you save him?" Pierson asked.

"He needs to be hospitalized. How far away is the ambulance?"

"Can you save him?" Pierson repeated emphatically. When the doctor looked at him, there was fear in his eyes.

Pierson called down to the agents waiting on the street to inquire about the ambulance. "They're in the lobby, boarding the elevator." He looked at Sullivan, who was sitting upright in a chair, attached to an oxygen tank. "How's Brett?"

"Bad," the doctor said. "Are there any other victims?"

Pierson looked at Sullivan, and, for the first time since he'd known him, saw panic in his eyes. Sullivan took a deep breath and nodded, removing the air mask. "There's another victim. She's on the bed. She...might be a maid."

The doctor looked at Pierson, both men understanding what he meant. Pierson glanced at his watch. "Where are the medics?" he said into the mic.

"One of the service elevators is locked out. We had to switch to the other one. We're four floors away," an agent answered.

"Aren't those elevators controlled by the Secret Service?" Lefleur asked Sullivan.

Sullivan nodded.

"Clarence, find out if one of the agents has control over that service elevator."

Pierson checked in with the other agents, but none acknowledged being in control.

Lefleur went to the phone and called the hotel operator. "Do you have locations on the service elevators?"

"One is on the twenty-third floor," the operator said. "The other is heading to the basement."

Lefleur hung up and darted for the door. "The assassin. That's how he's planning to escape." He pulled the door open, only to be stopped by the medical team. "Byrnes, you're with me."

Fielding stood to the side of the elevator doors as they slowly parted. He'd heard the radio traffic over the agent's radio, and he knew someone would be coming down to check on the elevator. Locking it off, he went to the elevator next to it and forced the doors open. Once they were parted, he grabbed a chair sitting outside the elevators and jammed it between the doors, propping them open.

He did a quick scan of the hallway. A housekeeper was folding and adjusting items on her cart.

"Where's the laundry room?" Fielding asked. The housekeeper looked at him, not understanding what he was saying.

"Donde esta la lavanderia?"

She smiled and pointed down the hall. "Left. Izquierda," she said in broken English.

Fielding strode down the hall, drawing the pistol he'd taken from the agent. Rounding the corner, he heard the tell-tale sound of an incinerator belching out heat as it destroyed the stained linens and huge amounts of garbage produced by a hotel this size. He stepped away from the hot metal and paused.

McLean stumbled out of the huge laundry depository. He was bleeding from his head, and his arm was hanging slack and dripping blood. Fielding pointed the weapon at him.

"It's over."

"Fielding," McLean said. "A lot of people thought I killed you in 2010, along with Kaczynski."

"Yeah, a lot of people thought I was dead. But ya know, like the bad penny I am..."

"But I wasn't one of the ones who thought about you like that," McLean said, backing away from him. "The people who employ me anticipated that it would be you who would try to stop me, so I took some preemptive actions to guarantee that you wouldn't follow through."

"There's nothing you can do to keep me from making sure you go to jail," Fielding said.

"Oh, I think there is. You remember Skip Larson, don't you, Ted? You got tangled up with him at a bar outside of Stonewall, Texas, back in 1949."

Fielding stopped and took a sharp breath. It had been almost seventy years since he'd heard that name. The barrel of the pistol dipped.

"Did you think that little incident had been forgotten?" McLean taunted. "The shirt? The knife? All safely kept away, but if anything happens to me, they go right to the Feds. You see, we haven't forgotten anything, least of all what you did in Dallas and Austin all those years ago. All those people are dead because of you. Tsk tsk tsk. If I go to jail, the whole world finds out exactly what type of man Ted Fielding really is."

Fielding felt as if he'd been punched in the gut. He'd thought that once Johnson died, everyone who knew about his crimes had either died or had been taken out by his own hand.

"I have to let you in on a confession, Ted," McLean said. "I always admired your work. The way you handled the whole Dallas and Austin thing...masterful." He smiled. "I learned a lot about you and tried to incorporate as much as I could in my own way. Hell, you made me the man I am today, and I just wanted you to know that I saw you as a mentor. I mean, I've killed attorneys and government witnesses. I even killed a Supreme Court Judge once. And the whole time I was thinking, 'Wow. Ted Fielding woulda been proud of the way I put them down.' So, thank you for your inspiration. Without Dallas, I would have never thought about doing what I did today."

For the first time in decades, Fielding was afraid.

CHAPTER FORTY-ONE
THURSDAY
NOVEMBER 21, 1963
DALLAS, TEXAS

Suite 8-F in the Lamar Hotel in Houston was a smorgasbord of Texas political figures. Fielding noted senators, congressmen, and celebrities rubbing shoulders with the presidents of industry. Each one glanced at the door every time it opened, as if afraid of being raided or having their location discovered.

Wolfe motioned to a small, compact man who was laughing and glad-handing various dignitaries in the suite. "Who's the guy playing host?"

"Jacob Rubenstein," Fielding answered.

"He looks familiar, but I don't recognize that name," Wolfe said.

"He goes by 'Jack Ruby' and runs that strip club on Commerce Street. You know the one—The Carousel Club. He's friends with a lot of the Dallas cops and local politicians and is supposedly tied into organized crime in the area."

"Another outstanding constituent," Wolfe said. "So, how did Kellerman take it when you told him you 'lost' your badge?"

When they'd begun planning the overthrow of the Kennedy administration, Fielding knew that if Whitman were to get involved, he would need Booker close by. The only way to get him into places they needed him to be was to 'make' him a Secret Service Agent. Fielding was able to create a passable ID card for him, but without a badge, it wouldn't fly.

"He chewed me out good," Fielding said. "I told him I must have lost it when we were traveling back from Atlanta last week for that campaign rally." He took a sip of his drink. "He made me write a report, then docked my pay twenty bucks to make up for it. Anyway, Booker is set. With his doctor's salary, I'm going to make Booker pay me back, if I have to take it out of his hide," Fielding said, deadpan.

The men stood quietly, surveying the room.

"Ever been here before, Ted?" Wolfe asked. They'd long since grown bored with the parade of dignitaries gathered in the large suite.

"Yeah," Fielding said, sipping his drink and lighting a cigarette. "I've been here a few times with Lyndon. He's met up with these folks so much the front desk started referring to their little cabal as 'The 8Fs.'"

"Where are the rest of the agents tonight?"

"They have a suite in the 'Rice'. If I know those guys, they're probably partying pretty heavily tonight, blowing off steam."

"That could play out in our favor," Wolfe said, sipping his drink. "If those guys aren't up to speed, then they're bound to mess up. We might just be able to pull it off." He patted his coat pocket. "Did you get your envelope?"

Fielding tapped his coat in return. Though neither Fielding nor Wolfe had a choice in planning and executing the operation, Johnson felt that their dedication needed to be rewarded above and beyond their expected service. Each man had been paid twenty-five thousand dollars cash up front, since Johnson had nothing to lose. If they didn't carry out their mission, he'd just use the evidence he had against them and destroy them.

They stood quietly, sipping their drinks and munching on sandwiches as their gazes wandered around the room.

It was here that the power brokers who would suffer the most under two terms of a Kennedy administration, and maybe more, met and plotted the best way to remove the Bostonian interloper. Some suggested publicly disclosing Kennedy's Addison's disease and other ailments or his extramarital affairs with various women, including Marilyn Monroe. But Lyndon didn't want to leave anything to chance, and planned on extending all his connections and influences with the current ruling class in the halls of Washington to maintain his position.

But Johnson's political clout wouldn't work on Kennedy this time.

Before leaving for Dallas, the President had been given a briefing by FBI director J. Edgar Hoover. Hoover relayed to Kennedy that on the Friday that he was in Dallas, at one in the afternoon, Washington time, a senate subcommittee was launching a corruption investigation, which had been instigated by Agriculture Secretary Henry Marshall before his untimely and suspicious death, which would implicate Johnson in several voter fraud allegations. Hoover stated that Johnson's former Chief of Staff, Bobby Baker, was the target and the most direct route to take down Johnson. Armed with this information, Kennedy had made his decision on his '643 campaign.

An hour before, Fielding had stood in the hall of the Rice Hotel, just outside the room where President and Mrs. Kennedy had been staying. The President had summoned Johnson to his suite. Although he couldn't make out the words, the tone of the conversation was less than cordial and, at times, heated. Their voices carried loud enough for Fielding to make out "Connally" and "political climate." After the meeting concluded, Johnson stormed out of the room, pushing past Fielding.

"Get me to The Lamar," Johnson ordered.

The Vice President was somber during the ride. He chain-smoked one cigarette after another—a habit that had increased to three packs a day. That wasn't his only bad habit. His weight had climbed to over two hundred and twenty-five pounds, and he drank too much. Despite this, he pulled a whiskey bottle from the limo bar and poured himself two fingers worth.

Fielding could tell by looking at Lyndon that he knew his career was about to come crashing down around him unless he made a serious choice.

"Ted," Johnson said, "if I ever had any doubts, I don't anymore." He took a deep drink of the whiskey. "Dealey Plaza. Tomorrow."

Fielding nodded.

As part of the advance team, Fielding and Wolfe had scoped out areas where possible assassins could hide and take a shot at the president during the motorcade. Contingency plans had been drawn up, so that in the event that the word was given and allocation named, they would have a provisional plan in place, to execute their orders.

When they arrived at Suite 8-F, Johnson saw Madeline Brown, his mistress for the last ten years, standing by the bar. After making eye contact, Lyndon stepped into the rear bedroom. Madeline soon followed and shut the door.

Fielding walked to Wolfe, who was standing with Booker. The men were deep in conversation. "It's on," he said. "Dealey."

Both men exchanged looks, which Fielding immediately picked up on. He quickly scanned the room and saw that Whitman was at the bar, alone, upending a beer. "What's going on?"

"It's Charlie," Booker said. "He's having second thoughts. I'm not sure he'll go through with it."

"Why? What's changed?"

"He watched Kennedy's speech at the Brooks Air Force base," Wolfe explained. "When he said that it was a time for American 'pathfinders and pioneers,' Whitman cried. He wiped the tears away, but not before I saw them."

"I asked him about what happened," Booker said. "He told me that Kennedy gave him hope for his future and the future of the country." He shrugged. "He doesn't want to steal that hope away."

"I don't give a damn about his feelings, Matt!" Fielding snapped. "We sprung him from the brig to do a job. I expect him to do it." He grabbed Booker by the arm and pulled him into the corner. "This is what you are going to do; you're going to use your medical hocus pocus on him and make him do this. I'm going to be there, to make sure you do it right. And once he's completed his mission, I want you to make him forget that he was ever involved."

"Are you talking about wiping his memory?" Booker asked, his expression tense. "I don't know if I can do that."

"Wipe it, suppress it, I don't care what you have to do, but damn you, you will try!"

"I can do this," Booker said, getting on board. "I can suppress his memory. Make it like it's a bad dream or a fantasy or something."

"That's not good enough," Fielding snapped. "I need some assurances that he won't ever remember his part in this."

"Ok. I can put in a secondary command. It's not that difficult, but I'm not really practiced in it."

"How does that work?" Wolfe had joined them, glancing around to make sure no one had noticed them talking.

"If he starts to remember even a part of it, a code phrase can trigger an irresistible urge to kill himself," Booker said. "He will become assailed with an overwhelming sense of guilt strong enough to push him into taking his own life just to put an end to the feeling."

"What sort of code phrase?" Fielding asked.

"Something out of the ordinary, like, I don't know, 'Strawberry Concrete.'"

Fielding heard the bedroom door open. Johnson stepped out, adjusting his pants, with Madeline following a few minutes later. Fielding noticed that her hair was still smashed down in the back.

Johnson headed to the bar and ordered a whiskey, then spotted Whitman. "Charlie, how are you tonight?"

Whitman looked at the Vice President with anger in his eyes. Just as he started to speak, Booker stepped between them.

"Charles, mind if I have a word with you?" Booker asked, looking over Whitman's shoulder at Fielding, who had secured the bedroom. Booker led Charlie to the room and closed the door behind them. Looking confused, Wolfe walked over to Johnson and whispered in his ear. Johnson nodded his approval.

A few minutes later, the two emerged from the bedroom. Booker looked at Johnson and nodded.

"Charlie," Lyndon began, "why don't you play us a song?"

Charlie nodded absently and sat down on the piano bench. He closed his eyes and began to play "The Battle Hymn of the Republic."

Fielding sipped his coffee and fought the pull of exhaustion. He was just one agent in a group of many assigned to the presidential motorcade and security along the route to the Trade Mart, where President Kennedy was slated to speak at twelve-thirty. They had gathered in a meeting room on the first floor of the Lamar, where they ate a buffet breakfast before heading out to their assignment.

Fielding yawned. The get-together at the 8-F had dragged on well into the night before it finally broke up. Though tired, he was in better shape than most of the other agents. Scanning the room, he saw a couple napping in chairs while others drank cup after cup of black coffee, trying to sober up from the night before. Fielding smiled to himself, thinking that he could make good money today if he charged for aspirin.

A feeling of disgust flipped his smile into a frown when Fielding remembered that he had the unfortunate duty of contacting Oswald to make him aware of the finalized plan. During his brief encounters with the strange man, he'd discovered that Oswald was humorless and morose. He was very abrasive and outspoken about his distaste for the current administration, and Kennedy, in particular, in his dealings with the Cuban situation.

"I read an article in the *Times-Picayune* a couple of months back," Oswald said. "It said that Kennedy and his people were plotting to kill Castro, and Castro called them out on it, warning them about taking any such action. The idea of Kennedy and his ilk trying to eliminate a sitting head of state because they don't like his politics made me angry, so I went to Mexico and tried to obtain a visa to Cuba, but it was denied. It just made me realize more than ever that I didn't want to live in a country where thugs like Kennedy run the government. Either I go, or he has to."

Oswald went on to tell Fielding that he was a Marxist and expounded his Communist virtues and beliefs, though Fielding had since learned that he'd been booted out of the USSR. But Fielding didn't care about any of his rantings. He was mainly concerned that Oswald would do the job he was hired to do. The only emotion Oswald showed was when Fielding told him that John Connally would be in the limo with Kennedy.

"Good," Oswald said. "He had the power to change my Marine Corps discharge to 'Honorable,' but instead, he wrote me a letter saying he'd already resigned as Navy Secretary to run for governor. He passed my request on, but nothing was ever done."

The more Oswald carried on, the more Fielding sensed that the man was all bravado and, under it all, he was a coward.

He couldn't trust Oswald to make the big play when the time came. He got the feeling he would freeze or just not follow through.

Despite this, Lyndon, Dulles, and the CIA were fully competent. Since the CIA had been monitoring and prepping Oswald, they had assumed the same about him as Fielding and had made a contingency plan. One that Fielding knew was time to implement. He slipped out of the room and went to the limousine, returning with a package, which he placed in an adjoining room.

"Lee," Fielding said, shutting down Oswald's latest rant. "You were a rifleman in the Corps, weren't you?"

"Yes," Oswald said, puffing out his chest. "I was a crack shot."

Fielding knew he was lying. He was mediocre at best, but he let it slide.

"I want to show you something. I'm thinking of buying from a friend. I'd really like your opinion on it." He glanced at Wolfe, who walked toward the back room. Inside a long cardboard box was a rifle. Fielding had mail-ordered it, using Oswald's alias, "A. Hidell." Oswald took off his coat and handed it to him, taking the rifle in his hands and grasping it firmly.

"Mannlicher-Carcano, six-point-five bolt action," Oswald rattled off. "A real piece of crap gun." He turned it over in his hands, worked the bolt action, and held it up to sight down. "I wouldn't pay more than twenty dollars for this piece of junk, if it fires at all." He held it out to Fielding, but Fielding waved him off.

"Just lay it in the box. I'll see if my friend will take twenty for it."

Shrugging, Oswald laid the rifle down and Fielding walked him out.

Before Oswald could go on another rant, Ruby put his arm around him and escorted him out of the suite. The two exchanged words before Oswald left.

The realization of what they were about to do settled on Fielding's shoulders like an anchor pulling him down to a watery grave.

He was on the verge of executing a plot to kill the President of the United States. He'd conspired with low-life politicians, who were supposedly upstanding giants of industry, and kooks with their own agendas who'd worked out a plan to take down a good man. A virtuous man. The most powerful man in the free world. So that a lesser, more villainous man could take his place. He had lied, killed, and destroyed others' lives in the service of the most corrupt person he had ever known.

And the worst thing about it was that he could live with that.

"All right," Rufus Youngblood began, "you all know your assignments. I expect you to be on post thirty minutes before the motorcade passes your position...sober and alert!" He looked around the bleary-eyed group. "Does anyone have any questions?"

"I have one," an agent said. "Have they decided who will be in the President's limo? I heard that Connally and Yarborough were in a pissing match over it."

Fielding, like the rest of the Secret Service detail, had been apprised of the running gun feud between the governor, John Connally, and the mayor of Dallas, Ralph Yarborough, over who would ride in the jump seat of the presidential limousine. Yarborough had lobbied to the point of whining to Johnson for the position. Johnson, in turn, attempted to use his political capital in Texas to influence Kennedy.

However, Kennedy had spoken with J. Edgar Hoover before they left for the Texas trip. The FBI Director had privately advised him that his agency was opening an investigation against Johnson, stemming from the voter fraud allegations the Secretary of Agriculture, Henry Marshall, had begun, before his untimely and suspicious death.

"In fact, Mr. President," Hoover said, "Bobby Baker is the focus of the investigation. As Johnson's former Chief of Staff, he will be the most direct route in bringing Lyndon down."

The meeting in the presidential suite at the Rice Hotel didn't go well.

"Lyndon, Connally is in the lead car. End of discussion," Kennedy said. "You're a political liability to me. Once the Senate's investigation becomes public knowledge, it will severely hamper my re-election bid, and that means anyone who throws his hat into your ring will be tainted as well. I need you here in Texas to keep solidarity in the party. Ralph Yarborough may be a good Democrat, but he's not a good Kennedy Democrat. Connally is." Kennedy pulled a cigar from his coat pocket and lit it. "Connally stays, Yarborough rides with you."

"Connally will be in the limo. Yarborough is in the follow-up car with Volunteer," Roy Kellerman said.

Fielding found Wolfe over on the far side of the room and joined him. "Is Charlie ready?"

"Yeah," Wolfe said. "Apparently, whatever Booker did to him was effective. He's standing by in the basement of the depository, ready to deploy."

"What time?"

"At twelve-fifteen, he will make his way to the stockade fence and get into position. Since it's been raining all morning, he's wearing a raincoat, so concealment isn't an issue."

"And Booker?" Fielding asked.

"He's already in the plaza," Wolfe said. He leaned in closer. "Ted…"

"I know, I know. You don't trust him. But it's late to do anything now. I think once this is over, you need to stick with him. Make sure he carries out his part and gets Whitman back to Lejeune. If you feel he's going rogue, take care of the problem."

The phone rang, and Kellerman answered it. "Fielding? Yes, sir. Hold on." Kellerman motioned to Ted. "Phone call. It's Volunteer."

Fielding tossed the empty coffee cup in the trash and looked at Wolfe. "I'll get it in the other room, sir." He walked into the bedroom of the suite.

"How does the detail look this morning?" Johnson asked. He was too cagey a politician to ask outright if the plot was proceeding as planned. He knew Fielding would understand.

"Yes, sir. Dallas PD has officers standing by in the basement of the depository. At twelve-twenty, they'll be in position," Fielding said. "Since it's been raining all morning, they'll be wearing a raincoat. The other assets will be in position before the motorcade makes Elm Street."

"Good," Johnson said. "Don't let me down, Ted. This trip has to be successful, if we are going to continue…"

"I understand, Mr. Vice President," Fielding said. "I have no doubts everything will work out."

"I won't forget that," Johnson said.

Fielding heard the click on the other line and hung up the phone. Stepping out of the bedroom, he watched the other agents head out the door. They had no idea that today would change their lives forever.

Lincoln, Garfield, and McKinley had all died at the hands of assassins. Today, John Fitzgerald Kennedy would join that very elite group.

CHAPTER FORTY-TWO
FRIDAY, NOVEMBER 22, 1963
TWELVE-THIRTY PM

Fielding stood on the sidewalk on Elm Street and watched the crowd as all eyes fixated on the corner of South Houston Street and Elm, awaiting a glimpse of the limousine carrying President Kennedy and his party. He scanned the plaza until he located Wolfe and Booker. Glancing over his shoulder, he surveyed the crowd behind him. A husband and wife, along with their two sons, shaded their eyes, straining against the pounding Texas sun. On a pedestal near the knoll, a balding man in a black suit adjusted the lens on a handheld video camera. A woman stood next to him, helping to keep his balance. Beyond the couple, standing on the other side of the stockade fence, a police officer stood in the shade, eyes trained on the intersection.

The limo slowly turned onto Elm from South Houston. The crowd began to shout and cheer, many flooding the sidewalk where Fielding stood, trying to get a closer look at the young president. Fielding scanned the crowd, looking for anything out of the ordinary—anything that might interfere with the plan.

A man opened an umbrella as the limo approached, the **movement** catching Fielding's eye. He started to move toward the man when the first shot cracked the Dallas sky. His gaze shifted from the man to the limousine. Fielding watched Kennedy's arms go up as he grasped his throat. A second shot followed, and he saw Connally react to being struck in the back. He knew what was coming next.

From his vantage point, he knew he could jump onto the side of the limousine as it passed, effectively putting himself between what he knew was to come and the President. He could be the recipient of any further shots and possibly save the man's life.

As he contemplated this, he watched the chaos inside the car and saw the pain on both Kennedy's and Connally's faces. If he leapt forward, he could save them both.

But Fielding didn't move forward. Instead, he crouched down on the sidewalk, giving the shooter a clear field of fire as the final shot tore through the air just to the right of him. At the sound of the shot, he prostrated himself on the grass.

Even though he'd known what would happen, he gasped at the brutality. Kennedy's head exploded, spraying blood, brain, and skull fragments inside the limo and onto the trunk. An agent caught up with the limo just as it accelerated, grabbing onto the support bar and pushing Mrs. Kennedy, who had crawled onto the trunk, back into the vehicle and covering her.

Jumping to his feet, Fielding shook off the shock and drew his revolver. He looked back toward the stock-ade fence and ran toward it. As he approached, a Dallas police officer pointed his weapon at him.

"Drop the gun!" Charles Whitman, clad in a police uniform, said loud enough for anyone within earshot to hear. Beneath the heavy raincoat, the Texas heat—and the fear of being caught—caused him to sweat profusely.

Fielding played along, just as they had planned. "Secret Service," he said, slowly raising his hands. "I have my ID in my inside coat pocket."

A small crowd began congregating around them.

"Set your pistol down and slowly remove your ID," Whitman said, playing the part of the conscientious policeman. Fielding laid the pistol down and slowly drew his leather ID case, holding out the badge for Whitman to read. Satisfied, he nodded, and Fielding collected his pistol.

"Find anything?" Fielding asked.

"Nothing here," Whitman said, sticking to the pre-rehearsed script. "I was standing post when I thought I heard shots coming from over here." Several people nodded their agreement.

"Yeah, we heard shots too!" some said.

Fielding peered over the fence, scanning the area and ensuring that Whitman collected his shell casings and obscured his footprints.

"I think there may have been echoes," Whitman said, raising his voice above the crowd and dampening their comments. He pointed across the plaza. "Seems like everyone is going toward the schoolbook building." He and Fielding waved off any other comments about the shots coming from the area of the stockade fence.

Fielding was walking around, making a show of investigating, when he saw that a small piece of the fence had been knocked off the top of the wood. He raised a questioning brow at Whitman, who shrugged, acknowledging that he must have knocked the piece off when he'd fired the rifle. Fielding tucked it away in his pocket before anyone could see.

Together, they made their way toward the depository. Fielding looked across the plaza and saw Booker standing in the street, looking in the direction the limousine had fled. He seemed to be in shock. Fielding, fearing that Booker had lost his nerve, made his way toward him. Before he could reach him, Booker snapped out of his trance and spotted Wolfe waving and motioning for him to meet him at the depository. Booker nodded and grabbed the first person he saw.

"The shots came from there!" he exclaimed, wide-eyed, pointing at the seven-floor building. The cameraman pointed his camera at the building while Booker yelled to others, pointing them toward the building. He was working on blending in with the crowd when Fielding, Whitman, and Wolfe joined him.

"Ted, what am I supposed to do?" Booker asked, a tremor in his voice.

Taking in his pale features and trembling hands, Fielding grabbed him by his arm and shook him, pulling him close enough to speak into his ear. "Hey, I don't need you checking out on me now," he growled. "We have a job to finish, and I expect you to uphold your part. Understand?"

Booker wiped his face with a handkerchief and nodded. "All right. All right." He worked to compose himself. "I'm fine." He pulled a cigarette from a crushed Chesterfield pack and lit it before realizing that he already had one in his mouth. He flicked the older one out of his mouth and replaced it with the newly lit one.

"All right. This is what I need you to do," Fielding began to tell Booker. He took Whitman by the arm. "Take this man away from the scene and speak to him privately. Make sure he tells you all he knows. Then, find out where they took Lancer and check his condition. When we're done here, Wolfe and I will meet you there. Now, move!" Spotting Wolfe, he sidled up to him as they moved closer to the front of the depository.

Booker escorted Whitman to a corner where they would be undisturbed. "Are you all right, Charlie?" he asked. "Any nausea or headaches?"

"No, I feel fine," Whitman said. "I just need to get out of this raincoat. I'm sweating to death."

"Okay, we'll take care of that. Go with Mr. Wolfe. Change out of your clothes and put on the suit that's in the back seat. Do you understand?"

"Yes, I understand," Whitman said.

Booker turned him around to the waiting car and opened the door. Charlie climbed into the back seat and spotted the clothes. He quickly removed the raincoat, with the rifle hidden inside, as well as the police uniform, and handed it to Wolfe, who placed it in the trunk. It was Wolfe's job to get rid of the evidence.

Crossing the street and turning onto South Houston was Lee Harvey Oswald.

"Get him back to the hotel," Booker instructed Wolfe. "I'll join him shortly."

Wolfe slowly pulled out and turned with the outgoing traffic while Booker jogged back toward the plaza. He was sure that he could catch a ride, but he paused to walk through the crime scene. He moved toward the curb opposite the grassy area and saw something shiny lying on the asphalt—a cylindrical item, about the length of his finger. Leaning down, he pitched the butt of his cigarette to the ground, crushing it with his toe, and picked up the item, holding it up to the sunlight.

It was a slug from a high-powered rifle. It was sticky to the touch, and Booker realized that it was coated with the blood and brains of the Chief Executive of the United States. Looking around to make sure no one was watching, he pulled out his sweat-soaked handkerchief and wrapped it inside, tucking it away.

Looking for transportation into the plaza, he struck out when he noticed an officer sitting in his car near the rear of the depository. Walking over, he flashed his doctored credentials, which supported the lie that he was part of the Secret Service.

"I need a ride to wherever they took the President."

"Parkland Hospital," the officer clarified. "Get in."

SUNDAY, NOVEMBER 24, 1963

All had gone well with the flight from Dallas to North Carolina. Booker and Whitman had been housed in a safe house just outside of Dallas, keeping them out of sight until they were ready to fly out the next day. Booker knew it would be easier to switch Whitman out with the double who'd been taking his place in the cell over the weekend. He'd hypnotized the shift sergeant in charge of the brig a few weeks before when he'd offered to help him stop smoking. Once the man was under, Booker had slipped in a post-hypnotic suggestion, a "fail-safe" phrase he could use to regain control over him.

Booker spent his time in the safe house preparing Whitman to receive the post-hypnotic command once they arrived in the cell. Whitman's replacement, who had been confined to the solitary cell for the past twenty-three days, was another patient of Booker, as was the Marine in charge of checking on the prisoner. All three would be under his control.

It was a good thing he had the time alone with Whitman. The young Marine showed overwhelming grief over the President's death. Booker found him sobbing in his room.

"What's wrong, Charlie?"

Whitman glared at Booker, tears streaming from his eyes. "What the hell do you think?" He walked into the living room and pointed at the television. The news channels were broadcasting the story continuously. "I killed him, man. I pulled the trigger, and his freaking head exploded!" He sat down heavily on the couch and buried his face in his hands. "I killed the President. I killed the United States of America. This country will never be the same. I did it! God, damn me to Hell, I did it."

Whitman walked to the bar and reached for a bottle, but Booker stepped into his path and pulled out his pocket watch, passing it before Charlie's eyes. He placed him under hypnosis, blocking the memory of his involvement with the President's murder. He let him sleep, knowing that when he awoke, he would be sad over the death, but that his level of grief would be like the thousands of others in the country who shared the same burden.

Booker saw Wolfe pull into the driveway of the safe house and went out to greet him. "Charlie's been wiped. Don't mention anything about the President."

At the prison, Booker approached the Marine guard and pulled out his Marine Corps ID, showing it to the sergeant. While the guard checked the ID, Booker spoke some key phrases, which immediately caused the man to slip into a deep sleep. Sitting him down, he crossed over to the filing cabinet and, in short order, found Whitman's file. Booker removed the impostor, Dennison's, photo from under the paper clip and replaced it with Whitman's true photo. He retrieved the keys to the solitary cell and unlocked the cell door. Dennison rose and turned toward Booker, who spoke a set of commands to him. Dennison began to take off the prisoner's jumpsuit as Whitman unbuttoned his shirt and removed his tie. Within five minutes, both men had dressed in each other's clothes, and Whitman took a seat on the bed. When Booker leaned over and spoke a command, Whitman closed his eyes.

"Charlie, you have spent the last month in this cell. You have written in your diary every day. The handwriting looks different because you hurt your hand. It is healed now. You have never left the brig. You will remember nothing about what happened over the past three weeks. You were told about the assassination while in your cell. It made you sad, and you cried. If anyone mentions the assassination to you, your knowledge is that Oswald was the only person involved. Should you think otherwise, you will become sick to your stomach." He then turned to Dennison. "You have been in the hospital for the past three weeks, due to a jeep crash. You are back on duty, but it is difficult to remember any details of the crash. Should anyone challenge you, I will verify your version of events" Booker turned back to Whitman. "Lie down, Charlie. Sleep."

Booker stepped back into the main office with Dennison, who was still under hypnosis, and attached the set of keys back on the Marine guard's belt. Looking at both men, Booker spoke once more. "Awake."

The guard shook his head and rubbed his eyes, then stood up.

"Are you all right, Sergeant?" Booker asked, feigning concern.

"Yes, sir. Sorry, sir," he answered, frazzled. "I just felt dizzy for a second."

"Perhaps you stood up too fast. I need to see Private Whitman."

"Certainly, sir." The marine wrote Booker's and Dennison's names down and looked at his watch. He shook it and looked at the clock on the wall, surprised to find that they were the same time. It was twenty minutes later than he thought. "Uh, down the hall. Second cell on the right." He led the way and unlocked the cell, finding Whitman asleep in his bunk.

"Whitman," the sergeant loudly called out. "You have visitors."

Whitman rose from his sleep, and, when he saw Booker and Dennison, he stood and saluted.

"At ease," Booker said.

The sergeant left the cell, pulling the door behind him.

Fifteen minutes later, Dennison was driving Booker out the front gate. They pulled onto the main road, and Dennison drove by the coffee shop where Wolfe was waiting for Booker to return. As they passed, Booker glanced in and spotted Wolfe reading a newspaper.

"There's the coffee shop, sir," Dennison said, nodding in its direction.

"Keep driving."

"Yes, sir. Where to, Captain?" Dennison asked.

"Get me to the airport," Booker said. Twenty minutes later, Booker exited the car and approached the American Airlines check-in counter.

"Can I help you, sir?" the man at the counter asked.

"When is your next flight to Indianapolis?"

The man looked through his flight manifest. "One is leaving at two thirty-five."

Booker looked at his watch. Forty-two minutes. "I need a one-way ticket." He showed the man his Secret Service ID and paid him twenty-five dollars for the ticket. While he waited for his flight to board, he headed to the coffee shop and bought a cup of coffee.

Wolfe put down the newspaper and looked at his watch. It was twelve-twenty. He glanced up at the television that the cafe had set up in the corner of the room and watched the news report on the transfer of Lee Harvey Oswald to the county jail.

Fielding, Booker, Whitman, and Wolfe had stayed behind after the other Secret Service agents on the Presidential Detail had forcibly removed the President's body from Parkland Hospital and loaded it onto Air Force One to get him back to

Washington. Fielding had been informed that Johnson had been sworn in before the plane had left the ground and was now in the position he had coveted since 1960.

They learned that the Dallas Police had apprehended Oswald after he had shot a policeman. He had put up a fight, and, from the looks of his face on TV, he had been beaten down by the Dallas cops. Oswald had stated during a press conference that he was "a patsy." Wolfe looked at Fielding.

"He's not going to keep quiet, you know," Wolfe said. "If he's pressured, he's gonna name names."

"It's already handled," Fielding said, without elaborating further.

Wolfe watched the crowd of reporters who'd gathered in the basement of the Dallas Police headquarters. The NBC cameraman focused his camera on Oswald as he emerged from a set of glass doors flanked by two Dallas detectives. Wolfe had just taken a sip of his fresh cup of coffee when he saw a man cut through the crowd of reporters and cross the lower right part of the TV screen, rushing Oswald. Wolfe saw the gun in the man's hand and heard the shot as he fired into Oswald. Oswald screamed in pain as the officers and a handful of reporters swarmed the shooter, taking away the pistol and taking him into custody. As pandemonium reigned in the basement, an ambulance moved in and Oswald was loaded onto a gurney. His arm flopped weakly off the stretcher.

Wolfe had seen enough dead people in his career to know that if Oswald wasn't dead, he would be soon.

He continued to watch the news. The name "Jack Ruby" was mentioned by a reporter. At that moment, Wolfe realized what Fielding had meant when he'd said, "It was handled."

Wolfe reached into his pocket and removed the check for twenty-five thousand that he and the others had received for pulling off the...situation. He, Fielding, and Wolfe had received their payoffs. Oswald and Whitman wouldn't see a dime, since Whitman was hypnotized to forget that he was ever involved, and Oswald wasn't a mercenary, but had wanted to do the job as a political statement.

Wolfe had been so engrossed in the news and his thoughts that he didn't realize the time. He looked at his watch.

Two forty-five.

Booker had told him that the entire exchange shouldn't take more than an hour, and that they would be boarding a three-thirty flight back to Washington.

He walked to the pay phone and grabbed the phone book, flipping through the pages until he found the listing for Camp Lejeune. He dialed the main number.

"I need to speak to whoever is in charge of the brig," Wolfe said. The line clicked as the operator plugged his call into the exchange for the brig.

"Sergeant Allen," the Marine guard answered.

"I need to speak to Captain Booker," Wolfe said. "It's very important."

"Sorry, sir," Allen said. "Captain Booker and his aide left the prisoner Whitman and signed out at twelve-forty-five."

Wolfe looked at his watch and cursed. Booker had been gone for two and a half hours.

He hung up and opened the phone book once again, turning to the page that listed taxicabs. When the cab arrived, he slipped the driver a twenty and told him he needed to be at the airport in fifteen minutes. The cab made it in twelve. Wolfe went to the American Airlines counter and pulled out his ticket and ID.

"You're the second Secret Service Agent I've served in the past two hours," the clerk said.

"Who was the other?" Wolfe asked.

The clerk flipped through his manifest and found the name. "Booker, Matthew."

"For the Washington DC flight at three-thirty?" Booker was relieved. Apparently, Booker had forgotten about picking him up from the coffee shop. He smiled to himself. *Maybe with all that hypnosis, he caused himself to forget,* he thought.

"No, sir," the clerk said. "He left on a flight to Indianapolis at two thirty-five."

Wolfe crumbled his ticket and threw it down. He thought about the dossier he had read on Booker, and then remembered where he had come from. *Booker was heading to Fort Wayne, where his family was.* "When is the next flight to Indy?"

"Not until eight o'clock," the clerk said. "But there's a flight to Chicago leaving in ten minutes. I can reserve a flight from Chicago to Indianapolis for you."

Wolfe nodded, grateful when the clerk was even able to transfer the fee he had paid for his Washington, DC ticket to offset the new flights.

Twenty-five minutes later, Wolfe was sitting back in the airplane seat, a plan already formulating about what he would do with Booker when he found him.

Wolfe sat behind the wheel of his Hertz rent-a-car as he tore down Interstate 69 in search of the '63 Ford Fairlane that Booker had rented from the same place half an hour before. He stopped at an Esso station on Jefferson Boulevard and asked for directions to Third Street and Wells. The attendant gave him concise directions, and Wolfe found Booker's rental car parked out front of a small two-story house.

Wolfe hunkered down in his car and waited for Booker to leave, drifting off somewhere around midnight. He awoke around six o'clock and made his way to a diner a block away. He used the facilities and ordered a quick breakfast before returning to watch the house.

At eight fifty-five, Booker left the house and got into his car. He pulled out onto Wells Street with Wolfe a block behind him. Five minutes later, he pulled into the parking lot of a men's suit store. The name on the sign read "Wolf and Desseur." Half an hour later, Booker walked out, wearing a new suit and highly polished shoes. Glancing around, he brushed off his shoulders. Quietly, Wolfe crossed the lot and came up behind him before he had a chance to reach his car.

He pressed a pistol into his ribs while checking Booker for a gun. He wasn't carrying one.

"W-Wolfe?" Booker stammered. "What's going on?"

"Get in my car," Wolfe ordered. "We need to talk."

They crossed the lot, and Booker slid into the passenger side of the car. Wolfe kept the gun trained on him.

"What the hell are you doing?" Wolfe put the car in gear and pulled out on Washington Boulevard.

"I wanted to see my family, that's what!" Booker snapped. "I don't know when I'll get to see them again, and I wanted to make sure my wife got the money."

"You told her about the money?! What are you, stupid?"

"I didn't tell her anything, and I never mentioned the money. She'll find out about it next time she makes the baby's bed."

"You idiot," Wolfe said. "Don't you think she's going to want to know where you got that much money from and how you got it? What are you going to tell her then?"

"Look," Booker said. "What I do with that money is my own business. I did my job, and you are in no position to tell me what to do." He crossed his arms. "I was going to meet up with you guys in Washington when I was done here."

Wolfe switched his gun to his left hand and reached into Booker's coat pocket, yanking out an airline ticket. Booker objected, but Wolfe pushed him against the passenger side door. He looked at the ticket and frowned.

"Costa Rica isn't anywhere near Washington, sport," Wolfe said. He put the ticket in his pocket and tucked his .38 into its holster.

Booker breathed a sigh of relief, then took the opportunity to explain. "You don't understan–"

"SHUT UP!" Wolfe snapped, and Booker slumped down in the seat and remained quiet.

They traveled an hour without speaking.

"I want to know why," Wolfe said, breaking the silence

"I told you. I wanted to see my..."

"No," Wolfe cut him off. "I want to know why you went along with the plan. I mean, you're some sort of head shrinker. Why did you agree to pretend to be a Secret Service agent and be in the plaza? What the hell is Johnson's hold on you?"

Booker looked at Wolfe, fear painting his expression. Wolfe cut his eyes to him. "Look, Johnson has dirt on all of us, okay? You aren't alone. We're all his puppets."

He recounted his story about the crash and how Johnson had used it as leverage to get him to work for him. When he was finished, Booker looked relieved and smiled.

"It's good to know I'm not the only one," Booker said. "Fielding?"

"Yeah, he has his own issues," Wolfe said.

Booker lit a cigarette and took a long drag on it. "I was a prominent doctor outside of Austin when I had a...little indiscretion...with a married patient." He scratched his ear nervously. "She said I tried to rape her, but it was totally consensual, ya know?" He inhaled the smoke again. "Anyway, she and I got in a fight because she wanted me to leave my wife."

"So, he found out and was going to expose your affair? That doesn't seem like..."

Booker shook his head. "She killed herself in my office." He tossed the cigarette out the window and lit another one. "I was doing some counseling with Johnson, and I panicked. I called him and asked if he could help. He did." Booker paused. "The cost was my soul." He crushed the cigarette out in the ashtray with more force than he'd intended.

Wolfe looked knowingly at Booker and nodded grimly. "You got Whitman squared away?"

"Yes. He won't have any memory of his involvement. He'll feel sad, along with the rest of the country, but the memory has been buried deep enough so that there's only a slight chance it will ever come up."

"A slight chance?" Wolfe raised a brow. "So, he may remember his part?"

"That's not going to happen," Booker said. "I'm very good at my job. And if he does start showing signs of memory restoration, I told Fielding the phrase that will trigger the post-hypnotic suggestion that will lead him to take his own life, thus eliminating the problem."

"What phrase?"

"Strawberry Concrete."

Wolfe gave him a strange look and laughed. "Whatever." He drove a few more miles before speaking again. "Other than the money, do you have anything that could tie you to Dallas?"

Booker looked at Wolfe for a long moment. The piece of the President's skull and the spent rifle slug inside the glass jar that was tucked inside his sock chafed against his left leg, while the Secret Service pin dug into the flesh of his right. He lit another cigarette, more to disguise his trembling fingers than to calm his craving. "No," he said. "I want to forget that it ever happened."

They remained quiet as they drove, each man lost in their thoughts. Wolfe looked at the next exit. "Camp Simmons." He exited, and they soon found themselves in a quiet little town that looked as though it was starting to grow. He drove down Ferguson Street and passed an appliance store. Like many of the businesses throughout the United States, the store was closed in memory of President Kennedy. A black wreath was posted on the door. Behind it was an open field, which had been excavated for expansion. It was also secluded, which was ideal for what he had in mind.

"What are we doing here?" Booker asked. He looked at his watch. It was eleven fourteen. "Look, I need to get that rental car back."

Ignoring him, Wolfe reached over and fiddled with the radio, finding a station playing a rock and roll song. "I'm sorry," he quietly said.

Booker looked at Wolfe and nodded.

"What's that?" Wolfe asked, suddenly pointing out the passenger side window.

Booker jerked his head to the right, his eyes trailing behind the car, trying to see what it was Wolfe had seen.

Wolfe pulled a .32 caliber revolver from his pocket, a throw-down gun he'd taken off a thug, and placed it against Booker's head. For a small caliber, the gunshot was still loud and reverberated inside the car.

Booker jerked, slamming his left hand into the roof of the car and slumping over. He gurgled for a few seconds as his brain slowly seized up, and then he was quiet. Wolfe pulled behind a building and parked. He exited and opened the trunk of the car, then went to the passenger side. Gathering Booker up, he carried him to the back of the car and stuffed him into the trunk. He found some old newspapers and wrapped Booker's head in the papers, soaking up the blood.

Wolfe was exhausted. He got back in the car and drove until he found a hardware store where he bought a shovel and flashlight. After placing them in the back seat, he set out to find a motel. He found one a block away. He checked in, then drove to the room and backed his car up by the front door.

He glanced at his watch. It was right before noon. Wolfe stripped and climbed into bed. He slept for ten hours straight, rising to see that it was dark. He checked the trunk and found Booker still inside. Going back into his room, he dialed Fielding's number.

"Where are you, Abner?"

"Indiana. There was a problem," Wolfe said. He then laid out what had happened the day before and that day. Fielding was quiet when Wolfe told him about what he had done to Booker.

"I see that the Oswald situation was taken care of," Wolfe said.

"Yeah. It took a little bit of persuasion. Some of the southern crime families being investigated by Bobby and the Justice Department contacted Ruby and offered to take care of his family if he did the hit. But they also emphasized that if he didn't, 'taking care of his family' could have another connotation."

"Looks like it worked the way we planned," Wolfe said.

After the meeting at the hotel while in Dallas, the night before the assassination, Wolfe and Fielding had broken into the school book depository using the key Fielding had lifted off Oswald when he was examining the rifle and had taken off his coat. They'd made their way to the sixth floor, and after making sure no one was around to hear, Fielding had put on a pair of gloves and fired three shots into a box of books, leaving the shell casings lying near the window. He'd tucked the rifle behind some boxes, fresh with Oswald's palm print on the stock, and easy enough to be found by the investigators on the scene.

Oswald was supposed to have brought his own rifle to the floor, but Fielding had bet that he wouldn't. Instead, he'd known what Lee would do: he would chicken out, but when he heard about the assassination, he would know that he was being set up. With Allen Dulles' help, the intelligence apparatus had placed a sniper team in an adjoining building, setting up triangulation fire, with Whitman taking the head shot. Oswald realized this, and he knew that he had to get out of the depository as soon as he could, knowing that he was the prime suspect. His panic had worked against him, and he'd ended up shooting a Dallas policeman who'd stopped to question him.

On the other end of the line, Fielding was quiet for a long moment before finally asking, "What are you going to do with Booker?"

"The less you know, the better," Wolfe diverted. "I'm driving back to Indy tonight and taking an early morning flight back to Washington."

"Good. Hazelwood was asking about you. I told him that you were staying in Dallas to do some follow-up, and he was all right with that. He wants all hands on deck for the presidential funeral."

"I'll be there," Wolfe said. "I just have one more thing to take care of."

After hanging up, Wolfe drove to the rear of the appliance store and grabbed the shovel from the back seat. After half an hour of digging, he dragged Booker's body from the trunk and placed him in the grave.

He patted down Booker's pockets and removed the man's wallet to keep him from being identified, but missed the jar and Secret Service pin tucked inside his socks. He buried the doctor and drove off, stopping long enough to throw the shovel over the fence into a construction site, where it would blend in with the rest of the equipment left behind. Satisfied that all his bases were covered, Wolfe got back on I-69 and headed to the airport in Indianapolis.

CHAPTER FORTY-THREE
JUNE 6, 1964

Ted Fielding had always been fond of New Orleans. There was something about the allure of the town, the energy on its streets. The bawdy bars with their half-naked billboards tempting the casual observer to come in and check out their wares just added to the ambiance and seductive charm of the city.

Unfortunately, Fielding wasn't there for the bars or entertainment. He was there to see a man whom his boss felt had the potential to be a problem for his administration—former FBI agent and Assistant Superintendent of the New Orleans Police, PI Guy Banister.

After Oswald had been arrested for Kennedy's assassination, a flurry of questions began to arise regarding his movements over the past three years and with whom he had been associated. Two names that had repeatedly come up were Dave Ferrie and Banister.

Banister had an office at 531 Lafayette Street, which shared an entrance with 544 Camp Street. This wouldn't have any significance at all if the Camp Street address hadn't shown up on pamphlets for the "Fair Play for Cuba Committee," which were produced and distributed by one Lee Harvey Oswald. Information had made its way to Fielding that Banister and Ferrie, a known anti-Castro supporter, had worked with Oswald.

It was Fielding's job to wrap up the loose ends associated with Oswald and keep the public's attention on the Warren Commission's Report, which found that Oswald had acted alone; therefore, it was determined that no conspiracy existed.

Fielding had done his homework on Banister. Knowing that he had a bad heart, it wouldn't take much to push him into a full-blown cardiac arrest. Banister was a tough cookie, but with controlled blows, combined with a heavy dose of epinephrine injected behind his ear, he didn't stand a chance.

Pretending to be a potential client wanting his wife investigated, Fielding lulled Banister into a false sense of security before striking him from behind. Once he disabled the older man, Fielding removed Banister's nitroglycerin tablets from the man's coat pocket and held him down until the arrest ran its course. He then straightened Banister's office, taking care to spill the nitro tablets just out of Banister's reach before leaving. When the job was done, Fielding strode into the Louisiana sunshine, wiped his hands with a paper towel, and walked toward Bourbon Street, where he intended to consume several Hurricanes before heading to the airport and back to Washington.

DECEMBER 5, 1964

Charles Whitman stepped out of the gate at Camp Lejeune and took a deep breath. The guard at the shack nodded to him.

"Take care of yourself, Charlie," the guard said. Charlie nodded and considered saluting, but decided against it. "The Corp will miss you."

"Screw the Marine Corps," Whitman said. He hoisted his duffel onto his back, cinched his coat closed against the cold, and started walking down the road without looking back. He reached inside his coat pocket and pulled out the one document that allowed him to turn his back on the Marines and Camp Lejeune.

He looked at his discharge papers and smiled.

The past year had been rough. After serving three months in the brig, Whitman had been assigned as a quota clerk, gathering information on marines, their promotions, and discharges. He'd gotten along fine with his superiors, but his anger toward the Corps flared up at times. He was told by the captain in charge of the office that he was a good worker but wasn't cut out to be a Marine.

Then, there was the beating.

Two months before, Charlie had been walking home from a bar when he was cornered in an alley by several men. He recognized one or two of them as men he'd loaned money to and had had to threaten them at gunpoint to get his money back. The Marines had filed a complaint, which had landed Charlie in front of a Court Martial Board. He'd thought the ninety days he was sentenced to would have been enough to appease the men, but he'd been wrong.

Charlie never saw the first punch that knocked him to the dirty alley.

"I've been waiting to get you back, Whitman!" a man's gravelly voice sounded behind him. Charlie was struggling to get to his feet when a second man hit him with a pair of brass knuckles. Curling up in a fetal position, Whitman had tried to protect himself as the men beat him. He glanced up just as a steel-toed boot crashed into his left temple, slamming his head into the brick wall. His head exploded in bright lights and pain, numbing the pain of the next kick to his head.

Lying on his face, his ears ringing, Charlie had heard a whistle cut through the noise in his head, followed by the sound of running feet. A hand had gently pressed down on his chest, and a face leaned close to his ear.

"We're gonna get you to a hospital, Marine," a faraway voice said.

Charlie coughed, igniting his ribs in pain and sending his head into agony. He rolled on his back and slipped into blackness.

After spending a week in the hospital, Charlie had been released, but the pain in his head was still there. He was taking aspirin three or four times a day, but it only dulled the pain. The doctors told him that the pain would fade over time, but that he would have to deal with it for the time being.

After the incident, Charlie **had** returned to his clerk job. He continued to file the paperwork for other marines, but soon received news of his own discharge. Back when he'd been in the brig, Charlie had sent letter after letter to his father, asking him to use his connections and friendships with people in his political circle and press for his discharge. His father was less than supportive. In one letter, Charles Senior took Charlie to task about his request, saying that, after the incident at the University of Texas—as well as his court martial for Usury and Extortion—the best Charlie could hope for was a dishonorable discharge.

And yet, here Charlie was, staring down at an honorable discharge with his name on it. He held it up and looked at it. He ran his finger over the piece of paper and found that he'd lightly smeared the signature of the President of the United States.

Lyndon Johnson had personally signed the form.

Charlie looked at the signature, and an image flashed in his mind. The image disturbed him. He remembered that when the President was Vice President, he'd hosted Charlie and his wife at his ranch for a wedding party. But the image wasn't of Johnson. Instead, it was John F. Kennedy who'd entered his thoughts.

The image made him sick to his stomach. Here, more than a year later, Charlie still remembered the guard telling him the news in his cell (was he in his cell?) that Kennedy had been assassinated and Johnson was the new president.

But something about the memory didn't feel right. It just didn't seem...real. It almost felt manufactured.

Charlie shook the feeling away. He was sure that many people were still in a state of shock at the enormity of the assassination. He read the paper every day and saw more and more unrest and disillusionment from people his age, who felt that Kennedy's death had started the country down a slippery slope of anarchy. A slope that the United States might never recover from.

And with the Warren Commission taking less than a year to investigate the murder, releasing their findings barely three months ago, the majority in the country believed there had been a rush to judgment, specifically designed to sweep the matter under the rug so the union could move on under the current administration.

Charlie was in the minority. He believed that the Commission had come to the only correct solution: Lee Harvey

Oswald was the sole assassin, and no other parties were involved. Any time he thought there might be another explanation, his stomach churned. Like many in the world today, Charlie felt that the murder signaled that the United States had lost its innocence.

Kennedy had given the country hope and enthusiasm, dreams and aspirations.

Johnson had given the country a new war, and, though war might be good for the economy, it wasn't good for the people. Charlie watched as a bus filled with recruits who'd been drafted into service headed to Lejeune to begin their training. He felt like he was one of the lucky ones. He got out before this thing in Vietnam went into full gear.

When the outbound bus pulled up, Charlie gave the driver his ticket and shrugged his duffle bag onto the seat next to him.

Two days later, he was back in Kathleen's arms.

CHAPTER FORTY-FOUR
DECEMBER 5, 1965

Fielding sat in the waiting room just outside the Oval Office, sipping a cup of coffee. It had been a little over two and a half years since the President took office and kept him busy settling old scores and tying up loose ends. Since Johnson had summoned him personally instead of going through channels, he figured there must be someone else whom he needed to remove.

The door swung inward, and Lyndon patted Deputy Attorney General Ramsey Clark on the back. "So, I can count on you to have a draft of the Voting Rights Act on my desk by this time next month?"

"Absolutely, Mr. President," Clark affirmed. "I'll have my staff make it a priority." The men shook hands, and Johnson turned his attention to Fielding. "Come on in, Ted."

Fielding followed him in and took his place in front of the President's desk. Johnson stepped behind it just long enough to cut off the recording device kept in the drawer. A usual occurrence whenever the two planned to discuss one of Fielding's "missions." But Fielding was caught off guard when the President stepped out from behind the desk and went into the bathroom, off the Oval Office. Dropping his pants, Johnson squatted on the toilet.

Fielding had heard of the "Johnson Treatment." It was usually reserved for people who had fallen out of favor with the administration, or for those whom Lyndon needed to show just who was in charge.

Whatever his reasoning, Johnson made sure that Fielding was there for the full display.

"We have a problem in Austin, Ted," Johnson said. "Our boy, Charlie, is becoming worrisome."

"How so, sir?" Fielding kept one hand over his nose to try and block the odor.

"I've received some reports that he's been abusing his wife," Johnson said. "Big old boy like that beatin' on that little ole girl just ain't right." Fielding nodded. "Back when he was in the Marine Corps, he got the snot kicked out of him by a bunch of disgruntled soldiers who Charlie cheated out of money. He's been having severe headaches, and I fear the worst is yet to come."

"What do you mean?"

"Well, we know that Booker hypnotized Charlie to forget certain things..." Johnson said, open-endedly. "But he also said that he told you about a back-up plan, in case Charlie started to remember."

"Yes, I recall," Fielding said. "So, you want me to go down and remove the problem?" It surprised him how easily the words rolled off his tongue. Fielding liked Whitman. He was a bit coarse around the edges, but for the most part, he was a good kid. Killing him without any consideration for how he felt about the man just showed how far Ted had fallen as a human being.

"This is gonna take more than just that," Johnson said. He wiped and flushed, then pulled up his pants and washed his hands. Fielding took the opportunity to retreat into the Oval Office to wait. "Ted, I want you to take a leave of absence from the Secret Service."

Fielding was stunned. "A—leave, sir? But why? Haven't I served you and done whatever you've asked?"

"Ted, you have excelled more than I could ever dream, son," Johnson said, placing both of his large hands on Fielding's shoulders. "But, with Booker out of the picture—if you know what happened to him, I don't want to know—you are the only one left who can control Charlie."

"I still don't understand," Fielding said.

"This is the situation," Johnson began. "I've already spoken with your old chief at the Austin Police Department. He's putting in a good word with Chief Miles so that you can go back to work with them as an investigator. Once you've settled in, I want you to approach Charlie."

"Once I make contact with Whitman, then what?"

"I want you to tell him whatever Booker had hidden in his brain to shut him up and then make sure that he doesn't leave anything behind that could be embarrassing."

"But what do I tell Kellerman? He'll want to know the reason."

"I'll take care of your bosses," Johnson said. "We'll just say that we had an old-fashioned Texas disagreement, and I thought it best that you put some distance between the two of us."

"I'll have to let Wolfe know," Fielding said.

"Probably a good idea."

Fielding started to turn to leave, but turned back to Johnson. "Does this mean you've relieved me of my obligation?" His voice held a hint of hope. Johnson still had the torn, bloody shirt and knife coated with Skip Larson's blood.

"Hell no, son," Johnson laughed. "I still have your peter in my pocket. Don't forget that now."

Fielding looked at Johnson's smiling face, and, for the thousandth time, wished he could bash it in.

JULY 28, 1966

Charlie Whitman rested his hand on his chin as he gazed out over the panoramic view of downtown Dallas. His brother, John, family friend, Jim Poland, and himself had decided to make a week-long road trip, checking out the sights and tourist spots of Texas.

Charlie had felt drawn to Dallas. He had never been there, but something about the place felt familiar. Even though John was afraid of heights, Charlie talked his brother and Jim into accompanying him to the observation deck located on the 50th floor of the First National Bank. He walked around the deck, stopping at different points and gazing over the concrete railing.

"This is the highest I've ever been," John said. He cautiously edged toward the railing and tentatively gazed over.

"This is almost twice as tall as the bell tower on the UT campus," Charlie said. "We'll visit that when we get back to Austin."

"Hey, Charlie," Jim said, putting his hand on Charlie's shoulder, "I think I can see Dealey Plaza from here." He pointed off in the distance, where the interstate with three distinct interchanges could be seen. "Want to go see where Kennedy was killed?"

Charlie stood up and backed away, brushing Poland's hand away. "I don't know. That's kinda morbid."

"It's not morbid," Jim countered. "It's history."

"Come on, Charlie," John said. "We may never get the chance again. Heck, they might shut it all down because of the tourist overload."

"That place...is sacred and evil," Charlie said. He wanted to stay away from the place, but something deep inside of him was urging him to go. He closed his eyes and rubbed his temples, squinting against a pain that was starting to surface. When he opened them, John and Jim were staring at him.

"You okay, Charlie?" John asked.

"Yeah," Charlie reassured with an unconvincing grin. "It's just that, because of that place, everything in this country has changed. We've gotten harder and less optimistic. It's like hope died that day." A strange rage clouded his features. "That damn Oswald..."

"Well..." Jim dragged the word out, thinking of some way to soothe his friend and still go to the site. "We can leave some flowers or something. In remembrance."

Charlie nodded, and the three men descended the elevator. They parked in the School Book Depository parking lot and walked to the plaza. Charlie took several photos of the plaza and the street the motorcade had traveled.

Charlie's unease resurfaced, heightening when Jim and John walked over to the stockade fence and around to the back side, which faced the rail yard.

"So," Jim began, "some folks say the actual shooter stood behind this fence and fired the shot that killed Kennedy." He took the camera from Charlie and moved him toward the fence. "Hey, Charlie. You were a crack shot in the Marines. You tell me...could a sniper have hit Kennedy from here?"

Charlie started to walk forward but stopped. A wave of deja vu swept over him. Grabbing the fence to steady himself, his fingers ran across a section of the fence that had been broken off.

"Hey, Charlie, smile!" Jim said, snapping two quick shots with his camera. "It's Charlie Whitman...Sniper!" Jim laughed.

"I was in the brig at Camp Lejeune when it happened!" Charlie snapped. He stormed off, walking back toward the car.

"What's eating him?" Jim asked. "I was just joking."

"I don't know," John said. "He's been moody as hell lately." John took the time for one more look around. "Let's get out of here."

JULY 31, 1966

Sergeant Ted Fielding wrote the last line in his report and set it in the tray. He yawned. The night before, he'd worked a paid uniform detail at a local theater, which had started showing a campy version of "Batman" a week before. It was strange that a film would premiere in Austin, but since a prop, nicknamed "Bat-boat," had been built there, the studio decided to have its first showing locally, rather than in some big Hollywood to-do. Fielding had let some of the hubbub die down before taking the evening off and watching it.

When he'd shown up in Chief Miles' office seven months prior, he was surprised by how seriously the chief had taken the President's recommendation. Miles not only started Fielding at an investigator's pay and position, but he also promised Ted that he would promote him to sergeant and crime scene investigator after just six months on the job. True to his word, on June 15th, Fielding had been promoted to Investigator and was one of the crime scene photographers on staff.

Cruising through downtown, Fielding spotted the clock tower, set on the University of Austin, its twenty-seven floors towering above the trees.

He'd always liked that building. Something about it just stood out in his mind as a sentinel, a beacon, calling for all who wished to learn and grow their minds to come and see. Fielding had seen its rival in very few places, but none called him home like the UT clock tower did.

But even the pleasure of the tower couldn't mitigate the enormity of what he had to do.

He glanced at his watch. He had ten minutes to meet Charlie at the diner on East 8th and Guadalupe, and it looked like he was going to be late.

Once Fielding was hired at the Austin PD, he began researching Charlie's activities. After discovering that he was working as a surveyor for the Texas Highway Department, Fielding made it a point to run into him while on the job. This led to the two men having drinks at a local bar and catching up.

Fielding was taken aback at Charlie's appearance. He was at least twenty pounds heavier, and stress lines were embedded in his face. His eyes darted from side to side, as if paranoid of being followed. But more than anything, it was his eyes.

They were hard and unforgiving, seething with anger.

Fielding was careful to stay as general as possible and avoided any mention of Dallas. For his part, Charlie was glad to see Ted, though he never became informal enough to call him anything other than "Mr. Fielding."

"So, what have you been doing with yourself, Charlie?" Fielding asked, sipping on his beer.

"Been doing odd jobs, mostly, sir," Charlie said. He slowly tore a napkin into smaller pieces, letting them fall to the table. "I was a bank teller at Austin National. Did some bill collecting for Standard Financial. Finally landed a job with the THD, as a traffic surveyor."

Fielding was aware of the hiring practices of the Texas Highway Department. They weren't very selective. "Traffic surveyor" was a fancy name for a construction flagger. He felt a little more hopeful when Charlie said that he'd also followed up on his training as an Eagle Scout, seeking to be a scout troop leader at a local Austin Boy Scout troop.

But underneath, Fielding could see that Charlie was a volcano.

"I'll be frank with you, Mr. Fielding," Charlie began. "I've been a failure as a Marine, a failure at school, and a failure as a husband. My dad won't leave us alone. He keeps sending Kathy gifts and money, like I can't take care of my own family," he said. "I've let myself go. I can't keep the weight off. I mean, I know Kathy doesn't say anything about it, but she's noticed. I love that woman to death, but I don't feel like I'm worthy of her, ya know?"

"Well," Fielding said, "just keep showing her love and affection, and I'm sure she'll appreciate that."

"I've done some things I'm not proud of. I started.... hitting her. It wasn't much, at first, but it's gotten worse." Charlie looked at the table and squeezed his beer glass so tightly Fielding was afraid it would shatter in his hand. "I've seen my father hit my mom. I-I don't want to be like him."

"You can be your own man, Charlie," Fielding encouraged.

"In May, my brother and I went back to Florida and moved our mom away from our father," Charlie said. Tears welled up in his eyes. "He was so mad, we had to call a policeman to stand by while we loaded her things in the truck."

Ted had read the police report that Charlie's mother had filed against his father for the harassing phone calls.

"We got her set up in an apartment not far from here, and now my father calls every day, trying to get her to move back." Charlie kneaded his temples, as though trying to pull the pain from them. "And my head hurts all the time. Ever since those guys jumped me and knocked me out cold."

Charlie reached into his pocket, removed a couple of aspirin, and tore two Dexedrine tablets from the tin foil package, which he quickly downed with his glass of beer.

"Those amphetamines will blow you apart. Maybe we can get you to see a doctor. One who deals with this sort of thing," Fielding said.

"No, sir," Charlie said. "I went to a shrink on campus. I told him about this dream I've been having. Crazy dream. A dream so vivid it's like it isn't a dream at all. More like...memories."

"What sort of dreams?" Fielding asked cautiously.

"It's one main dream," Charlie said. "In my dream, I'm shooting at someone—someone I can't see clearly. I'm in an elevated position, you know, like, higher than they are. I'm shooting with this rifle. People are running, car tires are squealing as they run from me." He continued to rub his temples. "You know, Mr. Fielding, this whole country has gone to Hell ever since Oswald killed Kennedy. I mean, I saw those pictures in Life Magazine. I saw what that bullet did to the President." He looked in his beer glass, focusing on the bubbles. "I'm glad Ruby shot that bastard. How could someone be so cold-hearted as to do that to a man who did this country so much good...and for what? To make a political statement? But a few days ago, my brother, a friend, and I went to Dallas on a road trip. We went by Dealey, and I was at the grassy area...and I felt like I'd been there and stood in that spot before. It was so real."

Fielding sat quietly, afraid to say anything that might spur Charlie to remember what had really happened–how it wasn't Oswald who fired the killing head shot, but Whitman himself.

"And even you, Mr. Fielding," Charlie said. "I mean, I remember when you came to my dorm room and a few other times we met, but there are like...gaps...in my memory. And I get this impression that I had pointed a gun at someone for some reason. I try and grasp it...and it slips away." Charlie rubbed his temples harder. "You, Mr. Booker, Mr. Wolfe, I see flashes of you guys. It hurts to think about it." He downed his beer. "Maybe I have a brain tumor or something."

Fielding had come to this meeting, torn about what he should do about Charlie. He wasn't sure to try and be a good friend and help him through the difficult times he was going through, or say the words that would trigger the post-hypnotic suggestion, ultimately leading the young man to take his own life.

Regardless, it was evident that Charlie was fighting with the demons attempting to unleash all of their hidden secrets and take control of his mind. And for this fact, Fielding decided that he'd seen enough evidence to do the latter.

Taking a deep breath, he looked Charlie in the eyes.

"Strawberry concrete."

Charlie stopped rubbing his temples. His face went flat and emotionless, his eyes glazed over as the MKUltra brainwashing took effect.

"You understand what you have to do, don't you?" Fielding asked.

Charlie nodded robotically. "Yes. I must die."

"You must do it quickly and not disclose to anyone why you are doing it."

Fielding then snapped his fingers, and Charlie's face returned to its same, pained expression.

"Thanks for the beer, Mr. Fielding," Charlie said, rising from his chair. He looked at his watch. It was a little before three. "Sorry to run off, but Kathy and I are meeting some friends for dinner around four. I would invite you along, but..."

"Don't worry about it, Charlie. I already had plans tonight," Fielding lied. He paid the check and shook Whitman's hand. "You take care now, Charlie. I'll see you around."

The two men went their separate ways, but Fielding glanced back over his shoulder to watch Whitman hustle down the street, heading in the direction of home.

Getting into his car, Ted wiped his hand across his face and found that he'd been sweating profusely. He glanced once more in the direction Charlie had gone, knowing that he would never see the man alive again.

AUGUST 1, 1966
11:25 AM

Fielding slipped the last roll of film into the crime scene envelope, sat back in his chair, and stretched. He picked up his coffee cup and swirled the lukewarm liquid around before tipping it to his lips, draining it.

He thought about what he had done to Whitman. The memory of it turned his stomach,

"God damn Johnson!"

He kept glancing at the phone, waiting for it to ring. He expected the call from a uniform officer who would tell him that he had responded to 906 Jewell Street and found a suicide–a young male who had taken his own life.

He had fulfilled the mission handed down to him by Johnson. Other than Abner and himself, Whitman was the last tangible link between President Johnson and the assassination of John Kennedy.

The small oscillating fan stirred up the hot air in the office, doing nothing to cool the stifling August heat. Fielding felt his shirt stick to his back as he sat up in his chair. He looked at the clock and saw that it was 11:30.

He was hungry. He thought about running down the street to the diner on East 8th and Guadalupe Street where he had met Charlie the day before, and grabbing a burger. He figured he would get it to go and come back to the office and await the suicide call. Easing out of his chair, he slung his jacket over his arm and headed out the door.

Charlie unloaded the battered footlocker from the backseat of his black Chevy Impala and looked up at the morning sun, squinting against its brightness.

Nearly twelve hours before, he had repeatedly driven his Marine Corps bayonet through the chest of his wife as she lay asleep in bed. A few hours before that, he had used the same knife and a pistol to remove his mother from this Earth. Afterwards, he sat down and wrote a letter, trying to explain what he had done.

While he was writing, his mind flashed back to the news interviews of Marina Oswald after Lee was shot. He gritted his teeth, confident that his actions had removed from the two most important women in his life the burden and embarrassment of having the news media dissect them publicly for the actions he was about to commit.

He paused in his writing. Something about Lee Oswald and the whole assassination nagged at the back of his mind.

He had felt it before. He dismissed it as the collective guilt of the nation for permitting an environment of hate that led to the killing of Kennedy. But, for him, it felt deeper than that. It was a personal thing; almost as if he'd had a hand in the whole thing.

Charlie shook his head, clearing his mind. He took three Dexedrine and four aspirin and washed them down with water from his canteen.

He had made several stops, gathering the weapons he would need, and headed toward the University of Texas campus.

He struggled to get the blue overalls on over his red plaid shirt and faded blue jeans and zipped them partially up before moving the ungainly locker onto the dolly. He walked toward the bottom stairs of the bell tower, a block-formed edifice which reached 307 feet straight up, situated in the center of the campus.

Charlie clipped the loading zone permit, identifying him as a research assistant, to his coveralls, while placing the placard on his dashboard, visible through the windshield. Obtaining the documents by lying to the security guard at the gates of the campus was the least of the sins which he had committed within the last twenty-four hours. He knew that this would allow him to park close to the tower, without raising undue suspicion.

An unrelenting headache pounded behind his eyes as he dragged his sleeve across his face and forehead, wiping away the sweat. The action just exacerbated the ever-intensifying pain. He glanced at his watch and saw that it was eleven forty-five. He balanced the footlocker and took a breath, pausing for a long minute.

He tried to shake off the feelings of impending doom but knew that no matter how hard he tried to stop himself, the compulsion was too strong...the urge overwhelming. He looked at his watch once again. A minute had passed.

Charlie hadn't slept at all the night before. He'd hoped that the compulsion to kill would have subsided after he had put away Kathleen and his mother, but instead it only grew. It became a monster that consumed his will and compelled him to do what he was about to do.

Charlie knew that he was going to die today.

He realized the fact after sharing a beer with Mr. Fielding. He didn't remember why, or what they were talking about, but something Fielding had said pushed Charlie toward the feeling he had kept buried deep in his soul.

He would die, but for the first time in his life, Charlie was a coward. He didn't have the courage to kill himself, despite the unrelenting urge to do so.

He'd put the German Luger in his mouth, but when he couldn't bring himself to pull the trigger, he decided to let his death be at the hands of the police. But before he did, he would rain down upon the people of Austin an ungodly fury that they would remember for the rest of their lives. If the country was willingly going to go down in flames, then Charles Whitman would be the one who lit the fire.

Securing the footlocker to the dolly, Charlie pushed it toward the front door of the tower.

AUGUST 1, 1966
11:48 am

Fielding returned to his office with his bagged lunch and sat down behind his desk to eat it. He was disappointed that they hadn't received a call to respond to Whitman's suicide, but he figured the call wouldn't come until Kathy had gotten home from work and found Charlie dead.

Just as he was about to take a bite, the squad room door swung open.

"Hey, Ted. Have you heard? There's a guy up in the UT bell tower shooting at people!" a detective announced. "At least three are confirmed shot, including a kid on a bicycle."

Fielding stuffed the hamburger in the bag and grabbed his coat. "I'm heading that way,"

He cut through traffic, making his way toward the campus. His car radio was tuned to a local station, which had a roving news car just a few blocks from the tower, giving a live accounting of what was going on and warning people to stay indoors and away from the campus area.

Several ambulances from Cook Ambulance Service passed Fielding on their way to the campus, ignoring the reports to stay away.

Fielding heard the shots before he saw them strike. He turned onto 24th Avenue at Guadalupe, and his windshield shattered as a spray of bullets struck his car. Parking the car, he ran around to the rear and opened the trunk for added cover. He pulled out a shotgun, knowing how useless it was against a sniper that far up. Still, it gave him a measure of security. He cut up 24th, crossing Guadalupe, and dove behind a concrete wall just off the sidewalk. Crouching low, he stayed behind the wall until it tapered off to about two feet above the ground.

Looking up, Fielding could see the top of the tower, which meant the sniper could see him as well. After the sniper fired off several more rounds in the opposite direction, Fielding sprinted to the safety of the Battle Oaks, a grove of trees near the auditorium, which offered him concealment from the sniper's scope. Moving slowly, he counted on the foliage masking his actions. When he thought it was safe, he bolted from under the canopy of the trees. The movement caught the sniper's eye, and he began to fire down a barrage of shots, tearing away limbs and leaves, which rained down on Fielding. He broke from the trees and took momentary refuge at the base of an ornamental light pole, catching his breath.

More shots continued, only these were coming up from the buildings and walls, instead of down. Fielding saw a man with a scoped hunting rifle firing at the tower from behind a tree. Utilizing the cover fire, Fielding darted out from behind the light pole and took cover behind a barrier wall on the patio of the student union. Crawling, he glanced to his right to see several students huddled in the stairwell on the back side of the union.

"Stay where you are. Don't move! You're safe there," he instructed.

One of the girls was crying, and Fielding could see that she was on the verge of hysterics. "Please, make him stop!" she begged.

"You're out of the line of fire. Officers are making their way to the tower to stop this guy. Just stay where you are. It'll be over soon." The students nodded and hunkered deeper in the well, hugging each other for support.

Fielding felt the sweat dripping in his eyes. "It has to be a hundred degrees today," he mumbled. He wiped away the sweat and made his way to the Hogg Auditorium, where the front door of the tower was visible. He saw a uniformed officer and a man in civilian clothes enter the door and disappear. A short time later, another uniformed officer went in.

Fielding knew that if he could circle around the rear of the union by way of the loading dock, he could keep out of the sniper's line of fire enough to make it into the tower. He crept along the wall, checking his position to ensure that he wasn't in the vantage point of the sniper, and ran across the loading dock to the union. He pulled open the door and saw around two dozen students huddled under desks and behind book racks. He flashed his badge and ran through the union, exiting out the door, which was directly across from the tower's door. The angle was too steep for the sniper to see him, much less shoot at him. He covered the twenty feet in record time and entered the lobby of the tower. Several other officers had gathered there, entering through the other side.

"Has anyone made it up there yet?" Fielding asked.

"Houston McCoy, another officer, and a civilian, a few minutes ago," one of the uniforms said. "We were just about to head up ourselves."

Fielding racked his shotgun and nodded. He, along with three others, headed toward the elevator, while two more took the stairs.

From one of the officer's portable radios, a newscaster announced that there had been a flurry of gunshots from the tower and now, someone, possibly the sniper, was waving a white cloth, as if to signal a surrender.

Charlie fired at everything that moved, but once he hit them, he didn't fire at them a second time. It was the code of the sniper: "One Shot, One Kill." It didn't matter to him if they were male or female, adult or child. To him, everyone was a target to be shot.

But then, something happened.

He looked through the scope at one man. He had brown hair, and he had just moved it with his hand, a subtle movement, nothing anyone would notice.

But Charlie noticed. And he remembered. He remembered standing behind the barricade fence in Dealey Plaza, looking through the scope, seeing the man holding his throat, a pained expression on his face. Leaning over, looking at his wife in the car next to him.

Right before Charlie pulled the trigger and blew the man's head apart.

The realization caused Charlie to fall back hard against the wall. He threw the rifle down and buried his face in his hands.

It all came back to him...the hypnosis sessions with Doctor Booker, meeting his double at the jail in Camp Lejeune, putting on the Dallas Police uniform, and Fielding handing him the rifle that he'd concealed under his raincoat, sighting in on the right side of John Kennedy's head.

The look of pain and fear in the President's eyes as he grasped his throat was seared into Charlie's brain as he squeezed the trigger. The recoil of the rifle, the smell of gunpowder, and the realization that the entire world had just changed, and history had been written.

Everything in the country—everything in the *world*—had been destroyed because of what he had done. But not just because of what *he* had done. Johnson and Oswald were also responsible.

And Fielding.

Charlie started to stand, when a shot from below struck the wall above his head. He ducked down and grabbed his rifle, angrily firing back at the ones below.

Momentarily stopping the barrage, he rummaged through his locker, looking for his notebook and ink pen. He had already written out a letter, requesting that an autopsy be conducted on him to try and determine why he had been demonstrating such erratic behavior. Now, all the memories of what Booker had subjected him to, the psychological conditioning, the hypnosis, all came flooding back. The door had been opened, and he remembered it all.

Scrambling inside the footlocker, Charlie found the Bic pen he had purchased earlier in the day. Pulling the top off with his teeth, he started writing.

"To whom it may concern: I have been compelled to do things that I do not understand. Strange thoughts have been running through my mind for weeks, and I haven't been able to figure out why. These thoughts and compulsions have led me to kill my wife and mother, to spare them the embarrassment of my actions. I had no idea why I did these things and felt this way.

Until today.

He wrote quickly, the words flowing out of him. Even as they appeared on the paper, the enormity of his message was not lost on him. Hot tears ran down his cheeks as he poured out his secret.

Charlie stopped writing when he heard the scraping of the dolly he had jammed against the door as a barricade.

He had scouted out the observation deck and determined that the best place to ward off an assault was tucked under the tower lights. Although Charlie knew he would die, his Marine Corps training kicked in, and he was determined to spread the maximum amount of carnage that he could before the police cut him down.

He heard the sound again, followed by a long commotion. Knowing that the police had gotten past his obstacle, Charlie dropped the notebook into the footlocker and slammed the lid shut with his foot as he grabbed his M-1 carbine. He positioned himself so that he could see the officers approaching, and waited for them.

Houston McCoy, followed by Ramiro Martinez, inched his way along the wall toward the sniper's position. Martinez, armed with his thirty-eight revolver, held it out ahead of him, cocked and ready to fire. They approached the last corner of the observation deck, painfully aware that the sniper would be waiting for them around the bend. Taking a couple of deep breaths, the two men exchanged nods and rounded the corner on the northeast side. The sniper had positioned himself against the wall, pointing down the southwest wall.

Charlie looked to his left and spotted the officers. For a split second, he thought about throwing the rifle down and surrendering to them. That would allow him to explain himself and the reason behind his actions.

The pain in his head stabbed at him. He knew he didn't have time to take any more aspirin, and it wouldn't stop the compulsion that pressed against his consciousness. Even though he knew that he'd been programmed against his will, the compulsion was still too strong for him to fight.

Charlie felt the futility of fighting against the pain. He knew he had to be punished for his sins against the country. Not only was he responsible for Kennedy's assassination, but he'd also shed innocent blood on the campus below him.

Charlie had been taken to church regularly by his Catholic mother. His father, who was not a religious man at all, slept in on Sundays, leaving the "weaker minded" to seek solace in a fairy tale. Charlie didn't remember much of what he'd learned in church, but one thing stood out in his mind: The wages of sin were death.

There could be no greater sin than the cold-blooded murder committed by an assassin. Charlie was that assassin, and the penalty was clear.

So, Charlie did the only thing he could do.

He raised the rifle to his cheek.

McCoy locked eyes with the sniper. Before the sniper could react, Martinez fired all six rounds while McCoy unloaded three from his shotgun. The shots struck the sniper in the face and chest, knocking him onto his back. Martinez rushed the downed, twitching gunman, and, grabbing the shotgun from McCoy, he fired one last round, point-blank at the man.

Fielding listened to the news report and knew it was over. He ran back to his police unit, replaced the shotgun in the trunk, and grabbed his camera and crime scene kit. He then sprinted back to the tower, pushing through the crowd that had started to gather around the mall at the base of the tower. He moved into the elevator and rode to the top of the tower with several uniformed officers.

When he arrived, a dozen people were milling around the deck. It seemed like every cop in Austin wanted to see with their own eyes that the sniper was dead.

Fielding saw that the deck was littered with shell casings and empty magazines. He looked around for someone in charge and saw a uniform with captain's bars. "Hey, Captain. Do you think we can get these people out of my crime scene?" They're kicking shell casings and messing up the evidence."

The captain seemed just as interested in the aftermath of the melee as the other officers, but reason prevailed. He walked to where the sniper's body lay. "All right, gentlemen. Unless you're directly involved in this, I need you to vacate the observation deck so that the crime scene man can do his job. Be mindful of the shell casings and bullet fragments." He turned to Fielding. "Anything else you need, Sergeant?"

"Leave me someone to guard the door. Don't let anyone else in. I'll need another couple of officers to help me collect the evidence after I've photographed the scene," Fielding answered.

The captain moved the officers out, assigning some to clear the building and look for more victims or anyone who may have barricaded themselves in their offices. He left two with Fielding and one to guard the doors. Fielding stepped downstairs and documented the victims in the lower office and the stairwell. After photographing them, he returned to the upper deck where the sniper lay.

He stared down at the sniper and grimaced. The man's face and head had been so disfigured by the shotgun blasts that he was unrecognizable.

One of the officers leaned against the wall, chain-smoking cigarettes. Fielding recognized him as one of the officers who had run into the tower shortly before he had.

"You're McCoy, aren't you?" Fielding asked. The man nodded. "You're the one who shot him?"

McCoy was quiet for about half a minute before he spoke. "Yeah."

"Good job," Fielding said. "Did you find any ID on him?"

"Hadn't checked." McCoy said. "Didn't want to get blood all over my shoes." He then pointed at the footlocker, which he closed with his foot. "Got a name on the top."

Fielding took a photo of the footlocker then looked at the name. When he read it, he backed up, swallowing hard.

"L/CPL Charles J. Whitman, USMC, number 1874634," McCoy read out loud. He looked at Fielding, who had begun breathing in short, gasping breaths. "You okay, Sergeant? You look like you've seen a ghost."

Fielding forced his breaths to slow. "I'm fine," he lied. "Must be a combination of the heat and elevation."

McCoy turned away, lighting another cigarette. Fielding bummed one from him and leaned against the wall, inhaling deeply. He looked down at the footlocker and opened the lid with the toe of his shoe. Lying on top of the boxes of ammunition and the foodstuffs was a Robinson Reminder notebook. He glanced up at McCoy, seeing that he was busy talking with someone else. Kneeling, he flipped the notebook open and read the last page. And froze.

"To whom it may concern. I have been compelled to do things that I do not understand. Strange thoughts have been running through my mind for weeks, and I haven't been able to figure out why. These thoughts and compulsions have led me to kill my wife and mother, to spare them the embarrassment of my actions. I had no idea why I did these things and felt this way.

Until today.

I realized that I had been subjected to mind-altering experiments, which led me to act as I have for the past few months. These experiments were conducted to keep me in the dark about what I have done in the past. A deed so awful that I am overwhelmed at the enormity of it, and its implications, now that I am able to recognize my part in it. I am confessing to being the rifleman who hid behind the barricade fence, on the grass area in Dealey Plaza, in Dallas, on November 22, 1963. I am the one who fired the shot that struck President Kennedy in the head, killing him. Because of what I did, I have destroyed the country that I love. The operation was conceived and carried out on the orders of then Vice President Lyndon B. Johnson and Secret Service Agent Ted Fielding..."

The rest of the letter trailed off, as though Whitman had been interrupted. Fielding looked around, making sure that no one else had seen. He closed the lid to the locker and threw the bolt on it. Hands shaking, he snapped several photos of the locker and the surrounding scene, including Whitman's mutilated body.

"I need a couple of guys to carry this foot locker down to my car," Fielding said.

One of the officers walked over and moved to open it. "What's inside?" he asked.

Fielding removed the man's hand and placed himself within inches of his face. "There's evidence in there, patrolman." His tone was condescending at best. "Evidence that needs to be documented and cataloged. And this is neither the time nor the place to do it." Fielding pushed his finger in the man's chest. "What you fail to realize is that for the next hundred years or more, people will be examining and re-examining what we do here today and why this man did what he did. They'll be asking what we could have done to stop it. They'll wonder where we go from here. Every nuance of this case will be dissected by experts and amateurs alike, picking this day apart and what we learned from it. Look at the President's assassination. It's been almost three years, and people still question what happened and if they were given the true story. Well, let me tell you something, mister. I don't want to have to defend my work and what I did here today for the rest of my life! Are we clear?"

The officer nodded, too stunned to speak.

"Good. Now, get this locker to my car, and I'll follow you down."

When they got off the elevator, a large crowd had gathered in the lobby, spilling into the mall. A frown tugged at the corners of Fielding's mouth when he caught sight of the coroner's assistant standing back away from the crowd, a stretcher situated between them.

Fielding stopped, stunned by how quiet the crowd was. With only an occasional whisper or an audible sob, the lobby was more like a funeral parlor. Some people standing close by reached out and let their fingers brush against the locker, as if they were touching a religious relic. Some murmured Whitman's name and gasped in recognition when they read it printed on the top of the box.

Fielding slowly walked ahead, parting the crowd. A few of the students patted him and the officers on the back, some quietly whispering their thanks as if they had been the ones to stop the evil which had rained down on them for the past ninety minutes. Fielding just nodded and smiled grimly.

When they arrived at the car, the locker was loaded and placed in the back seat. The officers nodded to Fielding, who dismissed them. Once they were out of sight, he opened the footlocker and saw the notebook. Turning to the last page, he ripped it out, as well as the two pages behind it, making sure no trace of the entry could be found. He folded them up and stuffed them inside his coat pocket, safe with him until he could dispose of them. Rummaging through the locker, he searched for anything else Whitman may have collected or written down that may have compromised or exposed his or Johnson's identities in the assassination, but found nothing.

Satisfied, Fielding closed the locker and returned to the tower to finish processing the scene.

When he arrived at the observation deck, the coroner was dropping the sheet over Whitman's body. The scene commander pointed at his cigarette at Fielding.

"Looks like you are going to have a busy day," the commander said. "Soon as you wrap it up here, you'll need to head over to the sniper's house and his momma's. Officers called in that they found this Whitman character's wife and mother stabbed to death. Looks like they died last night sometime. I've got my people and the coroner heading that way,"

Fielding completed processing the scene and collecting the other evidence, then descended the elevator to his waiting vehicle. He started the ignition and put the car in gear. He gave the tower one more glance before pulling out of the parking lot and pointing his car toward 901 Jewell Street, the location of Whitman's wife's body.

He wondered if he would find any more writings by Charlie, admitting his guilt.

The announcer on the radio was reading off the names of those killed and wounded.

He drove in silence, each name driving a nail into his heart. He felt the sob build up in his chest, finally coming to the surface as tears ran freely down his face.

Fielding considered the carnage that Whitman had wrought upon this city that he loved...and how he had been to blame for every ounce of their blood.

JANUARY 7, 1973
NEW ORLEANS, LOUISIANA

Fielding hunkered down behind the front wheel of the Chrysler. Glass from the driver's side window lay on the street behind him.

"Dammit. Another sniper," he muttered. It had been six years since he'd sprinted across the campus of the University of Texas, dodging the hell that reigned down from the bell tower, unleashed by Whitman. He'd been able to keep the connection between Charlie and Dealey Plaza non-existent for the past ten years—and had almost forgotten about him—until this Mark Essex guy stormed the roof of the Howard Johnson's hotel and opened fire on the cops below.

After Whitman had been killed, there was no longer any need for Fielding to remain with Austin PD. He resigned his posting and returned to the Treasury Department, where he was assigned to the Counterfeiting Unit out of New Orleans.

Fielding glanced back over his shoulder at his partner, Todd Henderson. Henderson was a deputy from the sheriff's office in Baton Rouge, who had arrived in New Orleans on the request of the Orleans Parish Sheriff's office to help in the capture of Essex. During the chaos, Henderson found himself separated from the others in his unit. Finding Fielding, the two paired up.

Mark Essex, who had gone on a rampage days before, shooting and wounding several New Orleans Police officers and at least one civilian, had barricaded himself in the Howard Johnson's hotel downtown. Once inside, he set a fire and then began shooting at responding officers.

When they learned that Essex had held up in the hotel as they were making their way there, Henderson was hit by a round in the knee.

"Stay calm, Todd. It isn't that bad," Fielding said, dragging him out of the line of fire. He applied his belt around Henderson's leg to help stop the bleeding.

Like Fielding, Henderson was positioned with the thick rubber of the car tire between himself and the sniper's fire. Henderson struggled to sit up against the pain. Fielding leaned close to him, relieved when he spotted an ambulance parked half a block away, the driver too afraid to come any closer.

Overhead, a CH-46 military helicopter moved toward the hotel, drawing the sniper's fire. Seeing his opportunity, Fielding slipped his arm under Henderson's and raised him to a standing position. Hobbling more than running, the two men covered the half block, falling into the arms of the ambulance driver. Henderson was placed on a gurney and then loaded into the rear of the ambulance.

"Thanks, Ted," he said. "I owe you one, man."

"Just get patched up, Todd. I'll check on you later."

As the ambulance pulled out, Fielding began walking toward the hotel, but froze when he heard the first burst of machine-gun fire coming from the helicopter gunship, directed at the roof of the hotel. He looked up, shielding his eyes, and grunted when he felt a heavy blow to the back of his head. Stumbling, Fielding fell between two parked cars out of sight of the rest of the officers on the ground, whose attention was drawn to the roof.

Fielding rolled on his back, holding his head. He felt the warm blood oozing between his fingers, dripping down his neck. Through bleary eyes, he looked up at his attacker.

Abner Wolfe knelt next to him.

"You?" he said. "Johnson sent you?"

After the death of Booker and Whitman, Fielding was aware that he and Wolfe were the only remaining members of the assassination team left alive. He had been careful of his surroundings, thinking Johnson might send someone to eliminate him as well.

He was just shocked that it would be Wolfe.

"So, you're the one he sent to kill me," Fielding said. A wave of dizziness passed over him, forcing him to lie back.

"Listen, Ted, we haven't much time," Wolfe said. You have to be taken out of circulation, but I'm not here to kill you. I'm here to make sure that you look dead, so that you can move on to another assignment."

"Another...assignment?"

"Yes...Mokroye Delos," Wolfe said. He glanced around, ensuring that no one was looking, before pulling out a semi-automatic pistol with a silencer and a syringe. "I have to inject you with a formula...and then shoot you. It'll look like Essex shot you, and, for all the world to know, you will be dead. I'm coming to get you from the hospital after you're declared dead, and then you are going into hiding."

"I-I don't understand,"

"You have to trust me, Ted. I have to kill you. It's the only way to save you."

He pushed Ted over on his belly and jammed the syringe into his upper arm. After dumping the contents into Ted, he glanced up at the helicopter, and when the ship resumed firing, he pointed the pistol at Ted and fired. The bullet entered the upper back, and, by design, stopped short of any vital organs. But with the combination of the injection and gunshot, it would be sufficient to make it look as if Ted had been wounded by Essex and would die on the way to the hospital.

"I'VE GOT A MAN DOWN!" Wolfe yelled to the surrounding officers. Some started emerging from cover, just as a pre-arranged ambulance pulled up. They loaded Fielding in and nodded to Wolfe, who climbed in the back with Fielding.

Although he was never officially listed, Ted Fielding's death was a footnote to the aftermath of the carnage brought forth by Mark Essex.

CHAPTER FORTY-FIVE
PRESENT DAY
HANCOCK ARMS BASEMENT

Fielding picked up a pillow from the laundry and fluffed it. "McLean, I'm only going to ask you this question once. If you don't answer it, I'm going to shoot you, but not kill you. No. I'm going to do something far worse. I'll turn you over to the police. Once they're done with you, there will be so many governments that will want your head, you'll never see the outside world again. I'm getting tired of playing your game." He wrapped the pillow around the pistol and pointed it at McLean. "Now, who hired you to kill the President?"

"You have to do better than that—" McLean didn't even get to finish his sentence before the first shot ripped through the pillow and struck him. He fell backwards, holding his stomach. "Y-you shot me."

Fielding tossed the ruined pillow aside and grabbed another. "I asked you the question. I'm not asking again." He held the pillow slightly away from McLean's face.

McLean looked at Fielding and smiled. "I meant it when I said that I admired you. Only someone as cold-blooded as I am would do this." He slipped a capsule from his pocket and tossed it in his mouth, holding it between his teeth. "Sarin gas tablet. The same thing I used to kill the President. My benefactor provided me with this little concoction in case I was ever caught." He twirled it on his tongue before holding it back in his teeth. "Enjoy what little freedom you have left. You just signed your own death warrant." He bit down on the capsule.

The effects were immediate. McLean started seizing and lost control of his bodily functions. Fielding backed away, the sight too gruesome to watch. He heard the elevator door chime, realizing that Lefleur and the others had arrived. Moving, he darted up the stairwell toward a door. He hit the crash bar and found himself on a busy sidewalk. Glancing around, he slipped into the throng of pedestrians just as Lefleur and

Byrnes emerged. Lefleur looked around, checking the faces of each passerby, but he knew that if Fielding didn't want to be found, he wouldn't be. He thought about calling him, but didn't want to give up his advantage to Byrnes. He figured that Fielding knew where he could find him when the time was right.

They went back down to the basement and found Pierson standing over McLean's destroyed body. Pierson was on the radio, dispatching other agents to the scene. He covered his mouth and nose with his hand and backed away. Pulling out his cellphone, he called dispatch.

"We're in the basement. We need to seal off this entire area and get a HazMat team in here!" Hanging up, he turned to the others. "Looks like he ingested some sort of nerve agent, but not before someone shot him." He looked up at Lefleur. "Any ideas as to who?"

Lefleur stared blankly, his emotions hidden behind a mask of detached professionalism. "I don't have a clue."

Lefleur sat in the interrogation room at the main headquarters of the Cincinnati Police Department. While waiting to be interviewed, he called Fielding's phone several times, but his uncle didn't answer. He checked his messages to find that he had five missed calls. Three were from his office, one from Reubans, and one from Gretchen's lawyer. The ones from the office advised him that he was considered AWOL and needed to contact Internal Affairs when he received the messages. Reubans was asking him what was going on with the case, and the attorney wanted to set up a meeting to discuss divorce proceedings. After listening to the messages, Lefleur was relieved when the door opened and Byrnes and Pierson walked in.

"Look, Jack," Pierson said, "we know you're holding back on us. Now, if there's some reason you're afraid to tell us, like, I don't know, your family is held hostage or someone else's life is in danger, then we need to know so we can help. I mean, right now, the story you're giving us just isn't holding up to scrutiny. Now, come on. Is there someone else involved that we should be looking for?"

"No," Lefleur said. "I told you. I received an anonymous call from a woman who told me that the President was going to be assassinated. She didn't give any details, other than it would happen at the hotel where he was staying." He looked at Pierson and Byrnes. "Wasn't there a woman found in the President's suite? Maybe she was the one who called. Did you consider that, or is her presence there a matter of 'National Security'?"

Pierson didn't answer, which Lefleur took as a direct hit to the Secret Service's cover story that a "maid" was found dead in the room. He had heard several unsubstantiated rumors about the President and his proclivity to cheat. Just as his uncle had done with JFK, Lefleur figured the current Secret Service also kept that secret close to their vest.

Byrnes stepped up to the table and laid a flat white object in front of Lefleur. "We found the original pass card that belonged to the deceased hotel security guard on 'Zack,' or whatever his real name is. We're reopening the investigation and looking at it as a homicide. The Secret Service, FBI, and CIA are running his prints and DNA through several databases to see if we have a hit on his true identity. Any ideas who he could be?"

"No," Lefleur said. "I wasn't told who the assassin was or anything about him."

"But you did say that this assassin had murdered someone the exact same way and made it look like an accident. How would you know that if you didn't know who he was?"

Lefleur held his silence. "The person who called me..."

"This *woman*?"

"Right," Lefleur said. "This woman told me that the President was going to be assassinated, and that the person had killed people before. One of the ways was by pushing someone downstairs and making it look like an accident. Then, she said that the President would be killed in a hotel in Cincinnati, during the presidential convention. I tried to get more information, and she said, 'Don't trust anyone.'" Lefleur leaned forward, resting his elbows on the table. "Look, Clarence, the truth of the matter is this: I was told that agents with the Secret Service, and possibly the Cincinnati Police, may have been in on it. The person who gave me the information apparently knew enough about the operations of the two departments and the presidential detail that they didn't feel that it was safe just relaying the information to someone over the phone." Lefleur leveled the man with a stare. "Had I known that it was you working the detail, I could have contacted you directly. I mean, we spoke earlier this week, and you didn't mention anything about the President's detail or that you were even on it."

"The Secret Service isn't in the business of broadcasting to everyone where we will be and when. Hence the name 'Secret,'" Pierson snapped. "Speaking of which, did that case pan out about the fifty-year-old body you found?"

"It's still under investigation," Lefleur said. "Clarence, if there were more that I could tell you, I would. And if I find out anything else, I promise to let you know."

Pierson stared at Lefleur for a long minute before glancing at Byrnes. "I don't have anything else," Byrnes said.

Lefleur rose and pulled on his coat. "Is there any word on the President's condition?"

"He's stable. Apparently, they got to him in time. It'll take a while for him to get back on his feet, but at least he survived. We lost Sullivan and Phillip Norris, the first agents into the room." Pierson said. "The... *woman*...hasn't been identified yet."

"How did the First Lady take it?"

"Stalwart." Pierson said. "She's a tough lady. Reminds me a lot of Nancy, when Reagan was shot."

Lefleur stuck out his hand and shook Pierson's. "Let me know if there's anything else I can do." Pierson held onto Lefleur's hand and looked him in the eye. "If I find out you're playing games with me, Jack, I will bury you."

Lefleur returned the gaze. "If I am, you have every right to." He then turned to Byrnes. "Sergeant, thank you for everything." She escorted him to the front door of the detective bureau and watched him drive away. Lefleur looked in his rearview mirror and caught sight of Byrnes staring at him, arms crossed and a stern look etched across her face. The image was burned into his memory.

By the time Jack made it to Fielding's apartment, Fielding was gone. The apartment had been furnished, so everything was still there. The only things missing were the laptop, computer equipment, and his toothbrush. He figured it was a waste of time searching the apartment for any clues to his uncle's whereabouts. Ted was too thorough to leave something behind. With a resigned sigh, Jack pulled the door behind him and headed to his garage apartment.

Four days later, Fielding pulled into the driveway of the small apartment he rented in Austin, Texas. He shouldered his bag, which held his laptop and a change of clothes, and placed it inside the door. He returned to the car, removed a box from the trunk, and set it on the kitchen table. Inside was the evidence that he had removed from Reuban's safe.

He walked down to the mailbox and checked the mail. He pulled out several envelopes addressed to the name that he had rented the apartment under: "John F Whitman." On top of the mail was a large, padded envelope without a return address. Suspicious of the package, Fielding held it by the corners and brought it inside. He took it to his bathroom and set it in the sink, on the off chance that it was some sort of letter bomb. He walked to his bedroom closet, removed a small case, and opened it. Inside was a portable X-ray machine. Setting it up, he picked the envelope up and placed it on the examination pad, which projected an interior image of the contents onto a high-resolution screen. Adjusting a knob, he looked at the screen and set back in his chair, placing his hand over his mouth.

The unmistakable outline of a switchblade knife was visible. Next to it was a folded piece of cloth and, what looked like, a small envelope.

Convinced there was nothing harmful in the envelope, Fielding tore open the package and realized that his hands were shaking. He upended the envelope, and the contents fell onto the bed.

It was the knife he had used to kill Skip Larson all those years before. The dried blood was still visible on the blade. Along with it was the bloody shirt with the piece ripped from it that he had worn that night.

Fielding sat down heavily on the edge of the bed, his breath coming in short gasps. An envelope protruded from under the shirt. With trembling fingers, Fielding picked it up and opened the flap. He pulled out a letter and began to read.

"John F Whitman. Really?

Is this what you do with your time, Ted? Beat yourself up over the past actions you were forced to take because of that fat, demented bastard of a Texan, Johnson? You go and hide under the name of the two most prominent people you were forced to eliminate?

Well, whatever gets you through the night, I guess.

I've always admired you. If you're receiving this, then I'm dead. Perhaps it was at your hand, perhaps the police. Who knows? Dead is dead. But even though I've done some heinous things in my career, I felt that I wanted to do you a good turn.

Sorry about Abner. He was getting senile, and I was afraid that he would spill the beans about you and the operations you two were involved in. Mokroye Delo. Interesting word. Wet works, spilling of blood, and such. Very dramatic. I like it. It's a shame I'm not around anymore to use it.

Anyway, more to the point. I found out a while back about the leverage that LBJ had over you and how he had passed it on to others so they could keep you under their thumbs. I used my unequaled skills and stole it from the last person who had it. I can tell you, both she and her husband were pissed to lose it.

Like I said, I always admired you for your integrity and for your ability to perform the work even though I'm sure it hurt you personally. If I were to die and you survive, I felt that you deserved a second chance. So, here it is. You can do whatever you want with it. No one has power over you anymore. All I ask is that you use your freedom wisely. Cherish it in your golden years. And, hey, maybe you can pay it forward somehow.

Your adversary and pupil,
Roger McLean

Fielding re-read the letter and felt the tension in his chest lessen and the strength return to his muscles. He picked up the knife and walked into the bathroom with it. A quick wash would remove both Larson's and his blood and DNA from the blade. A lighter set to the cloth would take care of the bloody shirt.

An exhilaration, a freedom, that he hadn't felt in decades rushed over him. Such small actions would eliminate any chance of him ever being caught. He would never face justice for the acts he had committed.

He looked out of the bathroom, past the bedroom, and saw the box with the evidence that Jack had collected.

He was proud of the man Jack Lefleur had become. He had taken a fifty-year-old case and had solved the greatest mystery of the twentieth century. It was a shame that, even though Fielding told him the whole story, he had nothing to corroborate it. If he went public with it, Jack would just be another kook with a conspiracy theory posted somewhere online. A theory with nothing to back it up.

He would end up broke and disgraced.

With a small smile, Fielding placed the knife in the sink and reached for the faucet.

CHAPTER FORTY-SIX

Lefleur entered the Internal Affairs office with his union representative and took a seat across from the lead investigator. After some preliminary matters, the investigator turned on his tape recorder and began his questions.

"The duty captain filed a report stating that you were advised that we were below minimum count, and you couldn't take the day off. Do you remember that conversation, Sergeant?"

"Yes, sir, I do," Lefleur said.

"But you took off regardless?"

"Yes, sir."

"Do you have a good reason why?"

"Did you read the account of the attempted assassination of President Kelly in Cincinnati?" Lefleur asked. "I went there to stop it."

The IA investigator leaned back in his chair and crossed his arms. He looked at the union rep.

"That's exactly what he told me." The rep shrugged. "I called Cincinnati Police and spoke with Sergeant Byrnes. I also talked to Clarence Pierson with the Secret Service. They verify his story, although they have questions of their own, which, apparently, Sergeant Lefleur didn't adequately answer."

"Okay, Sergeant. Tell me your side of it," the investigator addressed Lefleur.

Lefleur told him the version of the story that he'd told Byrnes and Pierson. Once again, leaving out any mention of his uncle's involvement. When he finished the story, he looked at the union rep, who nodded his approval. The IA investigator took in the tale and was quiet for a long moment.

"So, then, you admit to being away without leave, correct?" he finally said.

Lefleur exchanged looks with the rep and then looked at the investigator as if he had three heads. "Did you not hear anything I said?"

"Yes. Absolutely. You stopped the assassination of the President," the investigator said. "But you had to go AWOL to do it."

"Well, yes. But as I explained—"

"That's all I need, then, thank you." The investigator cut off the tape, then looked at the union rep. "The usual. It'll be typed up in a few days, and then the chief will make his decision." He cut his eyes to Lefleur. "Oh, and what have you concluded with that cold case? The guy found behind Werlin's? I understand from the coroner that all the evidence came up missing. Chief Gray wants to know the outcome. Something about a 'deal' you made with him?"

Lefleur had forgotten his conversation with Gray, but now it all came back to him. He had promised that if nothing came of the case, he would resign.

"Tell the chief I'll honor my agreement," Lefleur said.

"Well, if you do that, then I don't have to proceed with the AWOL case," the investigator said. "I'll tell the Chief to expect your resignation by the end of the day." He rose and walked out of the office. The union rep followed shortly afterwards, pausing at the door. "I don't know what you promised, but you should have come and seen us first. Now there isn't anything we can do to help."

CHAPTER FORTY-SEVEN

Ted Fielding walked into the main lobby of the Austin Police Department. Under his arm was a satchel.

"Can I help you, sir?" the receptionist asked.

"I'm Ted Fielding. I was an Austin Police Sergeant back in the '60s. Is there a detective I can speak with about a cold case?"

"How cold is the case?"

"It's an iceberg."

She smiled at his joke. "May I see your ID?"

Ted handed her his driver's license and old Austin Police Department Identification card.

"Thank you, Sergeant. Please have a seat, and I'll have someone speak with you soon."

Half an hour later, a young man with a badge clipped to his belt entered the lobby and stepped over to Fielding. "Sergeant Fielding? Sergeant Rod Brantson. Wow, what an honor, sir," the young man said, shaking his hand. "When they told me your name, I looked you up. You were here during the Whitman shooting, weren't you?"

A grim smile crept across Fielding's features at the memory. "Yes, I was."

"I saw some of your photos. Please, come with me." Branston led the way deeper into the building. Additions had been built on since Fielding had last been here. He was pleased to see that the detective bureau was still on the same floor. Brantson led him to a glassed-in interview room.

"Now, sir," Brantson began, "what cold case are we talking about?"

"May 9, 1949," Fielding said. "A man by the name of Skip Larson was stabbed to death outside of a bar on the outskirts of Austin." He reached into the satchel and pulled out a bag, sliding it across the table.

Brantson opened it and peered inside. Once he saw the contents, he reached into the desk drawer and removed a pair of latex gloves. Slipping them on, he slowly withdrew the blood-stained knife and blood-encrusted shirt. He spread them out on the table in front of them.

"This is the murder weapon?"

"Yes."

"And whose blood is that on the shirt?"

"Both Larson's and the killer's. He was wounded at the time," Fielding said. "It was self-defense."

"And how would you know that?" Brantson asked.

"Because I was there when it happened."

"So, you're a witness?"

"No," Fielding said. "I'm the killer."

Stunned, Brantson could only say, "Oh." Thrown off by the admission, he began preparing to interview Fielding for Lawson's murder. "I'm sure you, uh, know the drill," he stammered as he set up the recording and covered the required paperwork.

"I do," Fielding acknowledged.

"Uh, you don't have any other weapons on you, do you, sir?"

"I stopped playing with guns a long time ago, son."

"I'll take you at your word."

Branston nodded at Fielding. "Go ahead when you're ready."

Fielding adjusted the microphone and began.

Two and a half hours later, Brantson cut off the recorder and stretched. "I need a coffee. Can I get you one?"

Fielding nodded. "Black, two sugars."

When Brantson left the room, Fielding smiled and leaned back in his chair. He had played the doddering old man long enough to finish his dissertation on what he had done all of those years ago. But at last, his gamble had paid off.

Fielding had counted on the detective assuming that he was harmless after all these years and would forgo searching him before putting him in the interrogation room. Satisfied that he had answered all the investigator's questions, Fielding leaned forward in his seat and reached into the small of his back.

"Okay, so I lied." He drew the pistol from its hiding place.

Lefleur signed the resignation letter and set it on Chief Gray's desk. Gray picked it up and smiled.

"I never liked you, Jack," Gray said. "You seemed to always fall into crap and come out smelling like a rose, instead of working hard to get ahead like most people do. I knew, going into this, that you didn't have what it takes to close a case like the one you took. It takes dedication and a solid work ethic, which, I'm afraid, you lack."

Lefleur smiled. He had solved the most perplexing mystery that this country had ever seen, and, in doing so, gave explanation to another of the most defining events in law enforcement. After the Texas Tower incident, many departments saw the need for special weapons and tactical teams to combat snipers and barricaded suspects. Training flourished across the country, arming police agencies with higher caliber weapons and specialized training in dealing with active shooter situations.

He had solved it. To him, that was satisfaction enough.

"I'll go clean out my desk," Lefleur said finally. He walked into the Special Crimes Unit and found Peterson in his office. He thought about stopping in, but wasn't in the mood for chit chat or a pity party. He grabbed an empty copy paper box and began packing his stuff inside. He reached for his paperweight, but stopped when he remembered that Fielding had taken it, along with the Kennedy letter and the rest of the evidence of the Booker case.

Loading his desk, he walked to his in-office mailbox and grabbed the mail. On top was a letter from the Sheriff's Office. He tore it open and saw that it was a final notice of foreclosure. His house would be put up for sheriff's sale. The other letter was from his ex-wife's attorney, spelling out demands for child support. He dropped the letters into the box. Hoisting it under his arm, Lefleur gave his office one last look before heading out the door. He walked under the television just as a news story was coming on. Pausing long enough to see that it was something out of Texas, he ignored it and walked out of the office for the last time.

"Out of Austin, Texas, police detectives advised that a former Austin Police officer and Secret Service Agent has come forward and confessed to a murder from 1949. Once he'd completed his interview, the Agent drew a concealed revolver and shot himself to death when he was left alone in the interview room," the reporter said. *"Theodore Fielding was a detective with the Austin, Texas Police Department in the 1950s and 1960s and was also a Secret Service Agent under both Presidents Kennedy and Johnson. Fielding, 85, turned himself in after admitting to a stabbing death that had occurred outside of a Texas bar in May of 1949. A spokesman for the police department advised that an internal investigation has been launched to determine how Fielding was able to smuggle the gun into the interrogation room."*

CHAPTER FORTY-EIGHT

Jack looked around the small apartment and sat down heavily on the stained, second-hand couch.

"This is where I will spend the rest of my life," he told the empty room.

Jack had lost everything in the divorce. His wife had taken his kids and moved out of state. He had resigned, which meant he'd had to give up his detective car—his only form of transportation—and his income. His pension was vested, but he would have to wait two more years to be old enough to collect it. The house was in foreclosure and would be put up for sale the next week. He would have to declare bankruptcy and try to find a job to make ends meet. He'd thought about trying for another police department, but with the chief stating his true feelings toward him, he knew he wouldn't get a decent recommendation.

Even some of the people he'd considered friends had turned their backs on him. After he'd resigned, Jack had received an initial flurry of calls, but three days later, no one called, and no one stopped by to check on him.

Settling back at the kitchen table, he opened his laptop and began scanning through job openings in the area. After two hours, he realized that he would end up working as a night watchman at a foundry, making minimum wage.

Jack put his elbows on his knees and his face in his hands, feeling the despair close around him. His right elbow clipped his coffee cup and knocked it over, spilling coffee on him

He was broke, alone, and disgraced.

Jack thought about the Glock nine-millimeter handgun he had in the bedroom closet. It wouldn't be any effort to stick the barrel in his mouth and pull the trigger. Angled up, the bullet would travel through his brain, exiting out the top of his skull. An instant of pain followed by nothing. He would be dead before he hit the floor. His body probably wouldn't be found for days, until someone called in a strong odor.

He went into the bedroom, intent on finding a clean shirt, and saw the pistol there. He slowly reached for it, but something stopped him.

Jack had been a strong Christian back when he was married, believing in God and Heaven. He knew enough about the Bible to know that God often allowed His children to walk through the fire to teach them to lean on Him for strength. If he was honest with himself, his story was nothing in light of the story of Job, who'd lost everything except his life.

But the thought did nothing to ease the pain in his chest.

The way he saw it, he was one bullet away from being with God forever—and escaping the torment of this world. He reached for the Glock, but froze at the sound of a faint knocking coming from the stairway. Not sure of what he'd heard, he listened and heard another knock, louder this time. Jack opened the sliding door to the stairway and looked at the base of the stairs. A deliveryman was standing there. He saw Jack and waved a package at him. Jack met him at the door.

"Package for Jack Lefleur," he said. Jack acknowledged his identity. "Sign here, please." He signed the digital screen and accepted the package. Walking back up the stairs, Jack saw no return address on the package. He tore the top of the thick envelope.

A pile of hundred-dollar bills was looking back at him. He pulled them out and counted them.

Ten thousand dollars...and a key.

Jack swallowed hard and sat down on the bed. He looked back inside the envelope and saw a letter. Taking it out, he began to read.

"Jack,

Sorry I didn't stick around in Cinci or answer your calls. My work there was done, and I felt I needed to move on.

On to business. There's enough money here for you to get to Austin, Texas..."

CHAPTER FORTY-NINE

It had been a long couple of weeks for the Secret Service. With two agents dead in the wake of the Sarin gas attack against the President, the close-knit group had been shaken. The director reacted quickly, pulling several agents from the Treasury and assigning them to the presidential detail, even though some had never worked the assignment before.

Special Agent Todd Little was one of the men moved in. He was extensively vetted and rigorously researched before he was allowed in the East Wing. Having spent six years in the Marine Corps, where he'd obtained a master's degree in Homeland Security, Little had spent three of those years in Afghanistan. He'd seen plenty of death and had little fear of it. He'd had no problem dropping the hammer on any insurgents in the desert and felt prepared to do the same thing, if need be, to protect the President or step up and take a bullet to make sure the Chief Executive survived.

The presidential detail had been his dream ever since he'd visited the George W. Bush White House a dozen years back as a newly returned active service Marine. He began seeking active employment with the Treasury Department, intending to work for the Secret Service, and, ultimately, the White House.

But everything changed on June 4 when the President was attacked, and two agents died. Little was put on the fast track, and here he was, achieving his dream. Even though he hated the circumstances that surrounded his elevation to the White House Detail, at thirty-two years old, Todd Little felt that he'd earned the position.

The attack had left the President weakened, but still able to function. The Sarin gas had damaged his lungs, causing severe coughing fits. He was now on regular oxygen treatments to ease his breathing. The treatments required that he keep public appearances to a minimum. When he did appear, the appearance was very controlled and brief. His press secretary dodged as many of the media's bullets as he could, but the outlets smelled blood in the water and pounced whenever they could. Vice President Wells had stepped up and covered many of the campaign stops that Kelly was supposed to attend, and his approval rating had skyrocketed. First Lady Kelly attended the rallies with Wells, putting on a brave face and giving generic answers to questions about the President's condition. The united front that she and Wells put forth was beginning to show in the polls.

The Secret Service was still on edge about the attempted assassination. The investigation into Roger McLean led them to believe that he was a hired hand and that there was still someone out there who had financed the contract on the President's life. Without anything to tie McLean to a specific person or group, the intelligence agencies were still on high alert, concerned about another attack on either the President or the Vice President. Security had been beefed up in the White House, and the public appearances were scrutinized and examined from all angles before deciding if it was a safe venue for the President to attend.

The next morning, Little had been tasked with waking the President at six AM, the President's usual time. He was approaching the presidential bedroom when he saw one of the other agents, a few years his senior, posted in the hallway.

"First Lady was up at four thirty. She went for a swim in the pool," the agent explained. "She was careful not to wake the President. He's still sleeping."

Little nodded and stood outside the door. He watched his wristwatch, and, when it was straight up six o'clock, he knocked long and loud. After a polite interval, he knocked again and slowly opened the door.

"Mister President? Sir, it's six o'clock," Little said. The curtains had been drawn in the room, making it nearly pitch black. Little made his way to the foot of the bed. "Mister President?"

He stepped up to the head of the bed and reached for where he assumed his shoulder was. He gave him a light shake, but froze at the stiffness in the man's body. Sliding his hand up to his neck, he checked for a pulse. The President's flesh was cold and unyielding.

He fumbled with the light next to the bed. When it turned on, he gasped and stepped away from the bed.

President Kelly was lying on his back, his eyes fixed in a glaze, his mouth gaped open in a silent scream. A slight line of dried saliva ran down his lip and dripped onto the sheet.

Little's breath came in short gasps. He had seen dead men before. Most were killed in combat. He had never seen anyone die in their bed. Taking several slow, calming breaths to steady himself, he keyed the microphone on his lapel.

"West Four, West Four, I need a medic to the President's suite. Repeat, I need a medic to the President's suite," Little said, his hand shaking.

Within seconds, the door flew open, and the agent who'd been standing guard in the hallway burst inside. He rushed to the President and checked his pulse. Shaking his head, he looked at Little. "What happened?"

"I-I don't know. I came in to wake him and found him like this. I called for the medics right away."

"Medics aren't going to do him any good," the senior agent said. "The President is dead."

Little stared at the dead man until he heard the medical team, with their crash cart, burst into the room. The doctor placed his stethoscope on the President's chest and checked his pulse. He looked at the medical team and shook his head.

"We need to find the First Lady," the senior agent said. Little started to leave, but the agent stopped him. "You stay here and secure the room. I'll find her."

Little nodded and closed the door, looking back at the medics putting away their equipment. After they left, he stood beside the President's bedside and pulled the covers gently up over his head. He turned to walk to the door to wait for the First Lady, but looked back at the pillow lying on the opposite side of the bed. Walking around the bed, he picked it up and turned it to the light.

A wet spot, in the shape of a mouth, was barely visible on the pillowcase. The door opened, and the First Lady came in, her face distraught with fear and panic.

"Oh, my God! Oh, my God!" she exclaimed. She rushed to the bedside and fell on the covered form of her husband. "Oh, God, no. No!"

The older agent stood a respectful distance away, head bowed. A tear slipped down his cheek. He wiped it away and looked at Little, who was still holding the pillow and looking down at Angela Kelly. The First Lady caught Little's eye, and, in that split second, he knew.

What the assassin couldn't do with poison gas, Angela Kelly had done with a pillow.

CHAPTER FIFTY

Jack Lefleur walked into the First National Bank in downtown Austin. The news of the President's death was on all the TV and radio channels, and when he entered, everyone was talking about the story.

He approached a desk where a distinguished-looking gentleman sat. His suit and tie were Brooks Brothers and looked to be a custom fit. His name plate read *"Philip Davison."*

Jack pulled out the letter that Fielding had left him and read through it once more.

"There is no easy way to say this, so I'll just tell you outright. I'm dying. Pancreatic cancer. The doctors only gave me a few months. But before I leave, there are some things I need to do to make my peace with this world.

I didn't get to tell you what happened to Booker. After everything else you've found out, at least you should know that.

Fielding explained how Wolfe had executed Booker, fearing that he would be the weakest link in the group, and how Booker's body had ended up behind the store.

In the First National Bank in downtown Austin, there's a safety deposit box. The box is under your name, so all you will need is your identification. See Philip Davison. He will know what to do. I have enclosed the key. You will need to bring a large bag with you, preferably one that is long and deep. And I would recommend that you rent a car and drive it back to Camp Simmons. Some of the items in the box don't do well when transported on a plane.

Inside, there are items of historic significance, as well as financial value. I told you in the car that I am not a nice person and that I had done things I was not proud of. Some horrible, unforgivable things. Hopefully, in your hands, these things can help make amends for what I have done. Although I never told you, I am very proud of you and love you very much. Everything in the box is yours. It is my legacy to you. I plan on taking my own life and not letting the cancer eat me away, so this is goodbye. It was a pleasure working with you, and I hope only the best for your future.

-Your Uncle Ted

"Hi, Mr. Davison," Jack said, putting out his hand. "I'd like to get into my safety deposit box, please." He held up the key for Davison to see.

Davison grasped his hand and shook it. "And your name is...?"

"Jack Lefleur. But it may be under Jackson Lefleur." He presented Davison with his driver's license.

Davison typed in his name, and the account came up. "Yes, here it is." Pulling a key ring from his belt, he unlocked a drawer in his desk. He grabbed a set of keys and stood up, taking with him a wireless tablet. "If you will follow me, sir."

Davison led Jack to the rear of the bank, walking through the vault and into a room covered with deep-set drawers. He took Jack's key and inserted it into locker number 1122, along with his own key. Jack barely suppressed a smile at the historic significance of the numbers. November 22. The day of JFK's assassination. Davison turned both keys, and the door on the compartment swung open. He then reached inside and pulled out a long box, about four feet deep, and balanced it, setting it on a table in an alcove. Handing Jack his key, he stepped out of the room. "I'll leave you in privacy, sir." Before he left, he turned back to Jack. "This account has been open for a long time. A very long time."

"How long, if I may ask?" Jack asked.

Davison scrolled through the information and stopped, reading through the notes. "It was opened November 26, 1963, in your name, but you probably wouldn't have been born then."

"I was three at the time," Lefleur said. "Thank you, Mr. Davison."

With Davison gone, Jack opened the box. On top was all the evidence that he and Reubans had collected. It all appeared to be intact. There was a rifle that had been disassembled into two pieces lying side by side. Next to it was a pair of latex gloves. Jack found a sticky note on the barrel.

"Don't touch the stock without gloves. Whitman's palm prints are still on it. Check the jar with the bullet you recovered."

Jack shifted around the evidence until he found the jar with the bullet. It was still tinged brown and coated with blood. Another sticky note was on the jar.

"This is the round fired from the rifle. The round has JFK's blood on it."

Like the good crime-scene investigator he had been, Fielding was building the case for Whitman's involvement in the shooting. Jack pulled out his phone and began taking photos, carefully removing the contents of the box and documenting them.

He continued looking through the box. In the corner, folded and yellowing, were pages which had been torn from a notebook. Slipping on the gloves, he gently unfolded them. Another sticky was attached.

"This is Whitman's confession to the shooting of the President. There should be several sources online to make comparisons of his handwriting, to verify that it was he who wrote it."

Jack set the items in his bag, out of the prying eye of the video cameras mounted in the corners.

"Reubans will be happy to get her evidence back. And once you get a handwriting analysis done of Whitman's notes, you'll be able to prove that all the conspiracy theories about the assassination have been true all along. You will have solved the greatest mystery of the twentieth century."

The realization of that statement caused Jack's stomach to lurch. He remembered the website that he'd found, documenting the people who'd suspiciously died after their involvement with the assassination had been brought to light. Some were directly involved, while others were just on the periphery. He leaned back and passed a hand over his face, drawing it away and seeing that it was wet with perspiration.

Do I want to get Reubans involved any more than I already have? If we press on with this, could we be the next ones to die under suspicious circumstances?

Jack stared at the floor, taking in the enormous responsibility his uncle had dropped in his lap. "That bastard," he said aloud. "He knew he was putting me in a no-win situation." He pulled the letter his uncle had written him out of his pocket and ripped it to pieces. The act gave him little comfort, but at least he felt better that he had done something.

Emptying the rest of the box, he came across a thick portfolio. Jack removed the string that had tied it shut and pulled out the contents. Stock certificates from Apple Macintosh, IBM, Xerox, Motorola, Atari, and others were stacked up neatly, all in chronological order. Stapled on the front of the pile was a cashier's check. A handwritten note was paperclipped to the check.

"This check is for fifty million dollars. Just some of the dividends from the stocks I started investing in back in '63, in your name. Not bad for a twenty-five-thousand-dollar investment, eh? I'm too old to use it. Enjoy it for both of us."

Jack sat down heavily in the chair, staring at the check and stocks. He read the note again. His heart pounded in his chest, and his breath came in short gasps. Thinking about his prior heart attack, he began to regulate his breathing, calming himself down.

Breathe, Jack, breathe. Fat lot of good all this money will do you if you're dead.

When his breathing had finally settled back to a relatively normal rhythm, Jack held the check up and smiled. Then he laughed.

Dear Lord, this money will solve everything. I can pay off the house and set up college funds for the kids. I can start over and do the things I've always wanted to do.

Jack let the fantasy play out in his head for a few minutes, calculating what he would spend it on, when something about the note tugged at him. The amount Fielding had stated: twenty-five thousand dollars.

"1963. Davison said that the account was opened on November 26, 1963," Jack said to himself. "That would have been the first day the banks would have opened after JFK's funeral and a day of mourning." Jack's hand trembled as he let the check drop to the table. "The money Ted invested was what he was paid to kill Kennedy. All of this, the stocks, bonds, and cash. It all came from that one act."

Jack felt physically ill. He backed away from the table, rubbing his temples and pacing, while looking back at the check, stocks, and evidence stacked up on the desk. He saw the remnants of the letter he'd ripped up and picked up the pieces, spreading them out on the table. He scanned through it until he found the part he was looking for.

"I told you in the car that I am not a nice person and that I had done things I was not proud of. Some horrible, unforgivable things. Hopefully, in your hands, these things can help make amends for what I have done..."

Jack crumbled the pieces of the letter in his fist. He held his fist to his forehead.

"Damn you, Ted. Damn you straight to Hell!" Jack exploded, sweeping the contents from the safety deposit box onto the floor. "Every damn thing that you've done was horrible. And with your last dying act, you've dragged me down into the same hellhole that you wallowed in. Damn you!"

Jack heard several hurried footsteps coming down the hall. He stopped them before they entered the alcove. "Sorry. I dropped the box. Everything's fine."

Davison raised an eyebrow of disapproval and tried to peer around Jack, who steered him away. "If you need any help..."

"No. I'm fine. Just clumsy, I guess." Jack escorted him back toward the door and returned to the mess he had made.

He picked up the items from the floor, being careful to ensure the integrity of the evidence, and replaced them on the table. The last item he collected was the check.

He looked at it once again. So much good could come of it, yet it came from so much pain.

There were only two words to describe it. He thought back to just a few days ago when **Santiago Mendez had tried to give him an envelope of money to get him to change his testimony against Mendez's brother.** He wouldn't accept his money then, and had called it for what it was.

Blood money.

Jack closed the box and placed it back inside the vault. He dropped the key to the safety deposit box on Davison's desk.

"Here. Keep the key," he said. "I won't need it anymore." He then handed Davison the check. "But I think I'm going to help you have a really nice day."

Jack walked out of the bank, the evidence bag heavy under his arm. In his shirt pocket was a deposit slip and bank card from the First National Bank. He looked up at the sun and squinted. Slipping on a pair of sunglasses, he walked to the rental car and opened the back door, placing the bag on the rear seat. He settled into the front seat and gripped the steering wheel, unsure of where to go or what he would do next.

That's when he saw the blue folder lying half buried on the back seat.

It was the one that Ted had given him with the chief's information. Flipping through it, he realized that it was damaging enough to use against him and others if Jack decided to go public with it.

Jack had never been a vindictive or petty person, but the thought of holding the power to destroy the one man who had helped cause him so much pain was tempting.

Looking at the evidence that he had accumulated, a plan began to formulate in his mind. He pulled out of the driveway and aimed the rental back toward Indiana.

Lara Reubans stood against the stiff wind as it blew through the Lindenwood cemetery. She looked down at the grave of

Howard Booker as a Marine Corps Honor Guard fired off a twenty-one-gun salute. She looked across the casket at Matthew Booker, dressed in a suit, the sleeves long enough to cover the handcuffs. His escort from the prison stood next to him, while another officer stood behind the crowd, armed with a shotgun. Booker wiped the tears away while his sister sat next to their mother in the front row.

After Jack had called her and told her that he was unable to recover the stolen evidence, he instructed her to release the body to the family for burial without explanation and to move on. She asked him about Wolfe.

"I'll send you my final report. In it, you will find that Wolfe and Booker got into an argument over money Booker owed Wolfe, and Wolfe killed him in a fit of rage. He buried Booker, and later, in his guilt, he bought the land and watched over Booker's remains. Eventually, the weight of what he did, coupled with advanced age and a deteriorating mental state, compelled him to confess to where the body was buried. Since Wolfe is dead, that's how it ends."

Reubans was quiet for a long moment before speaking. "Is that really how it happened, Jack? What about Dealey Plaza and the assassination? What about the blood and the bone fragment?"

"Any evidence we had that tied Booker to the assassination is gone. If anyone challenged our findings, we wouldn't have a prayer without it."

"And Wolfe's death?"

"Accidental," Jack lied. "He knocked over the terrarium, and the scorpions stung him to death. That's it."

"I won't be seeing you again." Reubans declared, more as a statement than a question.

"No. It's better this way. Take care of yourself." Jack hung up. There was nothing left to say.

In a matter of days, Jack had ensured that Davison earned his commission. He took care of contacting the sheriff's office, arranged to pay off the house in full, and even found a real estate agent who would put it on the market for him. He also set up college funds for his kids and set up a trust for each of them to access when they turned twenty-one.

Three days after his first encounter with the lockbox, Jack was in Chief Gray's office, along with Peterson and Reuban, who were surprised to hear from Jack again.

"Okay, Lefleur," Gray said, closing the office door. "What's so important that you called this meeting?"

Lefleur stood against the wall and reached inside a leather satchel. He began handing a series of photographs to each of them. "A few weeks ago, I was contacted by my uncle—which is surprising, since I knew him to be dead for almost forty years." He pointed to the first photo. "After quite an adventure, he sent me a letter, which led me to a bank in Texas."

Lefleur recounted the story of the trip to Cincinnati, told of his stopping the assassin, and then what he had found in the safety deposit box. After he had provided them with all the information, he sat back and let them absorb it.

"My God, Jack," Reubans said. "You actually did it."

"Jack..." Peterson said. "This is incredible. I mean, people have been trying to find out the truth about the assassination for more than fifty years, and here you have it dropped in your lap. You are one lucky son of a bitch."

"Lefleur, we need to go public with this as soon as possible," Gray said. "Do you realize what a coup this would be for the department if we released this to the press? Having a detective from this agency solve the greatest mystery of the twentieth century? We would be internationally famous!" Gray reached for the phone. "How soon can we put this together for release? We'll need the actual evidence for the examination of course."

Lefleur began collecting the photos from the others and slipped them into the folder. "I'm not releasing this information."

Gray stopped in mid-dial and looked at Lefleur. "You're what?"

"I'm not releasing it," Lefleur said again. "I only allowed you to see this because I felt that you deserved to know the truth, and to know that the case has been solved. This is as far as it goes."

"Are you crazy?" Gray snapped. "This case is more than just about you. It's historic! This is something that can make us all famous!"

Jack fired back, "If we put this out there, and I can promise you that it will be buried amongst the thousands of other conspiracy theories that the internet generates. Even with evidence, it will still be called 'faked' or 'manufactured', and, instead of making the department famous, we will be made laughing stocks."

Peterson leaned back in his chair and nodded. "He's right, Chief. It doesn't matter how good the evidence is; it will be swept away with the other theories. And you know why?"

"People don't want to know the truth," Reubans said. "If they know the truth, they will have to admit that what they believe is wrong, and no one wants to believe they're wrong."

Gray looked at Peterson and Reubans in disbelief. "You're as crazy as Lefleur." He looked at Jack. "Lefleur, I am ordering you to turn over that evidence!"

"I resigned, remember?" Lefleur said. He looked at Reubans. "But I would like you to match the palm print on the rifle with Whitman, compare the ballistics on the spent round against the rifle I recovered, and match the DNA on the bullet with the one we have on file for Kennedy." He smiled. "If you don't mind a citizen's request to do it."

"Well, I'm not sure if the department will fund that work, since there is no active case involved with it," Reubans said

"If there's a funding problem, please let me know. I think I can handle that." Lefleur said.

"If you aren't going to release the information, then I will contest this to your superiors, and I'll have your job, Doctor Reubans." Gray snapped. Lefleur looked inside the satchel and smiled, his eyes going to Peterson and Reubans. "If you two will leave us alone for a minute, the Chief and I have some things to work out."

Peterson looked at Reubans and nodded toward the door. When they walked out, Lefleur closed the door and reached into his satchel, pulling out the folder with the blue cover. "I think we need to talk."

After a few minutes, the door to the office opened. Lefleur stepped out and zipped the folder closed. Behind him, Gray came out of the office, a stunned look on his face. Behind him, on the desk, lay the blue folder. Lefleur turned and faced him, lowering his voice. He nodded to the folder. "That is the only copy. I may be a lot of things, but I'm not a blackmailer," he said. Gray nodded and shook his hand.

"Peterson, meet your new boss," Gray said. "Jack starts back Monday as Lieutenant in command of the SCU."

"Am I being demoted?" Peterson asked.

"No," Lefleur said. "You're keeping your rank. We'll work something out about dividing the workload."

"Yes, sir, Lieutenant," Peterson said. "Good to have you back, Jack."

EPILOGUE

On a sunny Saturday morning, a memorial service was held for Jeffery Bailey at the Spring Grove Cemetery.

After realizing that Bailey had provided the vital information that allowed the Secret Service to respond and rescue the President from the Sarin-doused room, Jack had appealed to Detective Byrnes to recognize Bailey for his part in thwarting the assassination attempt, even after a preliminary investigation uncovered that the First Lady was behind the plot to kill Kelly. She had made a statement that she didn't want to be in the political arena anymore, and Kelly forced her to stay.

Jack was impressed at the turnout. Not only had the mayor, governor, and state senator attended, but also the newly sworn-in Vice President, appointed to the office by the former VP, now President Clifton T. Wells, had arrived as well, under tighter than normal security.

Vice President Courville led the speeches, ending with Trent Goldstein and the CEO of The Hancock Arms, who presented Bailey's family with a plaque—a duplicate of one that would be hung in the hotel lobby—describing Bailey's sacrifice and service to the city and country.

Clarence Pierson pulled Jack to the side. "This was a nice thing,"

"I didn't want this poor guy to have just ended up as some footnote in a dusty text. He didn't ask for his fate. At least he'll receive some recognition, and his death wasn't in vain," Jack said. He looked back at Bailey's family. "At least he made a difference."

After the ceremony, Jack went back to his small apartment. Soon, he would find a house to buy and start his new life, but for tonight, he sat at the kitchen table, with its torn laminated top, with a cup of coffee in hand as he opened his laptop.

With the conclusion of the case with his uncle, Jack felt an urge to put some of the stories down in writing, even if they never saw the light of day.

Jack's mind slipped back to Louisiana, and the major case he had worked. It involved a killer named, "The Barber". Digging through his closet, he pulled out the tattered box that contained the files he had kept when he left Baton Rouge. Those files documented his search for the killer.

Jack opened up the newly purchased laptop. Turning it on, he started at the blank screen. A passage from Shakespeare flashed across his mind. Smiling, he took a sip of the coffee and began...

"THE UNKINDEST CUT OF ALL"
BY
JACK LEFLEUR

THE END

Book One
"Unkindest Cut: Rise of the Barber"

Book Two
"If the Cause is Just"

Book Three
"Not Alone in the Fire"

Book Four
"Strawberry Concrete"

Book Five
"Unkindest Cut"

Author Scott Morales

About the Author

Some people grew up wanting to be writers.

I didn't. I wanted to be a cop. And I lived my dream for 32 years before retiring.

However, 9/11 changed my perspective on writing. After the attacks on the Twin Towers, I felt the need to reconnect with many old friends. In doing so, stories began forming in my mind. Ideas of "What if" and "If, then" pushed my imagination to take some of the lessons I'd learned in law enforcement and life, and craft tales encompassing both. From these thoughts and ideas, my books began to emerge, and the need to tell my stories.

When I retired in 2013, my career spanned from the state capitol of Baton Rouge, Louisiana, to the Erie Canal in Fort Wayne, Indiana. I worked as a dispatcher, jailer, medic, patrolman, crime scene tech, and detective. My career in police work, as well as my extended studies in criminology, investigative procedures, and tactics, have helped groom me toward a career in crime fiction. (And growing up watching *Adam-12*, Batman, and *Star Trek*, groomed me toward sci-fi and being a crime fighter.)

During my writing career, I have assisted at least a half-dozen authors in producing their stories and co-authored a few more.

Everyone has their own story, and it is my desire to see them published.

I'm the father of three sons and a daughter, have four grandchildren, and live in my hometown of Baton Rouge, Louisiana.

I can be reached at Writerscott.morales1496@gmail.com, on my webpage www.authorscottmorales.com, or on TikTok, X, Truth Social, Instagram, Facebook, Lemon 8, Pinterest, Rumble, Reddit, and WhatsApp.

www.ingramcontent.com/pod-product-compliance
Lightning Source LLC
Chambersburg PA
CBHW070527090426
42735CB00013B/2888